CONSTRUCTION CLAIMS

PRACTICAL CONSTRUCTION GUIDES

CONSTRUCTION CLAIMS
CURRENT PRACTICE AND CASE MANAGEMENT

BY
JEREMY HACKETT, FRICS, ACIArb

LONDON   HONG KONG
2000

LLP Professional Publishing
(a trading division of Informa Publishing Group Ltd)
69–77 Paul Street
London EC2A 4LQ
Great Britain

EAST ASIA
LLP Asia
Sixth Floor, Hollywood Centre
233 Hollywood Road
Hong Kong

© Jeremy Hackett, 2000

British Library Cataloguing in Publication Data

A catalogue record
for this book is available
from the British Library

ISBN 1 85978 553 0

Printed in Great Britain by
MPG Books Ltd,
Bodmin, Cornwall

PREFACE AND ACKNOWLEDGEMENTS

The last millennium went out with a bang in more ways than one, not least the unprecedented and feverish explosion since the Housing Grants, Construction and Regeneration Act 1996 of initiatives and legislation designed to change construction law as previously practised in the United Kingdom. The consequent frenetic activity—whether in respect of retraining of the judiciary, or legal commentary in the construction press, in the industry organisations who publish standard forms of contract, or in the mass of seminars offered by various bodies—has left us all feeling in need of a legislative holiday, preferably of a year or more.

But there are dark clouds blowing from the East. No sooner will we have got to know the new rules and procedures post Sir Michael Latham's and Lord Woolf's reforming efforts than someone in Brussels or Luxembourg is going to tell us that having changed direction we are now in breach of European Law—funny how "euro" sounds like something medical and unmentionable!

Anyhow "Adjudication" and "Access to Justice" are here to stay, and have already changed the landscape of construction litigation, albeit the latter has yet to prove that it can actually deliver affordable and manageable justice any better than the old pre-Woolf system.

As a construction industry professional, interfacing between specialist contractors, main contractors, design professionals, insurers, building owners, developers, funders, solicitors and the bar, it is fascinating to see how each element depends upon the other. Each has to run a business, yet few appreciate just how their advice or actions impact upon the others in the property cycle. When all is done, construction is but a service industry to the property industry and the wider investment market.

Hopefully this book will help to give a wider appreciation of how a dispute between two parties, like a stone thrown in a pond, creates ripples in all directions, and how any new rules or legal procedures must not be allowed to prejudice the rights of innocent third parties in the supply chain—least of all the employer or developer without whose initiative and willingness to invest there would be no project. Equally it must be appreciated that the small specialist at the very bottom of the supply chain is critical to the success of the whole endeavour, and must be protected from payment abuse.

Virtually all Construction Claims books to date have considered scraps between contractors and employers or sub-contractors, so in the first part of this book I have tried to give the wider perspective in discussing current practice in preparing and defending claims, bringing in funding, insurance and design team issues.

On basic Claims practice and case law I have usefully referred when in doubt to five main sources:

— *Berrymans' Building Claims Cases* by Diana Holtham and Paul Taylor.
— *The Management of Contractual Claims* by K.L. Scott.
— *Powell-Smith & Sims Building Contract Claims* by David Chappell.
— *Delay and Disruption in Construction Contracts* by Keith Pickavance.
— *Building* Magazine and the regular articles in the "In Business" Legal section.

In the second half of this book—entitled "Case Management"—I have attempted to bring together the basic knowledge arising from the principal post-1996 legislation required by practitioners (non-legal) for the everyday administration of projects, together with an outline of the options and risks when things go wrong.

At all times it is necessary not to lose sight of the most important person in any construction dispute: the Managing/Finance Director who is paying one's fees. It is his perception and commercial judgement which will determine whether the case—and the fee income—will continue. Unfortunately legal merits and strengths of case come second to cash flow considerations when one is struggling to continue to trade a business, and as will come out in the course of this book, bank managers can be very fickle friends indeed.

Undoubtedly Lord Woolf's Report, *Access to Justice*, set the scene for a long overdue reform of the UK commercial law system by identifying the limitations of the old system, but what does one put in its place?

In many ways the new Civil Procedure Rules should have been the easy bit, but these are taking an undue time to bed down and create confidence amongst the end users—i.e. solicitors who have to decide whether to throw their clients on the mercies of construction professionals sitting as arbitrators, or of the judges sitting in the Technology and Construction Court.

The much more radical reform came in the follow-up to Lord Woolf's Access to Justice proposals: the Lord Chancellor's Department's Consultation Paper, published in 1998, entitled *Access to Justice with Conditional Fees*. So far we have seen very little comment in the construction press as to how construction lawyers are responding to this very clear direction as to "the way ahead"—and the insurance industry has yet to come up with a sufficient choice of effective litigation expenses products, such that impecunious Claimants can generally afford justice, as envisaged by the present Lord Chancellor, Lord Irvine.

Certainly the construction cases that survive adjudication will need to be managed by all concerned, and commercial clients will be looking for solicitors and barristers who will be prepared to back their own judgement of case merits by undertaking those cases on a Conditional Fee basis. This will involve sharing the risks and the rewards now allowed under the new procedures, and those lawyers who presently earn their living from construction litigation will have to get commercial, or find their living elsewhere.

For the second part of this book, my thanks go to those several, mainly London, Solicitor practices who have over the years kept me regularly supplied with flyers covering the latest legal developments and case law. In fact, it was these flyers that gave me the original idea for this book—so much was happening all of a sudden that the construction claims scene would never be the same again. Someone, other than a lawyer, needed to try to make sense of it all.

Then over lunch one day with Tony Bingham—whilst the Housing Grants etc. Act was still on the drawing board—we were saying that there simply had to be a way of giving dispossessed sub-contractors (and all too often their Receivers) the means to pursue their abusers in court. This was in relation to a very large government-sponsored project which left a trail of insolvencies. When the government agency finally settled with the main contractor over £20 million could be seen going into group accounts—but with the method of accounting having been changed in successive years, no significant value could be identified as then having been disbursed to outside companies.

Tony's introduction led me into the world of litigation expenses insurance and Conditional Fee Arrangements, which unknown to me were shortly to be the main recommendation of Lord Woolf and The Lord Chancellor's Department's discussion paper, subsequently enacted as the Access to Justice Act 1999—so but for Tony there would have been no Chapter 12 in this book.

Importantly, my thanks are due to my publisher LLP Professional Publishing for having the confidence to engage me, a Chartered Quantity Surveyor, to tackle what is essentially a legal subject area and for providing me with the assistance of a legal "minder". To Ian Yule of Wragge & Co. my especial thanks are therefore due for the various corrections and suggestions made in the course of drafting and final proofing, most of which I trust I have adopted.

JEREMY HACKETT
25 March 2000

CONTENTS

CASES

CHAPTER 1

INTRODUCTION

1.1 AN ENGLISHMAN'S WORD

The world that we now live in, and in particular the construction world, has become a very fractious place, where the written word and proof of posting, or even time of transmission, can be everything when it comes to a contract dispute. With the inevitable progress to the exchange of information by electronic transfer the day of the paperless office, and even the paperless project, is promised by the disciples of Mr Bill Gates—but can that really happen I ask as I start writing this book "homeworking" on a laptop from the middle of peaceful nowhere in South West France?

One can always remember the hot summers of one's youth but my abiding memory of my father was his disillusionment with the rapid decline in business ethics when he returned to trying to run his own company after the Second World War in 1945: "... but in the thirties an Englishman's word was his bond. It was respected throughout the business world," he would say. For my father, written contracts, before putting the order in hand, were only for matters of real necessity, like buying or selling a house—and so he learnt the hard way with two bad debts in quick succession.

In the late 1950s my father used to sail at Shepperton with an architect who at one time lived on an old Thames barge and one day my future career was decided: "If your lad is good at maths and Latin, why not put him into quantity surveying—that is where the money is now, not in Architecture." A few years later I might have gone to Oxford or Dublin to study law, but funds did not permit and I enrolled at The College of Estate Management, then part of London University and located in Kensington, to study quantity surveying.

Having now visited various places in the world in the course of business I can look back on a colourful career, and have always had a keen interest in the legal aspects of construction contracts.

However, like the late Lord Denning, I have never accepted that lawyers necessarily know all the answers, or at least provide answers that acknowledge the requirements of justice in the real world. So with due deference to my various legal friends I apologise in advance if some of my

1

opinions in later Chapters are strong meat, but there has to be a dialogue between those of us practitioners, who have to operate major contracts, and those who advise how such contracts should be set up—or, when things go wrong, should have been set up!

1.2 THE COLLAPSE OF TRUST

When I started out as a quantity surveyor the JCT Standard Form of Contract 1963 was the "norm" in the building industry—with any specialist trade usually being the subject of a prime cost (PC) sum entered in the Bills of Quantities sent out to tender to secure the selection of the main contractor. The specialist work, when designed, would then be separately billed and tendered, and then the successful bidder would be appointed as a nominated sub-contractor—simple really, except they now call it "Management Contracting".

As work progressed all such nominated sub-contractors' work would be valued each month and the value declared on the back of the standard RIBA Interim Valuation Certificate, and this would be copied to the firms in question, i.e. they knew what had been certified each month, and when. Accordingly, if they were then not paid by the main contractor they could demand to know why not, and, in extremis, get paid direct by the employer.

This system worked very well for many years until in the early 1970s there was a minor recession and there were various nominated sub-contractor insolvencies. As such, employers and their Architects had to renominate, which not only went totally against the grain, but horror of horrors, more often than not Architects also had to grant Extensions of Time under the contract to cover the lost time whilst a replacement sub-contractor was appointed—usually at a premium cost. Usually, there would then be a claim for Loss and/or Expense.

The JCT in their infinite wisdom then tried to dump the sub-contractor insolvency risk on the main contractors and invented the obviously artificial dodge of the employer and the design team selecting a preferred specialist—with the main contractor then having a notional right of rejection before taking on the chosen specialist as their own domestic sub-contractor.

Thus specialist sub-contractors, typically cladding or finishing trades, were appointed as domestic sub-contractors, with no declared monthly work values on the back of the Architect's Interim Payment Certificate—so they had no better contractual status or better certainty of payment than the main contractor's own appointed domestic sub-contractors, e.g. groundworkers.

Having been appointed on a domestic sub-contractor basis, specialist firms often found themselves in what has been crudely described as a "mushroom farm" scenario, i.e. kept in the dark as to what had been certified for them and paid in good faith by the employer to the main contractor. All too often the sub-contractors were not paid until much later, and then only part paid without good reason, yet they were expected to perform as and when it suited the main contractor.

A simplistic statement no doubt, but one that increasingly came to reflect the frustrations of many genuine specialists. Such firms would often be kept at arm's length by main contractors as regards payment—when main contractors needed to protect their own overdraft position, particularly when the money supply became very tight in the major recession of the late 1980s and early 90s.

In short, for many an unscrupulous main contractor the temptation was too great, and with specialists' payments no longer declared on the back of the Architect's monthly Interim Payment Certificate, the specialist simply had no knowledge of what had been certified in his favour, or when. Accordingly, cash flow down the supply chain broke down on many projects. As projects increasingly overran on both time and cost, the employers, and in particular developers and funders, were the real losers and disputes proliferated—all because main contractors were quite improperly using sub-contractors as free banks and the previous basis of trust had broken down.

1.3 THE PROLIFERATION OF MULTI-PARTY DISPUTES

In the meantime the law had got itself into difficulties over who could recover what loss. This situation arose out of a series of cases concerning the duty of Local Authorities to properly consider the known history of sites when granting planning consent, and then when approving the design and installation of foundations under the Building Regulations to have properly inspected the work in progress.

In *Dutton* v. *Bognor Regis UDC* (1972) a second owner recovered the costs of major repairs when it was found that her house had been built on the site of an old rubbish tip, and in consequence the standard shallow strip foundations were inadequate. However, one of the Lords Justices in his speech volunteered the opinion—not directly relevant to the facts of the case—that had the Plaintiff claimed on the basis of diminution in market value, then he and his colleagues would have been in some difficulty, so setting the hare running concerning the principle of economic loss.

Then came *Anns* v. *Merton LBC* (1978) where a second lessee proceeded against the Local Authority, despite the fact that the builder retained the freehold, when major cracks appeared in his flat. Tried as a preliminary issue, the key question was: on the assumed basis that the Local Authority Building Inspector had been negligent in approving the foundation design, could he have reasonably foreseen that a second lessee might suffer injury or loss? Answer: Yes. The court followed *Dutton* v. *Bognor* and awarded full repairing costs to the Plaintiff against the Local Authority.

Presumably in total ignorance of the above cases, which took some time to reach judgment and publication, another houseowner, this time a first owner, on realising his property was affected by subsidence, obtained an estimate of £45,000 for the repairs. He then did the sensible thing: not wanting to live with all the uncertainty and mess he sold on, selling for £35,000 less than market value, and mitigated his loss by £10,000. Presumably the builder was not in business any more, so the owner then proceeded against the Local Authority for the lost £35,000.

So *Murphy* v. *Brentwood Council* (1991) came to court, the High Court finding for the Plaintiff following both *Dutton* and *Anns*, £38,777 being awarded—but the Local Authority appealed on the basis of the gratuitous opinion in *Dutton* concerning diminution in market value, and therefore the concept of economic loss. Unfortunately for Mr Murphy, or his insurers, the Court of Appeal and subsequently the House of Lords found for the Local Authority on the basis that:

1. Mr Murphy had only suffered "economic loss", as opposed to physical damage or injury.
2. Because the defects had become apparent before physical injury or loss to property had occurred, then no negligence had occurred sufficient to bind the LA under the previously established principle of foreseeable damage given a lack of duty of care.
3. To allow such a claim would create far too wide a class of action.

So the principle of economic loss was established and, importantly, the rule established that economic loss can only be recovered under the law of contract, and not in the tort of negligence. Thus if parties C or D (first and second lessees) in the development chain suffer economic loss due to the default of party B (the contractor), who was only in contract with party A (the employer), then there can be no right of recovery for C or D against B, either in contract or tort.

The consequences of this decision for the commercial property world have been profound. What if significant defects are found after completion, or after the development had been sold on, or after one of the links in the development chain had gone out of business?

So the Collateral Warranties industry was born, legally linking third parties to first parties, who otherwise were not in contract with one another, just in case an issue of economic loss should arise at some future date—but more about Collateral Warranties and third party rights later in the book.

As a direct result of the concept of economic loss being unrecoverable under the law of tort, but recoverable under the law of contract, the practice of alternative pleadings became the "norm", particularly in cases where the guilty party had yet to be identified.

1.4 ARBITRATION v. LITIGATION

Given that for every head contract between an employer and a main contractor there are probably 12 or more major sub-contracts—and that *each* of these is sourced by various labour or material purchase orders, even a relatively modest project has an extended supply chain. It follows that a dispute—usually about payment—can occur at any of the various links in the supply chain.

The main contract and the next level down of major sub-contracts will usually be secured with formally completed contracts, with back-to-back provisions concerning monthly payments. Usually these will also dictate whether any dispute is to be resolved by arbitration or litigation. However, at the next level down in the supply chain the placement of sub-sub-contracts is often relatively informal, i.e. no formal offer and acceptance in place, so when a dispute arises the first question is: arbitration or litigation?

In *Northern Regional Health Authority* v. *Derek Crouch Construction Ltd* (1984) the courts had come down firmly in favour of arbitration provided there was written agreement to an arbitration clause, so the existence of a completed contract incorporating such a clause was inevitably the starting point in any dispute. As such the existence of a written contract, and whether this incorporated an effective arbitration clause, often had to be resolved at considerable expense before even the forum for the main dispute could be determined.

Most disputes originate over claims for additional money or additional time, and the party trying to defend a position will naturally look to the next party up the supply chain, i.e. rarely will a dispute involve just two parties. Accordingly, there were often real problems of agreeing whether arbitration or litigation should apply if the middle party had an arbitration clause up the line, but no arbitration clause down the line.

Inevitably legal points on the existence or otherwise of a properly completed contract would be taken by the party wishing not to be parted from their money, and until the Arbitration Act 1996 there were few free-thinking and robust arbitrators who could handle a multi-party arbitration.

As most standard forms of contract, prior to the wholesale updates of 1998 prompted by the introduction by statute of Adjudication, provided only for arbitration, the perceived wisdom was that it must necessarily be the preferred option. Consequently, rarely were such standard arbitration clauses deleted in head contracts, and when a dispute arose litigation was often not an option—until *Crouch* was overturned in the courts in 1998.

In considering the relative merits of the two processes, prior to the late 1990s, one might have listed the following aspects:

— **In favour of arbitration**
   A private procedure.
   Parties had the opportunity to choose own "judge".
   Parties could choose own venue.
   Parties could in theory agree own timetable.
   Technical matters would be more familiar to a technical "judge".
   Arguably a simpler, quicker and therefore more cost effective process.
— **In favour of litigation**
   A public procedure—sometimes a tactical advantage to the party claiming money etc.
   A free court and a free judge—paid for by the taxpayer.
   More certain quality of decision.
   Defendants less likely to abuse timetable.
   Ability to handle multi-party disputes.
   Less likelihood of appeal or non-compliance with judgment.

However, there was one major disadvantage to litigation—the problem of getting a trial date allocated in the old Official Referee's Court on a first fixture basis, and then Counsel on both sides actually being available when eventually required. Usually one's case would get a provisional date allocated, on a double or treble booking system, given that other cases might settle in the meantime—so with a trial date often two years away one would get on with other business, leaving the dispute unresolved. Not only would the removal of pressure greatly lessen the incentive to settle, but one could never be sure that one's key witnesses of fact would still be available, with their memories as sharp, two or more years later. It also meant that as Claimant one had to carry one's alleged losses that much longer.

1.5 THE CALL FOR CHANGE

By about 1995 it was common ground in the construction industry that there had to be a more efficient way of managing the inevitable disputes. So often, cases had become trials of commercial strength. Under the pre-1998 court procedures the basic rule as to costs was that "costs followed the event", i.e. the net winner took all, and subject to court taxation the net loser paid both sides' costs. Whilst this remains the basic position under the new provisions, judges now have far greater discretion to disallow or to split costs, so costs are no longer all or nothing. Inevitably, the all or nothing costs risk of the old system militated against the smaller trader, often a specialist sub-contractor with a genuine grievance against a much larger sub-contractor or main contractor.

Under the old court procedures—and retained under the new CPR—a Defendant could apply for Security for Costs on the basis that the Plaintiff was effectively insolvent and the claim might well fail, in which event why should the Defendant be at risk of not recovering the costs of having to defend an unfounded claim? Thus any Plaintiff in litigation, or Claimant in arbitration, had to be very sure of their case to contemplate the risk of losing and also the possibility of being ordered to pay a significant sum of money into court as security.

All too often the dispute concerned alleged non-payment, so the Claimant party was operating on extended overdraft—and the party trying not to be parted from the disputed money could make life as difficult as possible by simply using delaying tactics, quite apart from threatening a Security for Costs application. Further, until the Arbitration Act 1996 arbitrators had no effective power to enforce a proper timetable that would deliver a result within six months if the Respondent didn't wish to co-operate.

So when the major recession of the early 1990s set in, there was no fair and effective, let alone prompt, dispute resolution procedure available to an aggrieved party in the construction industry. Payment abuse of the smaller company by the bigger company became the "norm"—particularly the practice of "pay-when-paid" and extended payment terms. As a result sub-contractor insolvencies proliferated, delaying many projects, but out of this very unhappy period came the cry for change—not only in the regulation of the payment procedures in the construction industry, but also in the need to revisit the whole basis of access to justice and the effective management of the legal process.

This book is therefore intended to give a practical insight into:

— how construction claims must now be approached when they are first conceived;
— how the aggrieved client needs to be advised, including how he can manage the financial risks of bringing a claim;
— how the courts or arbitrators will now require both parties to have genuinely tried to have resolved the dispute themselves.

Part 1 will therefore deal with the basics of construction claims, including the developing area of professional negligence claims against

Consultants, and current case law. Part 2 will then hopefully give readers a comprehensive overview of the several important legislative measures enacted since 1996, which collectively now present the construction industry with new opportunities for better practice in the new millennium.

However, an important and recurring feature of this book is that a construction claim is often part of a much bigger picture. Like conveyancing of domestic property, one transaction is but one link in a supply chain, and if that link should fail for any reason it is likely to have a ripple effect on both upstream and downstream parties. The commercial property world, which underpins so much of the UK investment industry, needs the construction industry to become much more efficient, both in terms of actual performance and in not wasting so much time and money on disputes.

From the author's experience, over more than 35 years, most disputes arise on non-standard forms of contract or incomplete written exchanges at domestic sub-contractor level. Most of these are relatively low value disputes concerning the operative terms of the alleged contract when a payment problem arises. Hopefully these will now be largely dealt with, as and when they arise, by virtue of the Fair Payment Provisions and the Right to Adjudication, as a first stage dispute option, incorporated in the Housing Grants, Construction and Regeneration Act 1996.

Certainly it was the author's experience that disputes referred to adjudication under the old "Green" and "Blue" forms of JCT sub-contract almost inevitably settled on the basis of the adjudicator's decision—the losing party taking the commercial view that it would be foolish to risk serious money in taking the matter on to arbitration or litigation, i.e. an 80% certain decision for 5% of possible cost may be rough justice, but it is what the commercial world requires.

However, it is always going to be the bigger value disputes which are hardest to settle, and these will inevitably be at the top end of the supply chain, e.g. where serious overruns have occurred, or where defects have come to light and the investment is dead in the water in terms of income stream. Accordingly the emphasis in construction claims of the future is likely to be those involving contract cost and time overruns, and defects cases, rather than Final Account disputes *per se*. Another trend in construction claims is likely to be the increasing use of litigation insurance, both pre-event and post-event, and conditional fee arrangements.

The cultural revolution in the processing of construction claims, heralded by the Latham Report of 1994 and the Woolf Report of 1996, is here to stay—the "rules" are now far better defined and all parties can now approach the process on a risk management basis, with litigation being a last resort, available only when it can be shown that the dispute resolution process has otherwise been exhausted.

PART 1: PRACTICE AND PROCEDURE

CHAPTER 2

THE STANDARD FORMS OF CONTRACT AND STATUTE LAW

2.1 THE JCT FAMILY OF CONTRACTS

For building contracts, as opposed to civil engineering contracts, the best known standard forms of contract are those published by the Joint Contracts Tribunal (JCT), a representative body made up of nominees from:

> The Association of Consulting Engineers
> The British Property Federation
> The Construction Federation
> The Local Government Association
> The National Specialist Contractors Council
> The Royal Institute of British Architects
> The Royal Institution of Chartered Surveyors
> The Scottish Building Contracts Committee.

The current JCT Family of Contracts as between employer and contractor, where the former is responsible for design, consists of:

— the JCT Standard Form of Building Contract 1998 Edition, Private or Local Authorities versions, with or without Quantities— SFBC 98;
— the JCT Intermediate Form of Building Contract for works of a simple content 1998 Edition—IFC 98;
— the JCT Agreement for Minor Building Works 1998 Edition— AMBW 98;
— the JCT Standard Form of Management Contract 1998 Edition— SFMC 98;
— the JCT Standard Form of Prime Cost Contract 1998 Edition— SFPCC 98.

These JCT employer design contracts are then supported by the following contractor/sub-contractor standard forms of contract:

— JCT NSC/A 98—Articles of Nominated Sub-Contract Agreement for use with SFBC 98, Condition 35.6;
— JCT NSC/C 98—Nominated Sub-Contract Conditions for use with SFBC 98, Condition 35.6;
— JCT NAM/T 98—Form of Tender and Agreement for use with IFC 98, Condition 3.3;
— JCT NAM/SC 98—Sub-Contract Conditions for Sub-Contractors named under IFC 98, Condition 3.3;
— DOM 1 1990 Amendment 10 (1998)—Domestic Sub-Contractor Articles of Agreement for use with SFBC 98, Conditions 19.2 and 19.3 (published by the Construction Confederation)—no design input by the sub-contractor;
— DOM 1 1980 Edition reprinted 1990 to incorporate Amendment 9 (1990), with Amendment 10 (July 1999) as looseleaf insert—Domestic Sub-Contractor Conditions for use with SFBC 98, Conditions 19.2 and 19.3 (published by the Construction Federation)—no design input by the sub-contractor.
— DOM 2 1981 Edition reprinted 1992 to incorporate Amendment 7 (1992), with Amendment 8 (July 1999) as looseleaf insert—Domestic Sub-Contractor Conditions for use with SFBC 98, Conditions 19.2 and 19.3 (published by the Construction Federation)—partial design input by the sub-contractor.
— JCT IN/SC—Domestic Sub-Contract Articles of Agreement for use with IFC 98, Condition 3.2.
— JCT NSC/T(PCC98)—Nominated Sub-Contract Conditions for use with JCT PCC 98.

The above JCT Standard Forms of main contract and Sub-Contract are summarised in tabular format at Appendix A.

It should be noted that the 1998 general updating of the JCT family of Standard Forms of Contract was in response to the major revisions required to comply with the Housing Grants, Construction and Regeneration Act 1996 (HGCR Act 1996—see Chapter 9). For example old JCT 80 is now JCT SFBC 98, and old JCT WCD 81 is now JCT WCD 98.

Whilst the above account for the majority of contracts placed each year, particularly in the lower value range, there has been a distinct move away from employer designed contracts since 1980, shifting the design responsibility to the contractor, and this is covered by the JCT Standard Form of Building Contract With Contractor's Design 1998 Edition—WCD 98.

With the exception of JCT PCC 98 and WCD 98, the common theme of the above lump sum contracts between employer and contractor, where the former is responsible for all elements of design through his appointed design team, is that they are fixed-price and fixed-time contracts, subject to change in price or time only if so authorised by the Architect or the Contract Administrator. Thus a contract claim, as opposed to a common law or an *ex gratia* claim by the contractor, can only arise by reference to express provision of the standard clauses dealing with "What if?" scenarios concerning money and time.

Further, careful distinction must be made as to what constitutes:

— a Variation to the contract giving rise to an entitlement, if relevant, to an adjustment of the Contract Sum;
— an entitlement to an Extension of Time, which in principle must be administered by the Architect, with or without notice from the contractor, particularly where the contract provides for Liquidated and Ascertained Damages (LADs) in the event of the contractor failing to complete by the prescribed Due Date for Completion;
— a Claim for Loss and Expense—i.e. actual costs suffered by the contractor, over and above Variations, and as a result of the employer not fulfilling his prescribed contractual obligations—there being no direct linkage between Extension of Time Claims and Loss and Expense Claims, albeit there are usually common facts and causation.

It is therefore very necessary to present a contractual Claim according to the relevant clause and sub-clause of the signed contract, the relevant clauses of the JCT family being:

— **Extensions of Time**:
 JCT SFBC 98—Condition 25
 JCT IFC 98—Condition 2.3
 JCT AMBW 98—Condition 2.2
 JCT SFMC 98—Conditions 2.12 to 2.14
 JCT WCD 98—Condition 25
 JCT PCC 98—Condition 2.5
— **Loss and Expense**:
 JCT SFBC 98—Condition 26
 JCT IFC 98—Conditions 4.11 and 4.12
 JCT AMBW 98—Condition 3.6
 JCT SFMC 98—Condition 4.6
 JCT WCD 98—Condition 26.

In the past too many disputes reached the Official Referee's Court or arbitration simply because of uncertainty of contract drafting, including imprecision in the JCT Standard Forms of Contract—the JCT Standard Form of Management 1981 (now 1998) being an example of a compromise document when it comes to key areas of risk allocation.

In consequence the practice of amending Standard Forms of Contract became widespread among Solicitors and Quantity Surveyors drafting head contracts on behalf of employers—and not surprisingly main contractors soon got pretty adept at amending Standard Forms of Sub-Contract; one judge remarking that the resultant contract was so one sided that he found it surprising it was written on both sides of the paper!

Typical areas of uncertainty in JCT contracts, and therefore regular areas for dispute, are:

— the need for contractor's notices as a condition precedent to entitlement to a claim for Extension of Time or Loss and Expense;
— the contractual status of the contractor's programme;
— the logic and criticality of key activities in that programme;
— the effect of instructed Variations on that programme;
— the definition of Practical Completion, especially if the employer insists on taking partial possession in order to carry out commissioning works, e.g. computer cabling installations;
— the dual role of the Architect as the person responsible for the timely issue of the detailed design and also as the contract administrator on behalf of the employer, certifying Extensions of Time and the Relevant Events, some of which are not Listed Matters when it comes to cost reimbursement.

Any form of contract, whether a standard form or a bespoke contract, can never provide for all eventualities and on the best run contracts either the contractor or the Architect will take the lead at the first post-contract project meeting in tabling procedures to cover the operational details, e.g. drawing release and design freeze dates, and whether Variations over a value limit need agreement of cost or time implications before they can be acted upon, etc.

However, all too often a project will get under way based on an imprecise brief, an inadequate budget and design information substantially short of "Approved For Construction" (AFC) status. Equally contractors regularly take an "us" and "them" attitude from the outset, deliberately setting up a claim situation by naming unrealistically early dates by which they supposedly need final design information.

When it comes to dealing with contractual issues of money or time few Architects have any aptitude for the necessary debate, and are often only too pleased to delegate the issues, usually unofficially, to the Quantity Surveyor, although the latter has no such power under the standard JCT provisions. In the past, when Architects did accept that the contractor was entitled to an Extension of Time under Clause 25 of the old JCT 80, it was remarkable how often the Architect cited the Relevant Event as Condition 25.4.2, i.e. "exceptional weather conditions", which was not a Listed Matter under Condition 26, so giving the contractor no entitlement to Loss and Expense. Thus the tendency was for the contractors to ambush the employer late in the project with overstated claims, whether for time or money, but usually both, supported with voluminous appendices.

On the other hand, an early and properly reasoned outline claim submission enables the Architect to deal with the issues with a fresher memory and hopefully a more open mind. It also enables the employer to allow for the additional funding in good time and for the contractor's Programme to Completion to be objectively reappraised.

Thankfully the JCT has taken the opportunity offered by the HGCR Act 1996, and the statutory requirement for adjudication, to carry out a comprehensive review of the standard clauses, rather than issue piecemeal amendments driven by evolving case law, and to incorporate most of the Latham Report recommendations—see Chapter 8.

As such, JCT SFBC 98 now offers standard provisions, which of course may be amended or deleted, covering:

— simple interest on late payments at 5% over base rate—Condition 30.1.1.1;
— an Information Release Schedule (Sixth Schedule and Condition 5.4.1)—which once agreed commits the employer to supplying agreed information by agreed dates, but still allows the contractor the option of changing his preferred construction sequence;
— payment for materials and goods off site secured by an "On-demand" Bond in favour of the employer—Condition 30.3.1;
— the option—Condition 13A—borrowed from the Supplementary Provisions of the old JCT WCD 81, of making the agreement of cost and time a condition precedent to the authorisation of a Variation;
— provisions for partial possession by the employer—Condition 18;
— the option of litigation or arbitration expressed by way of alternative clauses—Condition 41.

JCT WCD 98 also has a standard provision at Condition 30.1.1.2 allowing for an advance payment to be made by the employer, presumably in acknowledgement of the upfront design costs already incurred, and to be incurred, by the design and build contractor. This is payable only when the contractor has delivered an "On-demand" Bond, subject to agreed call notice requirements, which should be attached to the Bond.

2.2 THE STANDARD FORMS OF ENGINEERING CONTRACT

The most popular standard forms of contract for works involving civil engineering on UK projects are the ICE family of contracts, although it is to be expected that the New Engineering Form of Contract will gain ground progressively as more practitioners and lawyers come to know and trust it. The standard ICE Form of Contract for Works of Civil Engineering Seventh Edition, first published in September 1999, now provides for the statutory right of either party to a construction contract to call for adjudication following the HGCR Act 1996. Some clauses have been substantially amended and the running order of clauses has been revised in certain areas. It also includes a model form of Performance Bond, written in plainer English than most Bonds and applicable only in the event of insolvency or expulsion of the contractor from the site in accordance with the default provisions of the contract—see Appendix B.

Other standard ICE forms of contract are:

— ICE Design and Construct Conditions of Contract 1992;
— ICE Conditions of Contract for Minor Works: 2nd Edition 1995;
— the Engineering and Construction Contract 2nd Edition with Options A to F covering various procurement options, and The Engineering and Construction Subcontract;
— the Engineering and Construction Short Contract 1999;
— the Professional Services Contract: 2nd Edition 1998;
— the Adjudicator's Contract: 2nd Edition 1998—accompanied by Guidance Notes and Flow Charts.

Unsurprisingly the Engineer remains in his dual role of designer and contract administrator, and the old system of the contractor being required to refer any contentious issue back to the Engineer for reconsideration is also retained, before having the right to open an Arbitration. The question is therefore: how does this sit with the provision of the HGCR Act 1996 giving the contractor the statutory right to adjudication at any time?

The ICE 7th tries to take care of this question, but commentators are less than convinced that it could not be challenged. At Condition 66 the concept of a "Matter of Dissatisfaction" is introduced and then at 66(3) both parties agree that no dispute can arise until after the Engineer has had a further month to reconsider the matter.

As the dispute may well involve design or quality of construction, or temporary works, or permanent works about to be covered up, time may be vital. Equally it may be a payment dispute and the fundamental principle set out in the HGCRA 1996 of getting such disputes resolved by adjudication within 28 days to protect project cash flow is flouted if the adjudicator cannot even be called for until a full calendar month or more has elapsed. The betting must be on employer's solicitors when setting up the head contract amending Condition 66(3) to read "Except in respect of matters of valuation and payment ...".

The ICE 7th might also be criticised for not having taken cognisance of the Woolf reforms and the Civil Procedure Rules by only providing at Condition 66(5) for Conciliation or Arbitration—there is no option as in the JCT SFC 98 for litigation, short of amending the standard contract.

The New Engineering Contract (NEC) is a genuine attempt by the Institute of Civil Engineers to write a standard model contract with variants covering the various forms of procurement ranging from lump sum to cost reimbursable, with or without contractor's design. Its guiding principle, following the thinking in the Latham Report, was the identification of risk, and the allocation thereof to the party best able to quantify, price and manage that risk.

Unfortunately disaster struck, rather like the *Titanic*, on its first real test when the Austrian method of tunnelling collapsed, on a major project at Heathrow Airport. Luckily there was no loss of life, but substantial above-ground damage and disruption was caused, and thousands of tonnes of concrete were hurriedly needed below ground to make sure that there were no further collapses. By the time that the full remedial and diversionary works were complete the various claims and counterclaims were massive, and so eventually came to court—the contractor being prosecuted by the Health and Safety Executive.

Despite the best intentions of the ICE drafting committee, apparently the judge was critical of the contract arrangement, finding it very muddled as to allocation of design, temporary works and permanent works risks and the contractor was heavily fined for not having reported the matter to the authorities when it became evident that a collapse was almost certain, with the Piccadilly line tunnel only 75m away.

Finally it should be mentioned, considering the large volume of overseas civil engineering contracts carried out by the UK construction industry, that the first cousins of the ICE standard forms of contract are those issued by FIDIC—Federation Internationale des Ingenieurs-Conseils.

These now come in eight standard forms:

— FIDIC Conditions of Contract: 4th edition (Red) 1987

— FIDIC Client/Consultant Model Services Agreement: 3rd edition (White) 1998
— FIDIC Conditions of Contract for Electrical and Mechanical Works 3rd edition (Yellow) 1987
— FIDIC Conditions of Contract for Design, Build and Turnkey (Orange) 1995
— FIDIC Conditions for EPC Turnkey Projects: Test Contract (Silver) 1998
— FIDIC Conditions for Plant and Design and Build: Test Contract (Yellow) 1998
— FIDIC Conditions of Contract for Construction: Test Contract (Red) 1998
— FIDIC Short Form of Contract: Test Contract (Green) 1998.

2.3 THE LATE PAYMENT OF COMMERCIAL DEBTS (INTEREST) ACT 1998

Ever since the House of Lords' decision in *London Chatham and Dover Railway* v. *South Eastern Railway* (1893) it has not generally been possible to recover damages for the late payment of a debt. The courts had taken the view, in the absence of specific contract provision, that this was a matter of public policy and so it was for Parliament, not the courts, to change the law, if it was considered appropriate. Parliament has now so provided and has empowered the Secretary of State to set and revise the statutory rate of interest payable from time to time.

On the stated principle that "... to prevent the smallest of businesses suffering because they have to borrow overdraft finance to cover their late paid bills at a higher rate of interest than the base rate plus 4% as originally proposed" the initial rate set is the Bank of England base rate, plus 8%.

The Act allows parties to set their own terms for the date that interest is to run from, and for a rate to be agreed, but:

— if not expressly provided in the contract, interest is to run from the later of 30 days after (a) the date of provision of goods or services, or (b) the date of invoice receipt;
— any agreed rate of interest must represent a substantial remedy for late payment; and
— it must represent a deterrent to late payment.

There is then a proviso to the effect that it must be fair and reasonable in all the circumstances to allow the remedy—so here we have a whole new area for disputes!

For the JCT, who anticipated this legislation but have prescribed a rate of 5% over base rate, this could mean a further amendment dealing with the rate of interest, and the ICE will almost certainly be in trouble having prescribed a rate of interest of only 2% above base rate in their September 1999 published new 7th Edition.

However the Act's most profound influence on the construction industry will be at the next level down in the supply chain, where most sub-contracts are placed on anything but a standard form of contract. All of a sudden the boot will be on the other foot with a vengeance—why not borrow at base rate plus say 4%, and being sure of collecting at base rate plus 8%, why bother to chase a debt? Equally, if you are the paying party, why risk losing 4%? So why not pay promptly when paid yourself—i.e. a different version of the old pay-when-paid game?

It should therefore make good sense for employers to set up project Trust Funds, topping up the pot according to projected Interim Valuation figures, with an agreed minimum balance secured by an Advance Payment Bond. This will secure the main contractor's position. There can then be no excuse, or indeed commercial sense, in the main contractor not paying sub-contractors promptly, and in turn those sub-contractors passing the money promptly down the supply chain—at least in theory.

The Act sensibly contains various operative and phased provisions, including the following:

— Effective from 1 November 1998 it only applies to "Small businesses" (defined as employing 50 or fewer full-time or part-time operatives at the date of the relevant contract) chasing debts from "Large businesses" (conversely those firms employing over 50 operatives) or from public sector organisations.
— Proposed, but not yet enacted, it is planned to extend the scheme to "Small businesses" v. "Small businesses" in November 2000, and to all sizes of business v. all debtors in November 2002.
— Parties may not contract out or avoid the statutory provisions by setting artificially low interest rates or by setting extended credit terms.

How this is all going to be made to work in the construction industry and whether the JCT 5% rate of interest over base rate will be considered a sufficient remedy has yet to be seen. A key issue will be the date from which the debt will run, i.e. when does a payment become "late" and sensibly the JCT has opted for the "Final Date for Payment" as required by the HGCR Act 1996.

However, what is certain is that the test of the system will come bottom up in the construction industry, i.e. it will be the small sub-contractors operating under main contractors' bespoke contracts, and not JCT standard forms of sub-contract, who will be shouting the odds for payment of interest at base rate plus 8%!—and then calling for adjudicators when not so rewarded, but at the very real risk of not being invited to tender the next job!

This means that if the bespoke sub-contract is foolishly silent as to the right to interest on late payment, main contractors will have to fund any excess in the rate, over and above their rate of recovery under the main contract, i.e. the JCT proposed 5%. Thus the whole monthly valuation procedure will necessarily become a tightly programmed operation with predetermined dates for payment approval and cheque issue action points right down the supply chain. In theory we should then see the discontinuance of the present practice of the sub-contractors agreeing a contract sum with the main contractor and then each month allowing the main contractor to deduct 2.5% discount—supposedly for prompt payment! Inevitably the Act will lead to a new class of dispute, but overall it should be an improvement on the old system of non-transparency in the cash flow process.

With the almost universal use of computers there is no reason why the monthly valuation made by the Architect or Engineer, on the recommendation of the Quantity Surveyor, should not be published for all to see with coded Bill references and declared percentages of work done on the project—but no monetary values. Authorised Variations could be similarly presented in sub-Bill format. All sub-contractors, and in turn sub-sub-contractors, would then use the declared percentages, applied to their own unit rates, and submit their computer generated invoice accordingly. Thus the whole process would be transparent.

If the main contractor has any internal contra charges to levy he should notify them in reasonable detail at the same time, so the Notice of Withholding Payment should become the exception rather than the rule—with both parties able to discuss the merit of any contra charges in good time before the "Final Date for Payment".

The Quantity Surveyor, or the adjudicator if named up front in the main contract, could act as project cash flow policeman and ensure on a no-nonsense basis that all parties behave themselves, and in particular that any Notice of Withholding is properly reasoned and quantified.

Another potential problem area is whether a contractor might success-fully contend that the statutory right to interest at an arguably penal rate takes precedence over the statutory right of a sub-contractor to suspend work in the event of continued non-payment after due notice under the HGCR Act 1996 Fair Payment Provisions, as now incorporated in JCT SFBC 99. Seemingly the answer is "No" given the existing provisions, but one can just see a "No loss" argument coming, given the penal rate of interest payable—so why should the sub-contractor have a further remedy?

From the employer's point of view a culpable delay caused by the main contractor having a spat with a sub-contractor, who then suspends work, is bad news. So maybe the contract conditions ought to give precedence to the right to interest on late payment—stipulating that the right to suspend work can only arise after a prescribed period of non-payment, allowing the contractor the option of having organised an adjudication on the particular issue.

Equally is it a "dispute" between the employer and main contractor if the project is delayed, given the scenario above—and could the employer commence an adjudication requiring the main contractor and sub-contractor to adjudicate? Howls of legal protest seem likely, but the Late Payment of Commercial Debts (Interest) Act will make for interesting times ahead in more ways than one!

2.4 THE CONTRACTS (RIGHTS OF THIRD PARTIES) ACT 1999

This legislation, now in force since 11 May 2000, arose from the Law Commission Report (No. 242) published in 1996, which reviewed the doctrine of privity of contract, and has caused considerable debate ever since.

In the context of the commercial property world where developments are often traded on by the original employer, sometimes even before Practical Completion, it is essential that as many safeguards as possible are put into the head contract to protect the investment value and future income stream.

Apart from ensuring so far as possible that the project is built to time and budget it is essential to provide for the recovery of losses should the building not prove to be defects free and become unlettable. For example, a City of London office block that suffers a major curtain walling failure will not only incur very substantial direct costs in recladding, but also potentially even greater indirect costs in terms of loss of rental income, decant costs, alternative accommodation costs and general diminution in market value even when reclad.

The employer and his funder will therefore wish to protect their investment value by making sure, in the event that they wish to sell on at some future date, that the investment value is underpinned by the right of a future freeholder or leaseholder to recover against the contractor, his sub-contractors (contractors having been known to cease trading when major defects are discovered), or against the consultants as applicable.

Thus the practice of Collateral Warranties has evolved to get round the long established legal principle that only parties in contract with one another can have the right to recover damages from the other when things go wrong, i.e. the employer is likely to require that his position be ring-fenced by the contractor, principal sub-contractors and consultants agreeing to be bound in contract to a third party who may at some future date acquire a commercial interest in the development.

This Act should now make Collateral Warranties unnecessary, in theory, as it now provides that a third party may enforce a term of the contract where:

— the third party is expressly given rights of recovery in the construction contract;
— a term of the construction contract purports to confer such rights on a third party who is named, or identified by class or description.

This last provision for an as yet unidentified third party, who may not even be a trading entity at the time the construction contract is signed, is exactly what the property world requires, in order to guard against those latent defects which can so easily wreck an otherwise sound investment. There is also a rebuttable presumption of an intention to confer a legal right, but there is no prohibition on specifically excluding this Act by express provision in the construction contract.

The Standard Form of Architect's Appointment 1999 and the ACE Conditions of Engagement, being Consultants' standard documentation, have both seized on the lack of prohibition in the Act, and have specifically shut out Third Parties from the consequences of their members' future conduct.

In theory Third Party rights will be two-way traffic, down as well as up the supply chain, i.e. sub-contractors being given the right to sue employers if the contractor ceases to trade, subject to provisions guarding against double recovery. However, in practice the interests of sub-contractors will not be very high on the agenda of solicitors acting for employers when setting up development agreements and head contracts, so it remains to be seen to what extent obligations as well as rights in respect of Third Parties are provided for.

Generally speaking, property and construction lawyers are not enthusiastic about this Act, taking the view that the old red braces are more certain to do the job than the new unproven belt—so Collateral Warranties are probably here to stay for some time yet. Perhaps the solution is to focus on reality: what does the property investment industry actually need? A suggested "shopping list" might be:

— step-in rights for funders;
— the right of a Third Party to sue for design or workmanship defects;

— a prescribed net contribution clause to fairly limit consultants' liability.

At least this Act should put an end to the "No loss" defences put up by contractors and consultants, who, when sued for defects, claimed that the Plaintiff was a different company, albeit closely related, from the company with whom they had contracted—so lending weight to the Court of Appeal decision in *Alfred McAlpine Construction* v. *Panatown Limited* (1998).

2.5 THE CIVIL EVIDENCE ACT 1995

The previous rule was that "hearsay" evidence was inadmissible in both litigation and arbitration, and short of calling a potentially hostile witness there was no way of getting certain key evidence in. This caused particular difficulties to Rent Review disputes, where comparable market rental levels are usually the determining factor. Previously, the Agent who had acted in the review being relied on would have had to be called as a witness in the current Rent Review, but often he would be bound by a confidentiality agreement or other conflict of interest, so would not be available.

In construction disputes a similar problem often arises, particularly where sub-contractor A is pursuing the main contractor and he needs to bring in key evidence, freely obtained from sub-contractor B, on an informal basis. However as sub-contractor B is still hopeful of achieving a realistic Final Account settlement himself with the main contractor, or is looking to future business, he is often not prepared to give a witness statement or appear on behalf of sub-contractor A.

This Act therefore relaxes the old position on "hearsay" evidence, and gives discretion to judges and arbitrators, subject to six tests:

— Whether it really is unrealistic to call the original source of the evidence now being relied on.
— Whether the original statement was made contemporaneously.
— Whether the evidence involves multiple "hearsay".
— Whether anyone involved has a motive to conceal or misrepresent matters.
— Whether the original statement may have been an edited account, made in collaboration with another or made for a particular purpose.
— Whether the circumstances in which the "hearsay" evidence is adduced suggests an attempt to prevent a proper evaluation of its weight.

However, the "best" evidence will always be that given by a witness of fact from his own personal observation and "hearsay" evidence must always be carefully considered as to its true worth, bearing in mind the possible motive and credibility of the person offering it.

2.6 THE ACCESS TO JUSTICE ACT 1999

The main provision of this final part of the reforms called for by the Woolf Report deals with the reform of the previous legal aid system—which was rightly criticised on the one hand for assisting individuals patently well able to afford to pay their way in litigation (but employing "clever" accountants), but on the other hand for refusing assistance to many other oppressed individuals, who equally patently had no available funds.

As regards the construction industry, legal aid was not available to companies, so except in one case where a private individual managed to take on a major contractor with the benefit of legal aid, it did not feature— *Fakes* v. *Taylor Woodrow Construction Ltd* (1973).

Thus short of having purchased a "Pre-Event" litigation costs insurance policy a small sub-contractor, wishing to pursue a much larger company for payment of monies due and unpaid, was distinctly disadvantaged in that:

(a) The larger company could, prior to the HGCR Act 1996, give a multitude of excuses for non-payment and there was usually no way of disproving them.

(b) The larger company would often pay part of the sum due with a promise of full payment later (rarely honoured), and in the absence of an express right under the contract to suspend work, the smaller company had little option but to continue working, borrowing further funds, but with no right to interest on the debt.

(c) If the smaller company started litigation or arbitration the larger company could apply for Security for Costs, on the basis that the smaller company might not be able to pay the costs awarded against them should the Plaintiff not win his case—and if the application was granted the smaller Plaintiff company would have to borrow yet further funds (unchanged under the new provisions).

(d) The larger company could then use their Defendant position to put the smaller company to proof of their allegations using the old "White Book" rules, generally slowing the action and making the smaller company incur undue and unexpected further costs—all to the detriment of trying to keep trading their existing business.

(e) The larger company could then usually afford to employ more expensive, and arguably more able, legal advice and representation.

None of these disadvantages were lost on Lord Woolf, so this Act also sets out to provide, so far as possible, a "level playing field" between the parties—one example being the capping of recoverable costs, although there is no bar on either party spending what they choose to spend on legal advice, provided that they do so at their own expense, win or lose.

This Act then goes on to deal with how an impecunious Claimant may bring a case on the basis of a "No Win No Fee" or Conditional Fee Arrangement, but as these matters are very relevant to how a case might be managed by a Claimant with limited funds these are more fully addressed in Chapter 12.

2.7 THE HUMAN RIGHTS ACT 1998

This UK legislation was introduced as a result of having acceded to the European Convention on Human Rights and is very much concerned with giving the individual the right to protection from alleged oppression by the state or its systems. Starting with the right to life, the Articles go on to require "public authorities" to provide a fair and public hearing for individuals with grievances. "Public Authorities" are then defined as either:

(a) A Court or Tribunal
(b) Any person having functions of a public nature.

Arbitrations are undoubtedly within the definition of "Tribunal" and are of course not public hearings, so it remains to be seen whether the Arbitration Act 1996 will need to be amended, or whether an exception will be made to the Human Rights Act 1998. It also remains to be seen whether the requirements of the Human Rights Act conflict in any way with the drive for courts, rather than the parties and their solicitors, to manage disputes.

Similarly, will adjudication under the HGCR Act 1996 survive in its present form? Or will it be held to be a private process, and therefore non-public—despite it being only a first-stage process? Only time will tell.

CHAPTER 3

CLASSES OF CONSTRUCTION CLAIMS

3.1 SUB-CONTRACTOR CLAIMS

The supply chain on a construction project is rather like pyramid selling or a chain letter—the lower down the chain you are, the more there are of you. It also follows that the lower you are in the chain the more diluted the original message has become—typically terms and conditions will have been changed, inevitably in favour of the purchaser and not you, the supplier, of the service being sought. Quite possibly the actual definition of price will have changed, e.g. you may be asked to bid your minor piece of the overall jigsaw on a drawings and specification basis, whereas further up the chain price is defined by a Bill of Quantities.

Thus it is at the sub-contractor and sub-sub-contractor level on any project that there is the greatest potential for disputes, not only because there are more such agreements, but because of lack of definition and the fact that more often than not the sub-contract paperwork and the tender responses are being handled by individuals with little formal training, if any, in legal matters.

Almost inevitably disputes at this level concern proper value and payment for work done in the first instance—and typically time and quality only come into the picture by way of counterclaim and set-off defences, belatedly raised by the unwilling payer, upstream in the supply chain.

In the bad old days before the HGCR Act 1996 this unregulated system of domestic sub-contracting lent itself to payment abuse—the larger purchasing organisation having the superior bargaining position over the smaller supplying organisation, from tender right through to final payment. Main contractors became pretty adept at playing this game, and leading by bad example—so the practice of writing in "pay-when-paid clauses" and progressively increasing payment periods down the sub-contractor supply chain was common. This meant that the proverbial small "man and a dog" outfit, at the end of the chain, had no real prospect of seeing his money for work done until at least two, if not three months later—and that was assuming no other two parties further up the supply chain had in the meantime had a falling out and broken the chain, stopping the cash flow process.

The late Lord Denning was the son of a village draper and the law was in fact his second career. He first won a £30 p.a. scholarship to Oxford at the age of 16 and then got a first in Pure Mathematics either side of war service. Lord Denning then joined the staff of Winchester College teaching Maths and Geology for the salary of £350 p.a. and one day wandered into the public gallery at the Winchester Assizes soon realising his true calling was the law. So back to Oxford he went, in search of another scholarship, duly obtained from the Trustees of Magdalene College. A year later Lord Denning had obtained another first and then joined chambers in Lincoln's Inn. Not only was Lord Denning hugely determined, but above all, having done it the hard way, he was a realist who went out of his way to give legal decisions in the context of the commercial world wherever possible.

Many years later Lord Denning recognised the ills besetting the construction industry, long before Sir Michael Latham was appointed to write his Report of 1994, saying in the case of *Dawnays* v. *F.G. Minter* (1971): "There must be cash flow in the building trade. It is the very lifeblood of the enterprise." Lord Denning then focused on the plight of the unpaid sub-contractor. "He is out of pocket; probably has an overdraft at the bank. He cannot go on unless he is paid for what he does. The main contractor is in a like position. He has to pay his men and buy his materials. He has to pay his sub-contractors. He has to have cash from the employer, otherwise he will not be able to carry on. So once the Architect gives his certificate, they must be honoured all down the line."

Interestingly Lord Denning then continued: "One of the greatest threats to cash flow is the incidence of disputes. Resolving them by litigation is frequently lengthy and expensive. Arbitration in the construction industry is often as bad or worse."

Often in the past one would be consulted by a small specialist sub-contractor who started a project on the basis of quotation, negotiation, revised quotation and some form of informal written acceptance. Three months later, and after the project was well under way, a formal but bespoke main contractor's form of sub-contract would arrive out of the blue. Usually this would be from the head office legal or purchasing department, requiring immediate signature and sometimes suspending payments until signed and returned. Sometimes they were pretty good "look-alikes" for well known standard forms of sub-contract—even in one case being typed in the same typeface, and using the same paragraph numbering and same page layout.

However, when cash flow problems arose and the sub-contracts had to be examined in detail, they would inevitably turn out to be exercises in pure risk dumping, typically requiring:

— Pay-when-paid.
— Discount for prompt payment (but discount taken even if late paid).
— Design responsibilities inserted, although the project was fully designed by the employer.
— Liquidated and Ascertained Damages values at the full main contract value, irrespective of value or criticality of the sub-contract works.
— Sub-contractor to be responsible for co-ordinating his works with other equal status sub-contractors.
— Continuity of working not guaranteed, yet sub-contractor expected to perform to contractor's programme, as revised without notice.
— Sub-contractor to be responsible for checking accuracy of preceding trade's work—typically structural steelwork.
— Sub-contractor to be responsible for protecting finished work, even when work completed and with no site presence to safeguard the protection.
— Sub-contractor not entitled to release of retention monies, partial or final, until retention releases under the main contract certified by the Architect.

As previously mentioned the principal payment abuses occurred simply because domestic sub-contractors had no means of knowing what had been certified in their favour each month, and when—unless the main contractor chose to tell them. However, a group of main contractors and major sub-contractors, under the title of "The Construction Round Table" has now published a voluntary Code of Conduct committing themselves, *inter alia*, to:

— fair dealing with sub-contractors;
— acting as team leaders in the interest of the project;
— accepting prompt third party dispute resolution.

One can always hope, but whatever Chief Executives might say, usually for dissemination and personal profile in the construction press, the reality is that contractors are usually public companies, or family owned, so they have their shareholders to account to. They must maximise profits, so they will usually only do their minimal best, and at site level this means cutting corners and driving hard bargains, if allowed to by the professional team—just the same as it always has been.

By way of example I offer two major "scams" from my experience of acting for Receivers of failed sub-contractors. The first concerned a multi-storey City of London office block. The Management Contractor had utterly lost control of the programme and was being hit for £25,000 LADs each week by the employer. There were still four major Works Package Contractors striving to complete the project; therefore, advised by eminent solicitors, the Management Contractor notified each of the four that they were delaying Practical Completion and deducted 4 × £25,000 each week until such time as they sorted out among themselves who had delayed whom, pocketing the excess £75,000 per week!

Needless to say, two of the sub-contractors couldn't afford to play this game and after several weeks they called in the Receiver. However, the real loser was the employer, who suffered a major further delay whilst replacement sub-contractors were brought in. Six months later when all was due to be handed over an IRA bomb remodelled the front elevation.

The second "scam" was a major government research and military "know-how" sales facility, designed and built against an impossible deadline. Sub-contractors for the very specialised mechanical and electrical services were generally paid about 60% of monthly valuation submissions, and were promised full payment when the not-to-be-missed completion date was somehow achieved when the government would inject the necessary top-up funds.

In the event, the completion date was achieved by swamping the project with labour, and the main contractor duly received a settlement payment of over £20m. Unfortunately the main contractor, and his subsidiary mechanical and electrical company, then changed the basis of their company accounts, as advised by eminent accountants. No part of the £20m appeared to have been paid out to the various specialist sub-contractors, who had actually delivered the project against all odds, several of whom were put out of business—with houses and marriages being lost in the process.

In the author's opinion such practices are contrary to the public interest and should be reported to the authorities for investigation by the Fraud Squad, as they think fit. Hopefully the HGCR Act 1996 and the statutory right to adjudication will prevent such future abuses, but both of the above abusers were well respected, supposedly "best practice" main contractors.

Thus the most usual problem confronting sub-contractors when they need to bring a claim is proving the existence and actual terms of the sub-contract. They then have the problem of proving facts as facts—the larger organisation whom they are pursuing inevitably having greater resources to administer the project and maintain the necessary records.

On the other hand, the party being pursued may well have a claim of its own, against say the main contractor, and will have written letters and run arguments blaming the main contractor or the Architect for late release of information, etc. As there can but be one version of the truth the middle party is often caught facing both ways, both in terms of liability and in terms of existing correspondence, so it is often crucial to the Claimant to be able to obtain disclosure—the mere threat of applying for specific documentation sometimes being sufficient to promote an improved settlement offer.

By way of example, several years ago the author was the appointed Quantity Surveyor on a major shopping development and the main contractor asked whether, as he was seeking BS 5750 Quality Control accreditation, he could include his quality control documentation in all the finishings and fit-out package enquiries. Seemingly the contractor had trialled the documentation on another large project, so I asked to see the completed paperwork to assess its relevance from the client's perspective. This was duly produced on a confidential basis—and it measured nearly a metre high when stacked on the floor of the author's office.

Six years later the author found himself acting for an insolvent sub-contractor against the same main contractor on the trial quality control project. After obstruction in settling our delay and loss and expense claims we commenced arbitration. In due course we applied for Specific Discovery—top of our list was "Quality Control documentation measuring approximately one metre high, if stacked on the floor". All of a sudden we were invited to settlement talks, and came away having improved the Receiver's position by over £150,000!

In some standard forms of sub-contract the party receiving a claim, whether for money or time, undertakes to pass it to a third party up the supply chain—and expressly or impliedly undertakes to pass any benefit achieved back down the line. However, in the past this has been a wholly unsatisfactory process, as due to the sanctity that privity of contract has been held in, rarely has Party C ever been allowed to know when or where an arbitration between Party A and B was being held. Usually Party A and Party B had bigger and better arguments of their own, and Party C's claim was a relative sideshow. In these circumstances Party C had no right of attendance, let alone audience, at the arbitration, and clearly there could be little motive for Party B to press the claim of C.

It is therefore important that specialist sub-contractors do not accept any clause that limits their rights to bring a claim. If the purchasing party wishes to pass that claim up the supply chain he should do so in his own name, with or without the support of Party C, either allowing Party C full knowledge and attendance at the hearing, *or* settling separately with Party C, before proceeding against Party A.

However, the reality is that thanks to the HGCR Act 1996 the aggrieved sub-contractor can now call for an adjudicator as and when a dispute first arises. Assuming the adjudicator finds in his favour and the party up the supply chain has to pay and doesn't like it, the boot is on the other foot. The purchasing party must now institute arbitration or litigation to reverse the decision and recover his money. Alternatively he must pursue adjudication on his own behalf up the supply chain.

Thus it is at this lowest level of the construction industry supply chain that the HGCR Act 1996 is having the most beneficial effect—but there is still no substitute for sub-contractors, too small to employ qualified staff, taking proper professional advice when being invited to tender on non-standard forms of sub-contract, or when the all-important cash flow stops flowing.

For a relatively modest fee construction solicitors or claims consultants will be pleased to carry out a contract terms and conditions audit—and, if required, negotiate with the purchaser. In due course this could prove to be money very well spent. Similarly, it costs relatively little to obtain proper advice on how to bring an adjudication against a non-paying party, especially as the adjudication process is essentially a 28-day (maximum) dispute resolution process—see Chapter 9 for further details.

3.2 MAIN CONTRACTOR CLAIMS

The problem so often experienced on sub-contract disputes of fundamental contract uncertainty is less frequently found at the next level up in the supply chain. Inevitably the head contract for the build-out phase of the development will have been placed on a standard form of contract, usually one of the JCT Family of Contracts or one of the Engineering contracts referred to at Chapter 2, or a heavily amended variant thereof. Just occasionally will an employer be devious enough to insist on a bespoke contract.

Whichever standard form of contract may have been selected, it may not have been the correct procurement route or the most appropriate standard form, given the nature of the project, but at least both parties have so agreed and are therefore bound by a well proven set of rules. However, problems can arise on large schemes where there are several parties to a development agreement and wherein the construction contract is but part of the larger jigsaw.

Acting as monitor for the bank or other funder, the author has on various occasions been belatedly asked to look at contractual arrangements, inevitably as work is about to start, or has actually started on site. On one such negotiated brewery development scheme, to be procured on the old JCT WCD 81, there were:

— Solicitor A—representing the Developer
— Solicitor B—representing the Employer (Brewery)
— Solicitor C—representing the Contractor
— Solicitor D—representing the Funder.

All four were London practices, two with commercial property departments offering construction advice, and two having recognised Construction law departments.

On examining the heavily amended JCT WCD 81 Standard Form of Contract we had to advise the Funder that:

— The Preliminaries to the Bills of Quantities stated that a Bond was required and there was enclosed a tortuously worded draft Bond as an Appendix, which was entirely unclear as to whether it was intended to be an "On demand" or "Performance" Bond.

— Elsewhere in the documentation it stated "No Bond Required".

— There was no provision as to who would act as the all-important "Employer's Agent" administering the contract.

— The Supplementary Provisions requiring pre-agreement of Changes, both in terms of cost and time, had been opted in, but there was no provision for appointing an adjudicator—very necessary should the Employer fail to agree the Contractor's proposed additional cost or time.

— This was because no individual had been named as adjudicator in the contract and the appointment fell to be made by the arbitrator—but the arbitration clause had been deleted.

The old proverb about too many cooks springs to mind, but really one of the four supposed construction lawyers ought to have spotted the nonsenses—and of course we got no thanks when the funder told them all to think again and quickly!

In the author's experience Main Contractor Claims are more often brought as a defensive mechanism as against the risk of late completion, which gives the employer the right on most contracts to deduct Liquidated and Ascertained Damages (LADs to use the JCT terminology).

No doubt there are often genuine grounds such as the issue of Architect's Instructions or late release of required construction drawings, but equally many Extension of Time Claims are conceived because the contractor has problems of his own, which are so often the result of under-pricing the tender or lack of site control in the early stages.

The basic principle is that it is not for the employer and the design team to tell the contractor *how* to build the project, only *what* to build, so it is entirely up to the contractor how he delivers the project. Equally, it is a basic rule that the contractor is not late until he has failed to achieve the required completion date—as stated in the contract, or as extended by the Architect or Engineer according to the provisions of the contract. However, it is always advisable for the employer to take particular care in setting up project records to monitor the contractor's actual site performance and to entrust this task to the Structural Engineer or the Quantity Surveyor if there is no appointed Clerk of Works.

One such contract, which the author inherited from month 1 on site, had "trouble" written all over it; it was hurriedly let on JCT 80 (supposedly fully designed) to avoid a change in Value Added Tax (VAT) legislation, when a JCT 1989 Management Contract would have been the better option. The piling sub-contractor was also a subsidiary of the Main Contractor.

Demonstrably the piling sub-contractor opted for the wrong piling sequence, at least three successive labour-only sub-contractors jacked before the last pile cap was built and then the structural steel erectors took over the site. The Main Contractor was warned in various forms as to his site progress, but the reply was usually fairly blunt and disdainful. When the contractor's claim arrived in the author's site office at about month 12 we were ready—a typed outline counterclaim was in the bottom drawer, listing all the hours of site non-productivity, typically piling rigs not starting until 8.45 a.m. instead of 8.00 a.m. and 40 + steel erectors regularly taking an hour for breakfast in their own canteen before even thinking about work.

The other regular areas for main contractor claims are:

— Agreement of the proper value of Variations.
— Loss and Expense, i.e. disruption of the normal progress of the works resulting in financial loss not otherwise recovered under the contract.

As already touched on in Chapter 2 there is a general recognition that there must be more openness as between employers and contractors from before the start on site. Part of this openness is the acceptance that a standard form of contract, however detailed, can only be a framework agreement—the actual working details have to be bolted on according to the requirements of the particular project where the contract is otherwise silent.

Lack of certainty is the underlying cause of most disputes, so if both parties can agree who is taking which risk before the risk materialises, and put in place a procedure for early notification of problems the likelihood of claims arising must be substantially diminished.

On larger projects it is now usual to appoint a project manager who is responsible to the employer for delivering the project on budget and on time, but with no executive authority to instruct the contractor. Sensibly, the individual or firm appointed should be unrelated to any member of the design team, whose functions under the contract remain the same—although some Architects find this an uncomfortable relationship. Equally some contractors consider a project manager just one more member of the employer's team, kicking the ball their way most of the time. However, the real knack of being a project manager is to be the independent chairman, knowing what needs to be done by whom, and when—but resisting the temptation of doing it oneself. An independent project manager with a good grip on programming issues and able to run a business meeting, with minutes issued promptly thereafter, soon gains the respect of both the contractor and the design team, and is probably the best insurance of all against disputes becoming serious claims.

One further feature of contractors' claims is that it is not unusual for the employer to be commercially a smaller company than the contractor and this in itself can cause problems and lack of trust.

Some contractors have an undoubted policy of bullying the inexperienced or financially embarrassed employer, by deliberately threatening legal action to promote forced settlements of otherwise unmeritorious claims, knowing that the employer simply cannot risk committing itself to the unknown cost of the legal process.

On the other hand it has been known for a development to be undertaken by a Sole Purpose Trading Company, and when a major arbitration was brought by the contractor, SPTC Ltd made it known that, should they lose, they would cease trading—a real "heads I win, or tails you lose" situation, but within the law.

All the above only emphasises the need for pre-contract certainty and trust between employers and contractors—and the overriding need for the professionals, starting with lawyers, to think laterally, defining the rules and the risks such that they can be fairly priced.

As such, the old concept, no doubt born out of the need for public accountability, that the lowest price was necessarily right may well be counterproductive for commercial developments. For such developments there is a price to be paid for certainty of delivery:

— on time;
— to budget;
— defects free;
— and, probably most important of all, claims free, as contractors' claims are usually synonymous with problems of one or more of the above three.

However, even with well drafted contracts there still have to be safeguards as regards certainty of being paid for work properly done, and employers are not entitled to assume they can require contractors to put up Bonds, etc, yet offer no security the other way.

Hopefully the construction industry will see a greater acceptance soon of the overseas practice of advance payments by employers, issued against inexpensive Advance Payment Bonds, and in particular the restriction of contractors' bonds in favour of employers to the single risk of contractor insolvency. If this can happen, together with practical developments of the fair payment and statutory right to adjudication provisions of the HGCR Act 1996, contractors' claims should become the exception rather than the rule, and only the really difficult claims will need to reach the courts.

A further class of main contractor claim concerns Bonds—either "On Demand" or Performance Bonds, where the Bondsman has guaranteed the performance and continuing existence of the sub-contractor until a defined date. Employers usually require the main contractor to produce a Bond for 10% of the contract value, so why should the main contractor not seek back-to-back protection with each of his sub-contractors?

The immediate problem is that the project becomes effectively double bonded, with the premium costs being borne indirectly by the employer, but in practical terms Bonds simply don't work for the following reasons:

— "On Demand" Bonds are a nonsense unless specifically limited to insolvency of the sub-contractor.
— Performance Bonds are often written in old-style English and even when in plain English are subject to inevitable dispute as to what constitutes non-performance—unless they provide for certification by an identified and independent third party.
— Even then the bondsman may well resist paying out on the basis of:
  (a) non-disclosure of material facts; or
  (b) there being a claim situation which has prejudiced the sub-contractor's ability to perform; or
  (c) that he wishes to take over the sub-contractor's obligations and get the work completed himself using his own sub-contractor.

It would be very interesting therefore if someone could factually tell the construction industry what percentage of sub-contractor Bonds are called by main contractors in a typical year, and of those called, how many are paid out without recourse to litigation. The author's guess is less than 5% and less than 20% respectively.

3.3 EMPLOYER CLAIMS

Although the standard forms of contract are generally skewed in favour of the employer, and not the contractor, i.e. Retention Funds, Performance Bonds, and Warranties, employers are often caught up in claims and must themselves pass claims on to others.

Employers' claims can therefore take any one of the following forms:

— An action against the contractor for defects, usually discovered after Practical Completion.
— An action against the contractor for delayed completion, but only where there is no contractual provision for Liquidated and Ascertained Damages.
— An action against any member of the design team for alleged faulty design, lack of site supervision, or failure to properly administer their element of the project works.
— An action against the Architect/Contract Administrator or the Employer's Agent for wrongful certification of time, money or quality.
— An action against the Quantity Surveyor for alleged negligence in allowing the project to exceed budget.
— An action against the Project Manager, if so appointed, for allowing the project to overrun in cost or time.
— An action against a Bondsman in the event of main contractor failure, e.g. insolvency, and the Bondsman not honouring the Bond for whatever reason.

Inevitably when things do go wrong there is a hunt for the guilty party, but rarely can a finger be clearly pointed at just one party. It may well be that the contractor has full or partial liability, but until it is tested in a court of law, this is unproven and the employer has to issue writs against members of the design team as well, using alternative pleadings—typically along the lines that if the building defect, e.g. cause of fire, is subsequently held not to have been fully attributable to bad workmanship then the Architect or Engineer may have some partial liability, e.g. poor design or failure to supervise.

The more common scenario of course is that employers are Defendants in actions brought by contractors concerning alleged entitlement to time and money, but often the employer will be counter-claiming in respect of alleged defective work. Employers' claims therefore come in a variety of forms, the most difficult perhaps being where the Architect has issued a Valuation or Extension of Time Certificate and the employer has grounds for challenging the certification.

In fact the author's first instruction as a quantum expert witness was just such a case. A rich Middle Eastern employer had signed a £450,000 refurbishment contract for his London house, and had given specific instructions that the interim valuation certificates were to be paid immediately on receipt by his London bank if signed personally by the senior partner of an eminent architectural practice. One day the bank manager happened to notice that the gross value was over £1,000,000, i.e.

more than twice the contract sum, so he called Riyadh.

The quantity surveyor had prepared some basic but inadequate cost reports and somehow these had not been passed on to the client by the Architect. Quite rightly the employer demanded a recount, and refused to honour the Interim Valuation until it had been verified and the unsanctioned overspend accounted for. A draft Final Account was prepared but this failed our audit, the project having been uncontrolled and the contractor having essentially been allowed to operate on an unauthorised cost-plus basis. So we advised defending the contractor's Order 14 Summary Judgment application.

Based on the author's affidavit we managed to set legal precedent in winning the Order 14 application—*Aggad* v. *Marshall Andrew* (1983 Unrep.), the Interim Valuation being set aside and the matter being stayed to Arbitration. Two years later we then got an Award by consent, reducing the claimed and certified value of the works by over £350,000, as well as all the substantial defects made good. However, the employer's real complaint was against the Architect and Quantity Surveyor, and we were only having to go against the contractor in order to prove the employer's loss, as then advised by Counsel. For reasons best known to himself the contractor chose not to call either the Architect or the Quantity Surveyor—presumably fearing the damage to be done by cross-examination. Equally we had no control of what they might say if we called them, so we had real evidential problems. As matters turned out, the evidence we managed to find on discovery of the project files was sufficiently damaging, but it was a close call and only a very wealthy client like ours could possibly have contemplated this high risk and costly strategy.

Employers who find themselves having to defend contractor's final account or loss and expense claims are often faced with having to rely on their consultants, notably the Architect or Contract Administrator, for the facts, so they need them on side—and inevitably such consultants have a position and a Professional Indemnity policy to protect.

Nevertheless some claims situations are so complex that commercial reality dictates that a "deal" be done with the contractor, and if the employer's loss is substantial there is nothing to stop the employer turning on the Architect, or as in one recent case on the Project Manager. The question then is: can the employer rely on the "deal" done with the contractor as evidence of his loss? The law currently takes a very narrow view, as discussed in Chapter 4.7, but given the move towards proportionality in costs of proving complex construction claims, hopefully there may be some relaxation in the current case law, subject of course to persuasive evidence that the "deal" done by the employer with the contractor was in all the circumstances justified.

3.4 FUNDERS' CLAIMS

Just occasionally there are deeper problems and despite all the paperwork, including Bonds and Warranties, the funder is left without recourse. One such disaster occurred a few years back on a mixed social housing and high quality development of five blocks of flats overlooking a marina.

As part of the deal with the Local Authority the two social housing blocks had to be built first. These were built and handed over, but before the contractor got very far with the three private sector blocks major defects emerged in the first two blocks. The Design and Build contractor promptly called in the Receiver and when the author's company was asked by the funder to carry out a full contract and defects audit a horror story emerged—not only was structural steel sourced from seven different countries, but there was an incestuous company relationship between the contractor, the novated Architect and the firm retained as Employer's Agent, who hadn't renewed his Professional Indemnity cover!

Suffice it to say the funder was faced with a £5.5m loss, and the only professional left with a current P.I. policy was a Quantity Surveying practice, who had failed to question the contractual arrangement and had failed to notice something was amiss when delays and defects first arose. The contractual arrangement was so obviously flawed that the funder's solicitors should also have been in the frame, but in the end the funder decided to sell the half-built development to the Local Authority for a hugely discounted price—and avoid all publicity.

3.5 LIMITATION

A key issue in any claim situation, and particularly when the issue is defects discovered long after Practical Completion, is when the cause of action arose —and therefore when the guilty party can escape under the law of limitation.

For a non-lawyer like the author, who finds this subject so confusing that it is best left entirely to the lawyers, it is perhaps comforting to read the recent Law Commission Report *Making the Law on Civil Limitation Periods Simpler and Fairer*. This found, *inter alia*:

— the existing law to be "uneven, uncertain and unnecessarily complex";
— that "... there is considerable variation between the limitation periods applicable to particular causes of action and no readily apparent reason for that."

Pending the Report finding its way into legislation, the current position can be summarised thus:

— in contract—six years from date of breach, unless it is signed by deed, i.e. under seal, in which case it is 12 years from the date of breach.
— in tort—in theory six years from the date of the tort being committed, but as most torts require proof of damage, in practice this means six years from discovery of damage, unless it involves latent damage, such as in building defects cases; where the defect is not discovered within six years then there is a limitation period of three years from the date the damage was capable of reasonably being discovered, subject to an overall limitation period of 15 years.

An example of the problems this can cause in practice was brought into sharp focus for all professionals and their Professional Indemnity insurers by *Chesham Properties* v. *Bucknall Austin Project Management* (1996). On a preliminary issues basis, on the presumption that the Structural Engineer had been negligent in his design, the central issue was whether other design professionals, notably the Project Managers, had also been negligent in their duty to warn the employer, i.e. whistle-blowing. The court held that they had been negligent.

Next the court decided that the Project Manager had a *continuing* duty to warn the employer of the Engineer's default *right up to the end of a six-year period*, starting from the date of the Project Manager's appointment, which had been secured by contract signed by hand on the same day as the appointment of the Structural Engineer, which was also not under seal.

Now common sense suggests that if the Project Manager should have spotted the design fault, then he should have done so before it was built, or at least before Practical Completion. But the court seemed to think the Project Manager should have done so, even after the event, and then told the employer to pull the building apart and effectively start again!

In due course, the Developer's claim against the Structural Engineer failed in both contract and tort, six years having elapsed since the date of the appointment of the Structural Engineer. So the Developer commenced action against the unfortunate Project Managers on the basis that *the start date of the cause of action against the Project Manager was six years later—because the Developer only suffered damage when his right of action against the Structural Engineer became time barred*. The Project Manager was therefore responsible from year 7 to year 12, although his appointment had not been signed under seal.

One might well ask why the six years in respect of the Structural Engineer did not date from the time of design, or from the date that the Structural Engineer allowed the work to be built, or from Practical Completion, on the basis of common logic. One might also ask why the Developer should be allowed a second opportunity when he had six years to claim against the Structural Engineer direct.

The answer is that if the defective work manifests itself more than six years after Practical Completion, the employer cannot reasonably be aware of the problem before he loses his right to pursue the guilty consultant. So subject to the question of whether a normally competent Project Manager should have realised the design deficiency, the Project Manager and his P.I. insurer are the only remaining sources of potential recompense for the Developer.

In the light of the very real difficulties identified by the above and other cases, the Law Commission wishes to introduce a "Core Regime" on limitation periods, and whilst acknowledging Latham Working Group 10's recommendation of a 10-year period, whether in contract or tort, starting from the date of completion, it is unwilling to make industry-specific provisions.

The construction industry therefore awaits developments on clarification of the law of limitation and the betting must be on special consideration, given the present Government's high profile track record in implementing the main recommendations of the Latham Report.

3.6 ASSIGNMENT AND NOVATION

This is another area of construction law where the distinction between two basic concepts is often misunderstood. The basic starting point is that:

— *Assignment can only apply to benefits* arising under a contract, and essentially only concerns Party B and Party C, where Party A, usually the employer, has no interest in Party B's domestic arrangements.

— On the other hand, *novation applies to both benefits and obligations*, and as such requires the specific consent of Party B, if Party A wishes Party C to take A's place in the contractual arrangement.

An example of assignment might be where the contractor requires payments to be made to a subsidiary company for accounting reasons, but remains fully responsible under the contract for completing the project and attending to all defects.

Typical examples of novation are insolvency, where a substitute contractor is brought in to complete a development or where the design team who developed the concept brief on a JCT WCD 98 contract are then, by pre-agreement spelt out in the tender enquiry, switched to the selected Contractor's employment.

The novation of design professionals to contractors is neat in theory, supposedly giving continuity of design development, but in reality is fraught with potential problems, both for the employer and for the design professionals themselves. From the employer's viewpoint he presumably knows and trusts the chosen Architect, Structural Engineer and Services

Engineer but:

— The contractor is yet to be selected, so it is not known how the design team once novated will fit with the contractor's existing team, whether in-house or an outside consultancy.

— The project strategy must be clear as to how far the brief and schematic design will be taken before being tendered, and whether a single-stage or two-stage tender process is to be adopted.

— The project budget must be established and the design team cannot be allowed to go on a flight of fancy, writing a wish list for the contractor to design and price.

— Parameters must be established early, especially in respect of who will obtain Outline Planning Consent, and when, in relation to the tender programme.

— The duties of each design professional must be defined, i.e. at what point are they to commence their contractor advisory function and how will their obligations to the employer, yet be completed, be finally signed off?

— In particular, do they have an express or implied duty, or none at all, to report back to their previous employer, once novated, that their new employer, the selected contractor, is cheating on the contract specification—"whistleblowing"?

From the design professionals' point of view they have to be pleased to have obtained a new commission with the employer, but of course the real fees are to be earned with the design detailing and the post-contract supervision—or are they? The reality of most design and build projects is that the employer wants the best of both worlds: to develop a fairly comprehensive design for a minimal fee and then to expect every tenderer to fully check that design in respect of stated space planning and functional requirements as well as compliance with statutory requirements, i.e. means of escape and other key matters.

As such each contractor tendering has to commit not inconsiderable fees on this check process or, if the enquiry is a true performance specification and outline concept design only, to commit an even higher level of fees such that a partially developed design scheme may be priced. Either way the successful tenderer is likely to have developed a close working relationship with his first choice design team—particularly during the pricing and tender negotiation stages.

When the employer's design team then find themselves transferred to the "other side", it is only natural that they are looked upon with suspicion and that they themselves feel like uninvited guests. If the contractual arrangement can be structured to the effect that they are executive Architects, Engineers, etc, overseeing and taking responsibility for the work of the lower level project design team it can work, but the key question is: to whom is the responsibility owed?

Conflicts of interest are inevitable and it is perhaps artificial to pretend that in real terms their responsibility can be to anyone other than the person that pays them, i.e. the contractor. It is then for each of the novated design team to ensure that their terms of appointment, and the function they are requested or in fact allowed to perform, are in accordance with the prescribed novation scheme written into the tender enquiry.

If they are then compromised they must resign, an example being a novated Structural Engineer attending his first in-house design development meeting. The contractor proposed using a cheaper structural block but the Engineer disagreed, having broken the block over his knee! The contractor still insisted on using it, virtually telling the Engineer that he could speak when spoken to, so he left the meeting and wrote his resignation, with a copy to the employer.

All too often in practice novated design professionals find they have the worst of both worlds: they are used in an early speculative project concept role, followed by a nominal fee, by the employer, and then once novated they are always in the contractor's B team, with the design development already done by the contractor's A team, and all site supervision led by the in-house contractor's staff engineers. As such there is little money left for further fees, but plenty of responsibilities coming their way!

In the meantime, who looks after the employers' interests? The JCT WCD 98 requires the employer to appoint an Employer's Agent, but who can sensibly fill the void if the Architect, Structural Engineer and Services Engineer have been novated to the contractor? On most projects the key player at the brief development stage is the Quantity Surveyor, who advises on the contractual arrangement and tender process, but more importantly sets the cost parameters, including assisting in obtaining project finance. As such, when the design team are novated it is natural that most employers look to the Quantity Surveyor to act as the Employer's Agent under the contract, administering the project in the name of the employer.

However, there are two problems with this arrangement. Few Quantity Surveyors have any in-date professional training in building design and construction technology, and secondly, few will have Professional Indemnity cover for acting as quasi Architect or Engineer, Structural or Services, when it comes to design approval or site supervision.

As we shall see in Chapter 6 one leading Quantity Surveying practice made case law for all the wrong reasons; the individual acting as the Employer's Agent told the judge from the witness box that he had not inspected the problem roof because he considered it might be dangerous to climb the ladder. Suffice it to say it is difficult to know who was least impressed: the judge, the P.I. insurer or the equity partners.

CHAPTER 4

THE BASIC REQUIREMENTS FOR A CLAIM

4.1 BURDEN OF PROOF, DUTIES AND BREACHES

Causation must always be the start point in any construction claim, whether the claim is for time or money, i.e. *who* has done *what* (which they ought not to have done) to *whom*, and *how* has it caused the alleged *loss*? Quantification of the alleged loss, time and/or money, comes later.

The *who* and *whom* are the easy bits, assuming there is no dispute as to whether there is a valid contract, and the *what* should be just a matter of picking the relevant clause in the contract which covers the obligation on which the Claimant needs to rely. The tricky bit is the *how*.

Now it is a fundamental principle in common law as practised in England that "He who avers must prove", i.e. it is the Claimant who must make his case, not the Defendant who must prove his non-culpability *per se*. Because it is a civil, as opposed to criminal procedure, the burden of proof required is "on the balance of probabilities", rather than the higher criminal burden of "beyond reasonable doubt". It is also a fundamental principle that a Defendant is entitled to know the case being made against him, such that he may meet the case and defend himself, as allowed by the prescribed procedures.

Thus any claim must in the first instance state a case by:

— identifying the contract relied on;
— citing the obligations relied on;
— specifying the alleged breaches in skeletal detail.

Where there are multiple issues, e.g. defects cases, the above are usually then set out in a "Scott Schedule" with a multi-column format so that each item is summarised horizontally, starting with the Claimant's contention, the Defendant's contention, the Claimant's reply, the value or time claimed, the value or time allowed by the Defendant, Judge's notes, etc.

4.2 CAUSATION AND "ROLLED-UP" CLAIMS

The next test that a claim must pass is notification—again on the basis that the party alleged to be in breach is entitled to be put on notice as soon as reasonably possible, so that he can take steps to rectify his alleged default.

Different standard forms of contract have different requirements for notification of claims, but it is common to all that prompt notification is required, followed by notification on a provisional basis of the order of damage, i.e. time or money, when reasonably quantifiable, subject to a fully detailed submission later.

When it comes to the formal claim submission the key section will be the causation statement, i.e. the detailed linkage between the alleged, but as yet unproven, breaches, and the usual:

— actual Completion Date led time claim, or
— the cost ledger based statement of financial loss.

Hindsight is a fact of life; one cannot pretend one does not know the end answer, so the inevitable temptation is to try to make the alleged facts fit or lead to the known end result—not that there is anything wrong with this approach *per se*. The danger therefore is that all losses are attributed as if they were necessarily the result of the alleged breaches, taking no account of any possible non-attributable causes of loss, e.g. own site labour problems, defective work, etc.

Clearly any claim should therefore be up front in addressing one's own problems and failures and should give a deliberately generous credit so that it is demonstrably fair, rather than marginal and therefore arguable. However, the real problem of retrospective allocation of alleged losses to alleged breaches is that when the alleged cause of loss originated no one thought or had the time to sit on site, stop-watch in hand, carrying out a time and motion study. Indeed had they done so one can just imagine the comments and abuse it might well have provoked both from the main contractor's site management, and from the operatives themselves!

Almost inevitably the first line of defence the recipient of a claim takes is to say the claim is "rolled-up" and must therefore be better particularised if he is to answer it by way of granting an Extension of Time or making a payment—whether an interim payment or a full settlement. Whilst this might be a valid response to a preliminary or early claim notification it may well not be a valid response to a fully considered submission. Reverting therefore to the two fundamental principles outlined in Section 4.1 above, case law draws a distinction between "rolled-up" allegations and "rolled-up" losses.

In *J. Crosby & Sons Ltd* v. *Portland UDC* (1967) it was held that the arbitrator had acted correctly, the key passages of the judgment being:

— Where the claim depends "... on an extremely complex interaction in the consequences of various denials, suspensions and variations ... it may well be difficult or even impossible to make an accurate apportionment of the total extra cost between the several causative events."

— "I see no reason why he [the Arbitrator] should not recognise the realities of the situation and make individual awards in respect of those parts of the claim which can be dealt with in isolation and a supplementary award in respect of the remainder of these claims as a composite whole."

In *Merton London Borough* v. *Stanley Hugh Leach Ltd* (1985) it was held as a preliminary issue that the Plaintiff should plead each alleged breach by reference to the relevant condition in the JCT standard form of contract and then attribute loss to each head of claim in order to enable the Architect to make his award in accordance with the requirements of the contract, but only where such attribution was possible, the key extract from the judgment being:

> "If application is made for reimbursement of direct loss and expense attributable to more than one head of claim and at the time when the loss or expense comes to be ascertained it is impracticable to disentangle or to disintegrate the part directly attributable to each head of claim, then, ... the Architect must ascertain the global loss directly attributable to the two causes."

Wharf Properties v. *Eric Cumine Associates* (1990) concerned an action for breach of contract where the employer alleged non-administration of the project for allowing the project to severely overrun. The Defendant Architects applied to the court for a strike out of the employer's case on the basis that it did not particularise the period of delay attributable to each of the various breaches alleged. The court ordered the Plaintiff to re-serve by way of further and better particulars before discovery, but the Plaintiff claimed it was impossible to break down the cumulative delay by separate causes. When the case was repleaded it was considered "embarrassing" and an "abuse of process" and was struck out—the Plaintiff having had seven years to produce proper details!

More recently the necessary balance between particularisation of cause and effect was fully considered in the case of *Robins Holdings Ltd* v. *Specialist Computer Centres Ltd*, which was determined in the Court of Appeal in June 1998. Although it was not a construction industry case the basic plot is all too familiar. The contractor (SCC) was engaged by the employer (Robins) to design and build a computer system to provide a central service to their network of UK offices. In the event the product was found to be non-functional in various specified respects, was too slow, and was based on badly written software, but the real issue was quantification of loss—presumably because the contractor had joined in his various sub-contractors and consultants.

The Plaintiff set out his complaints fully, but was unable to offer a reasoned apportionment of his recorded loss, having had to pay for new, more powerful hardware, and for major modifications to the software, and no doubt having incurred substantial own staff time and business interruption.

The Defendant stalled, submitting two extensive lists of "Requests for Further and Better Particulars" under the old court procedure, but the trial judge was pioneering case management as we know it today. The Defendant then applied for a strike out on the basis that no direct linkage had been made out between the breaches and the claimed damages, but the trial judge was robust, stating that as he had had charge of the proceedings since inception he was not embarrassed by the present pleadings.

The Defendant appealed, but lost again—the Court of Appeal holding that:

— The overriding concern of the court should be the expeditious, fair and cost effective resolution of the dispute, i.e. the Woolf principles now enacted in the Civil Procedure Rules.
— It was necessary to strike a balance between essential facts and excessive particulars.
— The trial judge was the best person to strike that balance—particularly if, as in this case, he had been the case manager throughout.
— Although the nexus between the breaches and the losses was less than clear the nexus was nevertheless sufficient on the facts of the case.

In construction cases there are rarely single issues, so in practice when drafting a loss and expense claim there will be various heads of claim, and as one breach allegation may succeed and another may fail it follows that one must wherever possible separate the alleged loss on a factual basis as between each head of claim.

Sometimes one has to adopt the equivalent of alternative pleadings in structuring a claim. An example would be where the main breach alleged is severe and comprehensive disruption resulting in substantial loss of productivity and delays—the specialist sub-contractor having little option but to work overtime and pay premium rates in order to retain skilled labour.

In this situation one would claim the full labour loss expressed in terms of enforced loss of productivity, costed at tender rates, as the principal head of claim. If successful, this will take care of overtime hours (but not the cost of non-productive enhancement), and all time spent on variations, whether agreed or disputed. Credit would then be given for the agreed and paid value of authorised variations already recovered in the loss of productivity calculations. Under a separate head of claim one would then detail the unpaid cost of variations, but in terms of unrecovered material value only, reserving the position to the effect that, should the loss of productivity head of claim not find favour with the judge, then the labour element of the disputed variations head of claim, not now to be recovered under enforced loss of productivity, would need to be brought back into the claim equation.

The claim would then be completed by further heads in respect of non-productive overtime enhancement, if actually paid, and the premium costs of retaining labour. Additional Preliminaries (if applicable), Overheads and Profit, and Finance Costs would normally be further heads of claim.

Thus the basic rule for the presentation of loss and expense claims comes in two parts:

— Firstly, one must particularise the alleged breaches as far as possible.
— Secondly, one must then allocate losses on a factual basis to specific breaches wherever possible, but where the allocation becomes notional rather than reasoned, then a "rolled-up" balance of alleged loss might be acceptable as a claim submission. Whether it then survives as a matter of evidence is for the tribunal to decide.

Just recently a significant case covering three regular issues, i.e. "rolled-up" claims, the meaning of "ascertain" and whether Method Statements are contract documents has become available.

How Engineering Services Ltd v. *Lindner Ceilings Floors Partitions Plc* (1999) was a classic tale of ill-defined contract documentation and conditions, which were skewed in favour of the Construction Manager and passed down to Works Package Contractors, and down again to successive sub-contractors. Site planning and control was evidently other than under control, with the suspended ceilings going up and down like the proverbial "whore's drawers", the site being the major "Air Rights" redevelopment over Cannon Street station.

So an arbitrator was appointed—a well respected Quantity Surveyor arbitrator, who found substantially for Lindner. How Engineering appealed on various alleged points of law, including perceived bias, and if they weren't correct on the points of law, then they alleged misconduct. Par for the course—the two quantum experts didn't seem to want to agree anything either.

Central to How's case was that the arbitrator had allowed a "rolled-up" claim and had failed to "ascertain" the additional costs of the "substantial delay and disruption" caused by How's breaches. The arbitrator in his detailed award was very positive. He acknowledged case precedent concerning unparticularised losses arising from multiple causes, i.e. there was no factual basis for dividing proven losses, other than by professional judgement on the evidence adduced, but he maintained that he was required as an arbitrator to do just that. He even ordered a without prejudice experts' meeting, excluding lawyers, to try to get the two parties to narrow the financial positions, but How's solicitors stopped their expert appearing.

After close examination of the basis of tender, labour allowances in the tender and costs records, the arbitrator had had no difficulty in awarding substantial damages for Lindner, but had been quite strict in disallowing various other heads of claim. However, both in the arbitration and in the appeal hearing in the TCC, out came the dictionaries: What was the meaning of "to ascertain"?

How had contended this required a "rigid" test and that "... every figure appearing in the calculations is to be proven beyond any measure of doubt ...". The arbitrator was very firm. "When such a situation [delay and disruption] has been engendered by a Respondent and not by a Claimant, it would be common sense turned on its head to insist that the Claimant abide by an over-rigid interpretation of the contract requirement that, because of the engendered situation, is impossible of achievement." A welcome statement, which the judge was happy to endorse.

On the Method Statement argument, common sense again prevailed. The arbitrator decided that, if the tender enquiry required the successful tenderer to submit a detailed Method Statement for approval prior to commencing work, this was inevitably linked to the accepted Contract Sum, and accordingly had the status of a contract document by incorporation; i.e. impose restricted working and you invite an additional cost. Again the judge gave short shrift to How's counter-arguments.

Hopefully, this case and the clear decisions on these regular "old chestnuts" will be given wider circulation in the construction press. They will no doubt be welcomed by adjudicators faced with these same issues at first instance.

Finally on the subject of "rolled-up" claims, as touched on at the end of Chapter 11.3, it has been suggested by some commentators that the courts might conceivably relax the level of proof required between breach and loss, in line with the stated Woolf Report objective of "proportionality", i.e. the ratio of costs to the amount of damages claimed, if to insist on full proof, rather than balance of probability, would need disproportionate investment in time and fees.

This opinion would appear to be consistent with the recent decision in the *Robins Holdings* computer case, outlined above, but others are not so sure. At the time of writing we are therefore awaiting clear evidence from the judges in the Technology and Construction Court as to how they are to set "norms", and indeed cap costs on the basis of retaining the principle of "proportionality".

4.3 QUANTIFICATION OF LOSS—MONEY AND TIME

The last, but perhaps most relevant, element of any claim is the quantification of loss. If the claim is for additional money it can be on the basis of contract entitlement, e.g. a further seven weeks Extension of Time where the original contract Preliminaries are costed in detail in the accepted tender. It will then be possible to establish a weekly cost for time related Preliminaries. Alternatively the claim can be based on proven loss, provided the additional costs attributed to the breach are reasonably accounted for and are reasonable in all the circumstances.

On the other hand, if the claim is for additional time the assessment of entitlement will be by Programme analysis, plotting relevant events against the original programme intention, which can be shown to relate to the accepted tender.

The key to ascertaining loss—in both money and time claims—is being able to factually establish the baseline position, i.e. what was the contract agreement and definition of price, and how long was it all to take given the express terms as to how it might be achieved?

For this important reason it is essential that the method of estimating and the tender compilation show a clear audit trail—separately identifying the six essential elements of any contract sum, i.e. Labour, Materials, Plant, Site Costs (Preliminaries), Overheads (and what they include) and Profit allowance.

In this respect mechanical and electrical claims are often easier to prove as inevitably they are material led, i.e. the estimator starts with separately stated material purchase prices and then adds a labour constant—often from a published pricing book or from his own in-house computer database. Building works are more frequently priced on a composite unit rate basis, so labour allowances are not identifiable.

The other difficulty is that there is rarely any link between the tender sum and the contractor's programme other than in terms of weeks duration and the Preliminaries allowance. This is because tender sums are inevitably produced via a Bill of Quantities, either issued by the employer as a tender enquiry document or via builders' quantities taken from the tender drawings. On the other hand, the contractor's initial programme appraisal is usually focused on how to build the job in the stated time, what main plant is required, and how to pass the risks, i.e. either back to the employer by way of tender qualification or by way of sub-contracting.

In the days when main contractors carried most trades or had a shortlist of regular sub-contractors a Construction Programme was sometimes prepared on a labour resource basis, and the tender adjusted as necessary. In these days where sub-contracting is the "norm", based on lowest price, subject to re-bidding downwards once the project has been secured by the main contractor, there is rarely any factual link between the tendered sum and the contractor's programme, which can be of use when it comes to proving the baseline in terms of planned productivity.

4.4 EVIDENCE

By far the most certain way of achieving an acceptable claim settlement, short of litigation, or indeed proving loss if put to proof, is to be able to claim the moral high ground, i.e. be prepared to go "open book", from tender enquiry through to Final Account. This means that there must be no hiding place for key information and there must be an audit trail through the tender process. So often in the pressure of getting on with the next job the tender papers are not conscientiously filed and the files clearly labelled. Of course the majority of tenders are unsuccessful, most contractors being happy if their strike rate is one in four or better, so neat and tidy filing is not a high priority in most contractors' offices.

However, when the one in four comes up there is usually a panic as to how to staff the project and how to secure the key sub-contract packages—inevitably with an element of Dutch auctioneering to improve margins and to enhance the contractor's risk contingency. There is nothing wrong with this and nothing to hide, so records of sub-contract placement can be crucial, particularly arrangements made with labour-only sub-contractors. If the project subsequently loses its way for reasons outside the contractor's control there is nothing like being able to show that you could have purchased a key resource within the tender allowance, but because of site factors you had to work overtime, pay enhanced rates, etc—and to prove the extra over cost factor you need that baseline evidence.

In the meantime, the start of any project is a crucial period for filling in the missing details left behind by the contract conditions and resolving any uncertainties as to the required site procedures, e.g. who will chair the Site Meetings and how will the Minutes be signed off as a true record? Will Progress Reports tabled at the Site Meeting necessarily be accepted as a true record and incorporated as an Appendix to the Minutes?

A key area in any dispute will be the timing of information release and who had the responsibility for approving drawings for construction, so the keeping of a Drawings Register showing revisions and dates of issue is essential.

On most medium to large contracts the main contractor will be fast off the mark with his standard forms and procedures, and the professional team needs to climb in fast and establish just what is actually necessary— for the benefit of getting the project built on time and on budget, as opposed to what the contractor can subsequently use as a stick to beat the design team with.

The favourite contractor's standard form is the "Confirmation of Verbal Instructions" (CVI). Establish at the outset that only designated persons are empowered to give such instructions, on behalf of the employer, and that they are not to be acted upon until confirmed by counter-signature. Otherwise an unscrupulous contractor will often deliberately misquote an innocent conversation and then claim it has the status of a Variation Order because no one for the employer rejected it within seven days of utterance.

On one project the author was called in to audit by the employer the contractor had a neat trick: he would date the CVIs as if written out the same day as given, but then not send them to the Architect until the Friday before day 7, so several were technically out of time even before they hit the Architect's desk.

Correspondence is another vital area of evidence but should be used in moderation. If the project develops into a paper war, a law of diminishing returns sets in, unless of course you are a claims consultant or solicitor acting for one of the parties. By all means record and notify key events, as indeed you are probably required to do under the contract, but when correspondence on a particular issue has reached stalemate it is probably time to agree to differ and get on with building the project. Often what were hot issues at the time get overtaken by events, and bigger and better arguments.

Site management staff are of course key witnesses as to what happened at the time, albeit they obviously have a position to defend and a job to protect if still with the same employer. Generally the Site Supervisors are people who will tell it as it was, and any diaries kept at the time by them before they realised the project was in trouble will be most helpful. In particular these contemporaneous records will be "warts and all" and although they may contain facts unhelpful to the case you are trying to make out they will have two immediate benefits:

— They will identify case weaknesses and hopefully deter you from taking essentially bad points.

— They will give greater credibility to the relevant evidence on which you seek to rely if they are also critical in certain respects of your client's own performance.

Other essential contemporaneous evidence might be:

— Labour and Plant records, kept on a weekly basis.
— Dated photographs taken on regular dates from set positions and as necessary to evidence specific events or problems.
— Manufacturers' or suppliers' certificates, e.g. proof of stress grading of structural timbers, even if marked on the product; fire door certification, bearing in mind that colour coded fire door plugs can be purchased in certain areas; and glazing—and there is quite an industry in post-etching glass once fixed.
— Handover certificates, particularly relevant when the main contractor is running late and he wishes you, a sub-contractor, to start your package before the previous trade has substantially finished and that work has been checked for essential tolerances.

Most main contractors, and certainly the increasing ranks of so-called Construction Managers, are very good at project inception stage at selling their services to clients based on their in-house Quality Control systems and paperwork. However, the author's opinion is that when things get tough on site, the Quality Control system usually becomes one-way traffic.

The main contractor will use it to record all the faults he can find with the performance of his sub-contractors, but when they ask for Handover certificates as to when areas were released to them, or when they offer their work for Practical Completion the system is conveniently non-operational. For example, the hand-over of structural steelwork, properly surveyed and confirmed as plumbed, lined and levelled within specified tolerances, is a regular issue.

Thus if acting for a sub-contractor the project QA system as operated by the main contractor, or the Construction Manager, could well be vital evidence—and the other side's achilles heel.

Why do fewer and fewer projects have Clerks of Works? A good retired tradesman, with 25 years or more site experience, is not an expensive luxury for the independent watchdog role he can perform, if properly instructed. A vital part of such instruction is to check that the individual can actually read, and, more importantly, write. Dyslexic people are well practised at concealing their unfortunate disability—which could have been why they had to work on the tools in the first place.

It is also important to give them a specific written list of their duties including the spot checking of effective morning start times, and effective finishing times. They must also be specifically instructed as to their power to instruct the contractor, or otherwise, and in what detail their daily site diary is to be kept. This will be essential evidence in any dispute. On one of the author's audit investigations the ex-Clerk of Works agreed to meet us and to bring his diary. When we met and asked for his diary he produced a pocket diary with little more information in it than the date of his wife's birthday!

4.5 THE DUTY TO MITIGATE LOSS

It is an often quoted principle of English law that a party suffering a breach by the other party and incurring loss in consequence must mitigate his loss, but what does this mean in practice?

In *The Solholt* (1983) the judge said:

> "A Plaintiff is under no duty to mitigate his loss, despite the habitual use by lawyers of the phrase 'duty to mitigate'. He is completely free to act as he judges to be in his best interests. On the other hand, a Defendant is not liable for all loss suffered in consequence of his so acting. A Defendant is only liable for such part of the Plaintiff's loss as is properly caused by the Defendant's breach of duty."

Unfortunately over recent years it also seems to have become the unwritten law of English construction practice that the main contractor can require a sub-contractor to make a premature start, albeit later than the planned start, then to compete with other late running trades for access and use of promised site facilities. The sub-contractor then incurs further delays and loss of productivity, yet somehow is expected to miraculously accelerate and finish on time, or thereabouts—and without entitlement to additional costs for all his trouble.

Of course, this is a deliberately simplistic statement, but increasingly we are seeing such abuses by the more powerful party up the supply chain at the expense of the less powerful party down the chain. However, the HGCRA 1996 now gives either party the right to call in the adjudicator at any time, over any matter of dispute (excluding domestic and certain other types of process engineering contracts), and increasingly we will be seeing adjudicators called for over issues of time, as well as quantum and payment.

Whilst the delayed sub-contractor cannot use the enforced delay to his advantage, by the same token the main contractor cannot expect the sub-contractor to do more than he bargained for and to cut back the lost time without meeting any reasonable additional costs involved. A balance has to be struck therefore as to what is reasonable and what is unreasonable for the innocent party to do without pre-agreement as to additional payment.

Obviously it is much better if a properly defined agreement can be put in place, complete with future "milestone" dates to measure the redefined progress required, but all too frequently there is no clear break point from which the alleged breach can be sufficiently defined as to justify a contractual notice. All too often various factors combine and losses are incurred before a formal breach can be cited. The chances of the party responsible for the alleged breach putting his hand up and accepting liability without a fight are remote.

Even then there are no grounds for suspending work whilst a new price or compensation is discussed, so in effect what the unfortunate sub-contractor is being asked to do is to work less productively than envisaged at time of tender and then accelerate (overtime and at risk of inefficiencies and defects), both at his own expense. So again, intended productivity factors and records of site events together with actual productivity are vital when it comes to a dispute.

In practice it is probably desirable to increase resources, but only if available and only if it will be productive to do so, during the normal hours Monday to Friday. This should be accompanied by a letter confirming the additional resources being deployed in good faith, and reserving the entitlement to be reimbursed accordingly when the cause of the delay can be factually attributed.

Of course prior agreement to additional payment is the ideal, e.g. instruction to work overtime, particularly as the additional resources will need paying, but this rarely happens. So perhaps the answer is to voluntarily deploy the resources for a limited period and in the meantime run an adjudication to establish liability.

In any event it is probably best to back the situation both ways until liability can be established, as the consequences of being held liable for the delay could be the deduction of Liquidated and Ascertained Damages, often at a level bearing no relationship to the value of the sub-contract works.

Thus mitigation is best defined as taking reasonable steps to limit losses naturally flowing from a breach, but it is not necessary to take special steps to save the defaulting party from the consequences of his actions.

4.6 SET-OFF AND COUNTERCLAIMS

When a party to a construction contract receives a formal claim, whether in litigation or in arbitration he has essentially four options by way of defence:

— He can argue the case on its merits and establish the true measure of damages at a lower level than claimed.

— He can attempt a damage limitation exercise by claiming that on the same issues the Claimant caused him some loss, or contributed by his own default to the loss being claimed, i.e. a claim for Set-off.

— He can raise other issues and make his own counterclaim against the Claimant, proving loss, which is then balanced against monies he would otherwise owe to the Claimant.

— He can contend that, should he be held to be liable to the Claimant, the actual fault lay with a third party upon whom he, the Defendant, relied and so join him in the action as a third party or commence contribution proceedings against the third party.

Before the Civil Procedure Rules (CPR) of 1999 it was often a problem to agree what was a set-off and what was a stand-alone counterclaim. The fixation with costs, where in a counterclaim situation costs might be decided on a *"Net* winner takes all" basis, meant that set-off items were often wrongly claimed as counterclaims. Now that judges have greater flexibility on costs under the CPR it should no longer be a problem.

However, with the more robust approach of the CPR and the requirement for positively stated defences, rather than negative blanket denial defences of the old pleadings, it will be interesting to see if the courts are strict on what is a genuine defence and set-off, as opposed to essentially a different dispute on the same contract, i.e. a counterclaim, in its own right.

If a Defendant wrongly opts for set-off this could, in theory, open the door to summary judgment and costs being awarded on the claim, with the Defendant then struggling to be allowed to have the unpleaded counterclaim heard.

A leading case in respect of set-off is *Rosehaugh Stanhope* v. *Redpath Dorman Long Ltd* (1990) where the Construction Manager, Bovis, sought to rely on bespoke contract terms supposedly giving Bovis, as construction managers, the right on behalf of the employer to ascertain a *bona fide* set-off against the Structural Steelwork trade contractor on the basis of alleged culpable delays, notwithstanding that there were unresolved claims the other way from the trade contractor for an Extension of Time.

The Court of Appeal however were having none of it and invoked the *contra proferentem* rule against the Plaintiff. The leading judgment was expressed in terms which surely set the standard for legitimate set-offs:

"I absolutely decline, on the words of this contract, to impute to the parties an intention that the construction manager should have power to impose on the trade contractor a liability which is neither admitted nor proved to exist at the time, which may later be proved never to have existed at all, but which may in the meantime have brought him into bankruptcy, being a power which is not claimed even by the court on an application for interim damages where an arguable defence is shown."

Strong words indeed which should be music to the ears of many trade contractors caught up in similar Bovis-type Construction Management contracts where there is no independent third party certifier—and a strong lead for adjudicators to follow.

4.7 SETTLEMENT OF THIRD PARTY CLAIMS

Fighting a war on two fronts is very tricky at the best of times, particularly if your claim on Party A does not sit comfortably with your defence to Party C's claim against you. Even if you have no evidential embarrassment it is often commercially necessary to compromise your dispute with Party C, after going some part of the way in the prescribed dispute process, and then to seek to rely on that settlement as an essential element of your argument with Party A. Naturally Party A is not going to be too interested in your settlement with Party C and will inevitably seek to say there were different facts or issues. He is also likely to say, not unreasonably, that as he had no part in the settlement negotiations with Party C he cannot be bound in any event.

This problem came to public notice in *P & O Developments Ltd* v. *Guy's and St Thomas' National Health Service Trust* (1998). The project had been a nightmare for all sorts of reasons—not least that it had been let on the "soft" form of Management Contract, where all cost and time overruns of the Works Package Contracts usually pass through the Management Contractor and end up for the employer's account.

Unsurprisingly, given all the politics surrounding that unhappy project in which the author had a small part in the early stages, the Plaintiffs considered they had been put to considerable additional work as Project Managers and submitted a claim for additional fees. The contractor, Higgs & Hill Management Contracting Ltd, had complex and substantial claims for both money and time against the employer in the order of £100m.

The employer, not unnaturally and with major public accountability problems, took the view that neither claim was their responsibility, having paid good fees to both a *Management* Contractor and a Project *Manager*—so the battle lines were drawn. (Author's italic to emphasise the central issue of who should have actually managed the project.)

Sensibly the employer and contractor agreed to talk. An independent audit was carried out by eminent Quantity Surveyors called in by the employer, and eventually a compromise settlement was reached at £83.9m, saving very substantial legal fees as against going to court—the Project Managers having co-operated in the detailed investigation which had to consider a multiplicity of Works Package placements and what had happened on each Works Package in the course of the project.

However, no deal was done concerning the Project Manager's claim to additional fees. So *P & O Developments Ltd* sued the employer, and the employer entered both a defence and a counterclaim for £83.9m, as paid under considerable duress by the employer to the contractor.

Again, unsurprisingly, *P & O Developments Ltd* as Defendants in the counterclaim, together with the Services Consultants who had been joined in the counterclaim, cried "foul" and took a number of legal points including the following:

— Although the overall settlement may have been reasonable, how were they to know that each of the Works Package settlements was reasonable and attributable to their alleged fault, rather than any other causation?

— Was it necessary to enquire as to the actual values that the contractor had paid out to the various Works Package contractors, with whom the contractor had already reached compromise settlements?

— Was it safe to assume that the independent auditors had acted reasonably, and that therefore the employer was entitled to rely on their findings as evidence of loss?

As background to this dispute, it was relevant that a major recession was just starting at the outset of the project, and that during the project there were both supplier and sub-contractor insolvencies. Given that insolvencies inevitably cause delays and additional costs for the employer's account it must have been highly questionable how the £83.9m was made up, and therefore whether it was all attributable to the alleged negligence of the Project Manager and the Services Consultant.

The case was tried as a series of preliminary issues on the agreed premise that the case for negligence against *P & O Developments Ltd* as Project Managers would be made out at full trial, and it was duly held that:

— As a matter of principle, a settlement between Party A (the employer) and Party B (the contractor), however reasonable in the circumstances of that dispute, cannot be relied upon as exclusive evidence of the liability of Party C (the Project Manager) to Party A.

— It was not conclusive that the employer had relied on independent professional advice in settling with the contractor and had based its claim in negligence on that advice, but it was relevant evidence.

— This case was distinguished from the previous leading case *Biggin* v. *Permanite* (1951) as in that case the contractor's claim was purely based on issues which were directly attributable to the Architect's performance.

— Whilst in principle the courts encourage reasonable settlements, where strict proof would be inordinately expensive, the employer had to satisfy the court by way of evidence and cross-examination that the contractor's claim if tested by arbitration or trial would have had reasonable prospects of success in the value eventually settled.

— A settlement may be evidence of likely damages, but it is important to remember that the main purpose of a settlement is not always to assess legal liability.

As a personal footnote, if anyone has a copy of a video showing a man in a Beard Dove site helmet on a demolition site with high rise blocks all around, extolling the virtues of Quality Control and BS 5750 as the employer's best guarantee of getting the project delivered on time and on budget, then please let the author know.

If you have seen that video, that was the author in November 1990 on the site in question, under employer's orders to assist the Department of Trade and Industry, through the British Standards Institute, to sell Quality Assurance to the construction industry; I had received a copy of the Project Quality Plan only the morning of the filming and had not been briefed by management as to what I was supposed to say. I was never shown the resultant film because I was made redundant a few weeks later! Hence the appeal for a copy please.

It is ironic that the follow-on above-ground contract resulted in a £100m contractor's claim and then made case law!

CHAPTER 5

KEY ELEMENTS OF CONTRACTORS' CLAIMS—MONEY AND TIME

5.1 TENDER ANALYSIS

By definition any Loss and Expense claim means that a Claimant is contending that he has been put to additional expense over and above that which he allowed for in his tender, and that the cause of that additional expenditure was some act or default of the Defendant, whether under the contract conditions or at common law.

Thus such a claim is immediately open to two challenges:

— What *was* actually allowed in the tender?
— What *should* have been allowed in the tender?

Such challenges should therefore be anticipated when one sets about compiling a claim and in any event one needs to know that one's own client isn't the author of his own misfortune by having underpriced the tender, so was always going to make a loss—albeit not such a level of loss as now apparent from the cost ledger.

Consequently it is important that the primary information is available to show how the tender was arrived at and that it is logical as a pricing exercise. If it depends upon sub-contract quotations or major material elements, competitive quotations should be available, or at least contemporaneous evidence of market rates from current projects.

Unless the project in question is fitting-out, or is plant and equipment intensive, the balance in total price between labour and materials is likely to be strongly in favour of labour. As it should be possible to correctly estimate the total quantity of materials required, backed by known prices or quotations, it follows that the estimating risks lie under three heads:

— the level of labour resource required;
— the market availability, and therefore the market price of that labour;

— the management resource required to properly plan and manage the project.

Every project will have its own particular demands—accessibility, restraints, buildability options etc, plus the time available to complete the project which will need to be assessed to arrive at the level of labour necessary to meet the contract obligations.

Hopefully the Claimant's Planning Engineer or technical office will have carried out an initial appraisal, and will have made the strategic decisions as to *how* to build the project and the main plant required, e.g. tower cranes, hoists, scaffolding, sequencing, as applicable, flagging up to the estimator any particular problem areas. If this is confirmed by a Method Statement, so much the better.

If the claim to be prepared is for general building work, proving labour resource assessments can be problematic, particularly if the work required in the tender is less than adequately described. As a fallback, hourly rates of pay and labour resource requirements for recognisable items of work are provable from any one of three or more standard pricing books, or from computer based estimating systems, which are commonly used in the construction industry.

However, most claims for loss and expense are specialist sub-contractor claims and in such companies they will have "rule of thumb" or industry accepted "norms", i.e. productivity factors proven by past experience across a reasonably wide variety of projects, usually based on gang working. It is then just a question of deciding whether the particular demands of the project in question were more onerous than the "norm"; examples are whether the finished installation was particularly difficult or whether there might have been a market shortage of skilled labour, e.g. large projects, such as Millennium projects at the time of writing, competing with one another for skilled workers in key trades. If such special considerations applied at the time of tender it will be necessary to show what plus factor was applied and whether in a competitive tender situation, rather than with hindsight, this was reasonable.

It follows that starting with the agreed Contract Sum, usually based on Bills of Quantities, and working backwards therefrom it should be possible to factually show all labour hours allowed in the tender, as distinct from the material value and the allowances for Site Management (Preliminaries), Off-site Management (Overheads) and Profit. From this one can hopefully show the target productivity to be achieved on a composite basis, taking the dependent lineal items on an inclusive basis the main items, usually expressed in square metres. If this can be done without having to make too many assumptions, one will then have established a baseline position, not only establishing the adequacy of the tender, but also providing a basis for comparative assessment of what then happened on site.

If the Defendant still seeks to argue that your client should have priced the tender differently, i.e. higher, so mitigating the loss now contended, then one has two available responses open:

— That the Defendant sought competitive tenders on a "best price" basis and this is how the tender was compiled, given the contract and site conditions described in the tender enquiry.
— That the Defendant chose to accept your (the Claimant's) tender and took the benefit of it in either:
  (a) compiling the Defendant's own winning tender;
  (b) increasing the Defendant's own margin as against his previously secured tender, which was presumably based on a higher sub-contract tender price.

5.2 ORIGINAL RESOURCE PLANNING

When a tender enquiry is received in a main contractor's office the first action is to rip the Bills of Quantities apart, and decide how to package the job into sub-contract enquiries and then make multiple copies for each section of the works. Rarely is there any specific contract risk appraisal at this stage or consideration as to how to build the project—the priority being to get the sub-contract enquiries back as soon as possible and then build up a composite tender by the stated return date.

Before the general move away from general contracting to specialist sub-contracting some main contractors had systems in place where they would assess the labour resource required as part of the estimating process, and with the close co-operation of a Planning Engineer then create their own programme. If this did not fit with the employer's required time scale the contractor's programme would be revisited and amended if possible, the contractor then offering two prices:

— Price A—for the stated contract completion date.
— Price B—for the contractor's preferred, resource based, completion date.

Then through the major recession of the early 1990s tendering practice became lowest price dominant, as sub-contractors vied to win scarce work and main contractors likewise tried to stay in business.

Although at head contract level only 61% of contracts by value were (November 1999 Survey) placed by competitive tender, leaving 39% placed by negotiated tender, at sub-contract level procurement remains price led. Rebidding of sub-contract packages after the main contractor has secured the project remains common practice.

Sometimes a specialist sub-contractor will receive a telephone call asking for a cover price and then hear nothing until months later when his best price is required by return—based on a faxed copy of the Bills of Quantities extract only, and a statement of the likely start and finish dates. In such circumstances, the tender for the specialist sub-contract works can only be based on the stated quantities and an appraisal of the number of gang strengths required over the total stated duration.

If the project is defined by zones or stages then the resource planning can be matched to the individual quantities in each zone and a more detailed appraisal of gang numbers and strength made. Ideally this will then be shown on a bar chart such that a direct linkage is shown between the tender price and the total labour man weeks assessed.

Productivity factors in each zone can then be established—it being an implied term, given no other express statement as part of the tender enquiry, that there will continuity of working, i.e. that defined zones will be released to the sub-contractor by the main contractor in their entirety on pre-scheduled dates. Whilst there may be nothing contractual beyond the agreed price and the sub-contract project duration at this stage, it is nevertheless persuasive evidence should the project overrun in time and a claim need to be made for both an Extension of Time and Loss and Expense.

All too often the sub-contract works will be started in good faith based on a main contractor's Order Number or Letter of Intent, particularly where long-lead materials are involved, only for the full sub-contract paperwork to be produced by the main contractor's Head Office Buying Department weeks later. Almost inevitably the Buying Department will attempt to introduce a whole new set of terms and conditions, which may or may not be subsequently used to deny payment of the previously agreed price.

The advice to sub-contractors must be to keep it simple. If your quote has been accepted, if you have been instructed to start work *and have actually done so*, what else do you require? As time passes, the more the main contractor will need you. Further, if you don't get paid on monthly invoice then the law is now right on your side.

As we shall see in Chapter 9, the HGCR Act 1996 gives a party to a written contract (however basically recorded) the right to call in an adjudicator at any time to resolve a dispute on other than domestic occupier and certain process engineering type contracts. More relevantly, if the main contractor fails to issue a Notice of Withholding in response to a sub-contractor's invoice, he could well be in even deeper trouble.

The message to both sub-contractors and main contractors alike therefore is that the days of informal tendering and then hiding behind supposed but retrospective terms and conditions are doomed. Robust adjudicators, backed by the courts, will generally find that there is a contract, as evidenced by performance, so why not be open with one another at the outset—go for simple sub-contract documentation backed by a properly detailed tender, which if necessary can be opened up to show as a matter of factual evidence the originally assumed tender resource.

If this can be done it will not only reduce the level of sub-contract disputes, but will make any subsequent dispute that much more manageable—so make sure that that all-important labour resource baseline is in the company safe in its own right or as part of the tender build-up.

5.3 "PLANNED" v. "ACTUAL"—AND WHY THE DIVERGENCE?

This is the area where most claims will succeed or fail—particularly the rhetorical question: "Why the divergence?" It is to be assumed that the detail in the tender and the contemporaneous site records enable a factual comparison, conventionally in bar chart form, as to the "Planned" project progress and the "Actual" project progress to be made. On their own, bars on a chart tell one very little, other than giving an overview. What is all important is:

— the logic links from one activity bar to the next; and
— the duration allowed for each activity.

By definition, related to the law of gravity, there has to be a fundamental logic of what can't be built before something else has to be finished. Beyond that it is down to the expert knowledge of the Planning Engineer working in conjunction with technical support to determine what the optimum total project duration might be if the criteria are lowest price and minimal level of risk.

On a large project though it will be all about site access and how to get "muck away" or keep water out, etc, and therefore which end of the site should be started first. Continuity of working for all trades is vital, so most projects need to be zoned, preferably on an upward staircase principle— with the floor slabs offering safe working conditions and partial weather protection for following trades working below.

It follows that on any project the contractor must, for his own purposes, have an action plan or formal Construction Programme. Whether this is a contract document will depend upon the tender enquiry requirement, but usually it is not—on the principle that it must be for the contractor to decide *how* he builds the project and meets his contractual obligations. Nevertheless it is perfectly proper, indeed sensible, that as a contract requirement the contractor is to produce such a document before commencing on site—in whatever form as may be previously described in the tender enquiry, and using a named IT software package—for approval by the Architect/Contract Administrator. In this way key objectives or "milestones" can be defined, against which the project can be monitored, and most importantly the employer's required actions can be programmed and recorded, e.g. key drawing release and design freeze dates.

The prescribed form of Construction Programme should take care of identifying the assumed logic links and activity durations such that there is a demonstrable "Critical Path" through the project, i.e. where there are no options as to the sequence of activities and minimal flexibility in the time available to achieve them, and still achieve the contract completion date.

The tender enquiry should also have required the contractor to update his Construction Programme every so often, or when specifically instructed, incorporating the effect of any Instructions issued under the contract. On larger projects it is also helpful if the contractor is required to issue detailed Completion Programmes over the last scheduled six months.

In the way of the world, and the construction industry in particular, events conspire to upset the best laid plans. Sometimes these are sheer bad luck and neither party is in any way to blame, but because most contracts require an agreed end date, and some form of agreed recompense in favour of the employer if the contract overruns, there has to be a regime for administering delays.

Most contracts therefore have express provisions as to what events give rise to an entitlement to an Extension of Time, and where appropriate an entitlement to additional monies. The most usual event is that the employer, or one of his design team, have second thoughts and require changes to the tendered scheme, and these must be administered on their merits, both as regards money and time.

However, there has to be a starting point in considering whether any particular event has actually prejudiced the contractor's ability to finish on the agreed date, and that starting point can only be the original Construction Programme, even if it is not a contract document. Equally, any review of entitlement to additional time is very much dependent upon the detail available to explain the logic and necessary assessments on which the original was based.

Also, following the principle that any Construction Programme is the contractor's own, non-binding, statement of intention as to *how* he will meet his contractual commitment to complete on time, the onus must clearly be on the contractor, not the employer and the Architect, to demonstrate that any event:

(a) has actually delayed the progress of the works; or
(b) is such that it will now be unlikely that the works can be completed on time; and

(c) is an event that according to the terms of the agreed contract entitles the contractor to an Extension of Time.

It may well be that a delay to the project has been caused by some event within the control of the contractor—a culpable delay, e.g. changing the construction sequence, in which case it should still be noted as a matter of record, with the outstanding work reprogrammed to get the project back on track. Thus any divergencies, actual or planned, from the original Construction Programme are for the contractor to identify and reasonably prove to the employer or his Architect.

This is best done by preparing a sub-programme, or impacted programme, showing:

— when the event occurred or arose
— when it took effect on the Construction Programme
— the current progress of the works
— the consequences of delayed completion on those activities directly affected
— whether the additional time required on the affected activities necessarily affects the "Critical Path" activities and therefore impacts upon the required end date.

If it does so impact on the existing end date, it is then for the contractor to firstly show that it cannot be accommodated by reprogramming or controlled rescheduling of labour resources. If not, the employer should be given reasoned options, so that he can opt whether to accept the delay or take special measures at additional cost in order to retain the contract completion date.

The real problem comes however where there are not just one or two stand-alone events likely to jeopardise the end date, but a series of events, such as client instructions, etc. In isolation no one instruction might be said to threaten the end date, but collectively they certainly pose a problem.

The conventional way of graphically presenting such information is a "Dot Chart"—leaving the reader, or judge, to accept that as a matter of fact, rather like Custer's last stand, the position was inevitably overwhelmed by weight of numbers, but that as a matter of evidence it was impossible to determine which arrow actually killed Custer.

A leading building case on Extension of Time entitlement was all about Critical Path Planning and it is interesting to review the key paragraph of the judgment in *John Barker Construction Ltd* v. *London Portman Hotels Ltd* (1996). The case turned on the methodology used to analyse the cause and effect of the various events, or more precisely the lack of methodology employed by the Architect in making his assessment of the contractor's entitlement.

The judge found the Architect's assessment "... fundamentally flawed ..." on the grounds that the Architect "... did not carry out a logical analysis in a methodical way of the impact which the relevant matters had ..." and the Architect had formed an "... impressionistic, rather than a calculated assessment of the time which he thought was reasonable for the various items individually or overall".

Likewise in a leading civil engineering case *McAlpine Humberoak* v. *McDermott International* (1992) the judge at first instance found for the Plaintiff, dismissing the Defendant's case as "being a 'retrospective and dissectional reconstruction' by expert evidence of events almost day by day, drawing by drawing, TQ by TQ [Technical Query] and weld procedure by weld procedure, designed to show that the spate of additional drawings, which descended on the contractor virtually from the start of the work, really had little retarding or disruptive effect on its progress". However, the appeal judge took a radically different view saying in reference to the earlier rejection of the Defendant's expert evidence, "In our view the Defendant's approach is just what the case required."

Returning to JCT SFBC 98 and the Extension of Time provisions of Clause 25, an arbitrator was asked to decide whether the Architect in considering the contractor's application citing two alleged Relevant Events was restricted to considering the effect of the two events only, or whether he was entitled to go behind the two events claimed and assess the impact of other non-qualifying events cited by the Employer. The arbitrator's decision was appealed, so *Malmaison Hotel (Manchester) Ltd* v. *Henry Boot* (1999) came to court.

The judge decided that it was impossible "to lay down hard and fast rules", but on the wording of the contract there was no bar to the Architect looking at the facts cited by the employer and then deciding whether these events had already impacted upon the Critical Path, and therefore whether the two Relevant Events pleaded by the contractor truly had the effect in their own right, as claimed.

5.4 CONCURRENT DELAYS AND DOMINANT CAUSES

By definition, the Critical Path is the optimum sequence of construction activities compatible with meeting the required end date. There is therefore one route through the project at any one time, given fixed start and end dates, although it may well change and at times there may be parallel routes through a limited string of activities.

It is therefore essential to determine the impact of any event upon the existing Critical Path—adding extra time to any one activity may mean the end date cannot now be achieved, i.e. it impacts on the Critical Path, or it may mean that a string of non-critical activities runs later, but without detriment to the required end date. The latter scenario would constitute a Concurrent Delay. If the event relied on is shown to be a Concurrent Delay, then unless the other side can show that the analysis is invalid, such evidence would defeat a contractor's entitlement to Extension of Time.

When arguing liability for delays, and in particular when arguing for entitlement to Loss and Expense, the attribution of causation can be critical. This is because on most forms of contract some recognised events are valid grounds for obtaining Extensions of Time, but are *not* valid grounds for obtaining additional costs—on the basis that these events were nobody's fault, i.e. neutral events. Thus the contractor gets further time to complete and therefore relief from possible damages, but he has to stand his own prolonged Preliminaries costs and other extended indirect costs.

So, it is important that the "Dominant Cause" is factually identified, or more precisely that all employer and self-imposed changes are retrospectively "planned", i.e. that whenever some event can be seen to have occurred, the influence on the existing Critical Path is assessed and the Critical Path to completion either confirmed or re-plotted.

For retrospective analysis purposes there are two basic techniques: "windows" and "snapshots". The former is like a monthly visitor to a site—at regular intervals "Actual" v. "Planned" progress is measured and the current causes of delay recorded. With "snapshots" the reassessment is made, not at regular intervals, but is triggered whenever an event likely to have influenced the Critical Path occurred.

The problem is that, like Custer's last stand, it is the sheer volume of slings and arrows that overwhelm, not a recognisable event, so there is something to be said for retrospectively using a combination of "windows" and "snapshots". However, for those who need to know a whole lot more about the techniques and mysteries of Planning Engineering as applied to Construction Programming, both on live projects and as expert witnesses, I can but refer you to *Delay and Disruption in Construction Contracts*, by Keith Pickavance—quite the most informative, but readable, work on the subject.

A good example of a "Dominant Cause" was in a Loss and Expense claim the author inherited when the contractor had to call in the Receiver. Various Extensions of Time had been certified by the Architect under the JCT SFBC 80 contract, including one for delays to the roof structure of six weeks under Condition 25.4.2, citing "exceptionally inclement weather". This Condition has in the past been much abused by Architects and Contract Administrators since it is a "Relevant Event" for the purpose of additional time, but not a "Relevant Matter" for the purpose of letting in a contractor's Loss and Expense claim.

In my case the agreed Construction Programme showed that the last block of maisonettes making up the five-block development should have been roofed-in and weathertight by mid-October. However, major foundation design problems had intervened and an Extension of Time of four months had been awarded. Consequently the roofing activities had been pushed into the winter months, when a prolonged spell of ice and snow set in which stopped all steel welding on the roof and generally made roofing work unsafe. The Architect duly certified a further six-week Extension of Time for "exceptionally inclement weather" under Condition 25.4.2, and the contractor was not amused!

On the "What if?" test basis, it was clear that *if* the contractor had been allowed to build the foundations as originally designed, then it was reasonable to assume that indeed the roofs would have been covered in before the onset of the ice and snow, and therefore that all activities dependent upon having watertight working conditions could have been progressed four months *and six weeks* earlier, i.e. the "Dominant Cause" was the foundation design problem, not the ice and snow.

It is often argued that a delay causing sub-contract works to commence substantially later than planned at time of accepted tender, and then to run through the winter as opposed to summer months must *ipso facto* be grounds for Extension of Time and an adjustment of the agreed contract sum, on the basis of loss of productivity as between summer and winter working. Obviously this can only be relevant to "exposed" trades such as roof cladding or curtain walling, or the primary trades such as groundworks or brickwork.

However, there are two problems in making such a claim:

— Firstly the lack of necessarily relevant accredited information on productivity losses, winter v. summer.
— The fact that most estimators work on a "swings and roundabouts" basis, i.e. if a contractor's estimator was asked in court whether he took a different view of labour resources required to complete the same amount of work in winter as opposed to summer it would be exceptional if he answered "Yes"—and could prove it.

Again comparative analysis is required. The project base line is best established by reference to historic records obtained from the Meteorological Office for the nearest weather recording station and then compared with site records, weather often being very localised.

On one of the author's sites a whirlwind struck, and apart from extensive damage caused by scaffold boards being hurled around, a site helmet, complete with sub-Agent's name on it, disappeared—only to be found some time later on the roof of a supermarket eight miles away. According to the Met Office weather records, we had only had gusts up to force 6!

As mentioned, accredited information is very scarce as to the effect of weather on productivity factors, but the following sources might be of some use, if still in print:

— The Building Research Station Report—"Weather Conditions and Productivity"
— *Construction Journal*, Vol. III, No. 2 (June 1985)—"Climatic Effects on Construction Engineering and Management"
— *Building Technology and Management*, October 1975—"Evaluating the Costs of Adverse Weather".

Subject to the possible challenge of whether the estimator took a seasonal view, probably the best approach in making a productivity loss claim on the basis of being pushed into winter working is to prepare a comparative study of one's own as to trade practice. This would cover effective starting hours and available daylight hours at the end of the day, drawing upon your own client's experience across similar projects. Wind chill factor and demotivation in miserable weather are more difficult to quantify, but nevertheless are facts of life.

A good example of the interaction of complex arguments as to who or what actually caused which element of the total delay is the case of *Ascon Constructing Ltd* v. *Alfred McAlpine Construction (Isle of Man) Ltd* (1999). The Claimant was the reinforced concrete sub-contractor on a seafront development which overran and in consequence the Defendant contractor imposed Liquidated and Ascertained Damages. On the other hand there were claims for delay citing late information concerning the lift pit, failure to keep the foundations clear of sea water, acceleration to mitigate delay, etc.

At the end of the trial the Claimant was awarded 8 ex 15 days claimed for the lift pit delay, 6 ex 22 days for the sea water problem, a pro rata extension of site Preliminaries, nothing for the alleged acceleration and was held responsible for only eight days of the total project overrun. They also escaped the financial consequences of their eight-day culpable delay, as there was no evidence that the contractor had suffered the Liquidated and Ascertained Damages at the hands of the employer, i.e. there was no proven basis for the contractor having passed them down to the sub-contractor.

5.5 WHO OWNS "FLOAT"?

Firstly there are three types of "Float":

— The incidental spare time at the end of a planned activity which is not on the "Critical Path".

— "Critical Path" time, deliberately built in by the contractor as a periodic safety valve and expressed as a "Dummy Activity", or an excess duration knowingly ascribed to a particular activity.

— The spare time sometimes shown on the contractor's Construction Programme between his earliest possible (in theory) Finish Date and the required Finish Date under the contract.

In all these situations the contractor is making assumptions. He is backing his judgement and his money as against all the risks he is about to take on the employer's behalf, e.g. availability of labour at the cost level used for tender purposes, weather etc. As such, the basic presumption is that all types of "Float" belong to the contractor.

However, there always has to be an exception to every rule, and so it turned out when the author was called in mid-term to audit a troublesome project—and subsequently to act as Employer's Agent when the original appointee prematurely issued Practical Completion and then resigned.

The employer had required an 18-month contract duration in the tender enquiry, but the lowest Design and Build tender was for a 15-month duration. The Design and Build contractor was adamant that 15 months was achievable, provided the employer agreed to make necessary decisions and give appropriate approvals in time to service the accelerated programme. However, the employer was adamant that he did not require the building until the end of the 18-month period, i.e. July, as he had no staff capability to take it over any earlier, even if available.

So the contract had been signed on the basis that the contractor would complete by the end of month 15, and then put the building on a care and maintenance basis until the end of month 18, at which time Liquidated and Ascertained Damages would kick in if the building was not completed. As such, the contractor's accepted Construction Programme showed a three-month "Float" period at the end of the project.

At the end of month 15 the contractor was not complete, but his month 15 Programme to Completion showed that he would be complete by the end of month 18, and he had at that time lodged no Extension of Time claim, or notified same. Now at about this time he got into major disputes with both his plastering and decorating domestic sub-contractors, following which his electrical sub-contractor called in the Receiver. It also happened that he had only a few weeks before sought the employer's instruction as to the choice of a feature chandelier (Provisional Sum) to be hung in the entrance atrium from the underside of the second floor slab. This work of modern art had no less than 24 lightbulbs and fancy globes.

With only three weeks to go disaster struck: a fire had totally gutted the Italian workshop where our 24 globes were all packed awaiting transit to the UK, the chandelier itself being fabricated in England, but needing trial assembly off-site prior to final hanging. Trying to be helpful (a big mistake) we located an alternative source for the globes and the contractor ordered them, but they would not be available until sometime towards the end of month 20—two months late.

At the end of month 18 works were far from finished—plastering was still 20% incomplete and second fix electrics had only just started, using a replacement sub-contractor. Eventually Practical Completion was certified (quite wrongly given the outstanding works and tests) at the end of month 20, two months late. The contractor then submitted an Extension of Time claim—not for two months, but for six months—followed swiftly by a Loss and Expense claim based on having supposedly saved four months by virtue of acceleration.

By this time the author had taken over as Employer's Agent and the contractor's two claims got the shortest of possible answers. The employer then deducted two months Liquidated and Ascertained Damages, whereupon the contractor served notice of arbitration and an arbitrator was appointed.

The legal issue came down to whether under JCT WCD 1981 the employer's approvals of the contractor's drawings, or verbal suggestions, were Instructions under the contract and in particular whether such events, including the choice of alternative chandelier globes during the three-month "Float" period, gave automatic entitlement to an Extension of Time.

Clearly our Counsel had not been previously asked to advise on JCT WCD 81 as opposed to JCT SFBC 80, and gave an opinion based on his understanding of *Balfour Beatty Construction Ltd* v. *Chestermount Properties Ltd* (1993), a JCT SFBC 80 case, where the risks of information provision and programme control are significantly different. In that case it was decided that there was no bar to the issue of an instruction for further work after the Due, but unachieved, Date for Completion; and this did not, as Balfour Beatty contended, automatically stop the clock and wipe out the existing culpable delay. The likely effect on completion of every such instruction falls to be fairly and reasonably considered by the Architect, taking into account the existing state of the works and whether, but for the culpable delay, the instruction could have been incorporated without prejudice to the achievable completion date. This is known as the "net" or "dot-on" time adjustment method. Depending on the degree of culpable delay, such a method can legitimately result in a revised Completion Date preceding the actual date of instruction. As such, Counsel advised that our case turned on two issues:

— Whether we could rely on the contractor's Completion Programme issued at the end of month 15 confirming that he would be complete at the end of month 18—but then wasn't until the end of month 20, or arguably later.

— Whether our selection of replacement globes constituted an Instruction and whether this alleged Instruction, being issued after the contractor's intended completion date, gave entitlement to an Extension of Time *until the replacement globes were available,* and the complete chandelier could be finally hung and switched on— despite there being a prepared suspension fixing and a plug in socket.

Counsel further advised that should we not be successful in relying on the decision in *Balfour Beatty* v. *Chestermount* then the cost consequences would be unsustainable by our mutual client. So we had to compromise the action. The contractor later admitted that he knew he had no real case, but was deliberately playing legal poker up to the date of the hearing, in the full knowledge that our Further Education College client could not afford the costs risks of getting involved with arbitration or litigation.

More recently the basic understanding of "Who owns Float?" has been reviewed by the courts in *Ascon Contracting Ltd* v. *Alfred McAlpine Construction (Isle of Man) Ltd* (1999), as already discussed above. McAlpine's Construction Programme showed a five-week "Float" at the end of the contract duration and they contended that Ascon were responsible for the totality of the contract overrun. Ascon challenged this as clearly there had been interacting delays.

The court favoured Ascon, the reinforced concrete frame contractor, requiring the Defendant main contractor, McAlpine, to:

— prove that the sub-contractor's performance had not been in reasonable accordance with the main contractor's programme;

— show that following trades were delayed thereby, and thus the contract completion date had been delayed primarily by Ascon; and

— properly account for the use of the five-week Float, rather than arbitrarily use the Float to eliminate or reduce delays caused by their own culpable delay and those of their other sub-contractors.

This decision is, on analysis, common sense. It does not disturb the basic position that such Float is for the contractor's management risk and not for the employer's benefit to cover delays caused by late release of information, etc—it simply requires proper accountability and allocation of fault.

The foregoing raises another issue in that it is often uncertain what the contractual status is of Contingencies and Provisional Sums in relation to the time for completion. Obviously the expenditure of such values, reserved within the agreed Contract Sum, requires express authorisation by the employer, preferably by specific Architect's Instruction rather than by drawing issue, in good time for the contractor to attend to them.

If the contractor is not to know the type and extent of work required how can he plan such values as construction activities, with dependencies on other defined activities? Yet he has, in overall terms, agreed to carry out the Contract Sum within the required contract duration.

As such, when a contractor first tables his proposed Construction Programme, post acceptance of tender, there are two alternatives:

— agree a Dummy Activity somewhere on the Critical Path to allow for carrying out the undefined work value; or
— if the Construction Programme shows the last activity finishing on the Due Date for Completion then it must be a presumption that the durations assumed for the activities when viewed collectively allow time for carrying out the undefined work, e.g. if the undefined value is 7% of the whole, somewhere the contractor has allowed the equivalent time.

In this respect the Standard Method of Measurement for Building Works 7th Edition as published by the Royal Institution of Chartered Surveyors requires Provisional Sums to be entered in Bills of Quantities as "Defined Provisional Sums" wherever it is meaningful to do so, and by implication requires the use of "Undefined Provisional Sums" to be kept to a minimum—for the very reasons outlined above. Given these two distinct definitions, it is assumed that "Defined Provisional Sums" are allowed within the contract duration, subject to detail when instructed, but that "Undefined Provisional Sums" are not necessarily included.

5.6 ACCELERATION

When a project is running late, particularly a project sensitive to the commencement of a seasonal income stream, it is not unusual for the employer to request the contractor to accelerate. Almost inevitably there will have been an earlier exchange of views with allegations of default both ways, with the contractor firmly believing that he is entitled to an Extension of Time, which has so far been denied.

The employer may well be the developer of a large commercial retail outlet or a manufacturing plant where the opening date is vital to his competitive position in his particular market, and he has to account to the funder and the appointed project monitoring consultant as to why the project is running late. If so, he can hardly admit that he has changed his mind on some aspect of the project or that the design team have not performed to schedule, so the temptation is to blame the contractor, leaning on the Architect to write the necessary letters.

The contractor on the other hand might have problems of his own, so it is all too convenient to be able to point to some shortfall or delay in the information supply—or when a genuine variation is requested to deliberately overstate the time implications, quoting a modest additional cost, which is more easily checked and therefore likely to be approved.

Whatever the rights and wrongs of the situation to date therefore it is important to appreciate that:

— It is the contractor's site and the contractor's programme.
— Until the contractor fails to meet the contractual end date (or any contractual "milestone" dates) he is not in default.
— The employer may not, under the standard forms of contract, instruct the contractor to accelerate in lieu of granting any Extension of Time that may be due.
— The employer's remedy for late completion is usually the deduction of the stated Liquidated and Ascertained Damages.

Thus in any acceleration situation the employer starts as second favourite, and for acceleration to work the contractor must also need a new deal. This will inevitably involve "wiping the slate clean", i.e. not only settling all previous disputes, but agreeing a new programme to completion and a new price—usually based on overtime working, extended Preliminaries, incentivising the key sub-contractors and of course rewarding the contractor by way of a bonus if the new target is met. But herein lies further danger.

What if the problems of the past continue? Typically the Services Engineer might continue to modify his designs and in consequence the Mechanical sub-contractor cannot now meet the agreed services balancing date. The contractor has in the meantime increased his resources and already incurred substantial costs.

The above identifies the need for total commitment by all parties to any new deal. The remaining tasks have to be identified and allocated to either the employer or the contractor, i.e. under JCT WCD 98 it would be the contractor who would be biting the bullet, as he is in total control of the information release programme.

The key elements in any acceleration deal are therefore as follows:

— Good faith and a mutual need to close the project out.

— The definition and allocation of remaining risks.
— The agreement of a Programme to Completion and the identification of Critical Path activities.
— The commitment of the design team and the key sub-contractors to that programme.
— A pre-agreed payment mechanism directly linking the required performance to the premium price to be earned, e.g. defined "milestones".

It frequently happens in commercial developments that the employer's circumstances change—typically one part of the project is pre-let after commencement of the construction project and certain works have to be brought forward to enable early completion of the pre-let works, including the early commissioning of services and temporary access, etc.

Of the JCT family of contracts only JCT SFMC 98 recognises this situation, providing at Clause 3.6 for "Acceleration—alteration of sequence or timing". In this event the employer is expressly empowered to direct the Architect or Contract Administrator to give what is then rather quaintly termed a "Preliminary Instruction" to the Management Contractor setting out the employer's new requirements.

The Management Contractor must then state:

— any objection to carrying out the new requirements;
— in respect of each Works Contractor, the additional lump sum or basis of reimbursement required, together with the earlier Completion Date that can now be agreed, or the reduction in the Extension of Time that would otherwise be due.

Strangely there is no express provision for the Management Contractor to be able to state his own additional costs and fee for organising both the estimate and the work if so instructed, but that can probably be taken as read. However, the whole point is that nothing can happen without the consent and co-operation of the Management Contractor, and the prior acceptance by the employer of the premium price to be paid.

In effect, whether expressly provided for as in JCT SFMC 98 or not, as in the other JCT contracts, acceleration has to be by mutual variation of the original contract and is most likely to be successful once the employer, through the design team, has signed off the design, including all Provisional Sums.

So, what if the contractor has applied for an Extension of Time but the Architect has rejected the application and upheld the existing Completion Date? Can this be construed as a tacit instruction to accelerate and to what extent should the contractor respond?

Each situation must depend on its own set of facts, but in principle:

- The employer or Architect has no power to instruct acceleration— it must be consensual.
- The employer's remedy for late completion is damages, but subject to the duty to have ensured that any application for an Extension of Time was properly considered.
- The contractor must take all reasonable steps to mitigate, i.e. limit the alleged delay.
- The contractor's remedies in the event of the employer seeking to deduct damages and/or not granting an Extension of Time, which may well mean denial of additional costs, are:
  (a) adjudication (optional);
  (b) arbitration or litigation, depending on the contract provision.

The contractor who deploys additional resources and voluntarily incurs additional costs without a clear commitment from the employer, achieving the completion date by effective acceleration, does so at his own risk—so, to answer the question posed above in connection with the denial of an Extension of Time request, the answer is an emphatic "No".

However, all the above arguments, and the bad feelings that are usually engendered, should be avoidable with proper Planning Engineering expertise on both the employer's and contractor's side. Once the original Construction Programme has been established, not forgetting to agree with the key sub-contractors the essential sequences and what is possible, any disruptive event should be capable of being managed into the remaining contract duration; or if that is impossible then there should be no reason not to agree an Extension of Time on a factual and fair basis, citing the true contractual reasons and so allowing for recovery of any additional costs reasonably proven.

5.7 THE NEED FOR PROGRAMME INTERROGATION

Any contractor's programme, whether presented as a proposed Construction Programme for agreement as a statement of project intent, or whether presented as a claim submission for Extension of Time or disruption towards the end of the project, must be interrogated.

It is all too easy to assume that just because a long column or row of figures is computer produced it must be mathematically correct. There is every chance of an input, transfer or spreadsheet reference error—so take nothing for granted. And so it is with computer produced Critical Path programming, as two salutary tales will demonstrate.

Some time ago the author was presented with a detailed Extension of Time claim—computer produced with all the pretty coloured lines and boxes. Essentially what the contractor was saying was that, because the employer through the design team had instructed a late amendment to the amount of cruciform glazing in a large span vaulted roof over a shopping mall involving smoke vents etc, he was entitled to an Extension of Time of 13 weeks. Certainly six weeks were justified, but why 13 weeks? So off we went to the contractor's Head Office to see supposedly the very latest IT software in action.

Now "throwing darts" at someone else's detailed programme is good sport—but aim high. Having listened to the plausible spiel, the author suggested a "What if?" scenario. The proposition was: "What if, with no roof yet on the mall vault the present developer decides to change the mall to an up-market garden centre needing only a canvas tented covering over part of the mall, i.e. no fixed roof—when will the project now be complete?"

The whole thrust of the contractor's claim submission was that to accommodate the additional cruciform glazing all the roof secondary steelwork would need to be redesigned and re-ordered—hence the Critical Path delay of 13 weeks. However, after no less than three attempts at deleting the secondary steelwork as a required activity, the contractor's chief planner had to admit that the end date inexplicably remained unaltered. A month later the contractor binned that software package in favour of another.

The other tale was told to the author just recently. A claims consultant had been asked to prepare an Extension of Time claim on behalf of a contractor on a very large overseas civil engineering project. After some 6,000 activities and dependent links had been programmed in, the answer was that the overrun was culpable delay by the contractor, i.e. no contractual event could be shown to have delayed the project beyond the Extension of Time already granted by the Engineer.

Now this was not what the client had paid good money to be told, so it was quietly decided to make just one of the links a fixed link, i.e. one activity could supposedly not start until another activity had been completed. This radically altered the Critical Path and supposedly justified a further six weeks Extension of Time!

The moral of these tales is therefore that incompetent supposed "Planners", and clever cheats, can all too easily prosper using readily available software packages—so there is no substitute for employing professional Planning Engineers, either for preparing an Extension of Time claim or perhaps even more importantly in interrogating the additional time claimed by the contractor.

Inevitably litigation will become ever more dependent on evidence created by information technology, such as described on the overseas civil engineering project referred to above. Accordingly forensic investigation of the other side's computer disks may well be needed to see just *when* and *how* someone may have resorted to some selective editing in order to make their client's case, as well as what may have been deleted.

Construction Programming is therefore no longer an art form for Architects, Engineers and Contract Administrators. Either in-house or out-house someone must have the detailed "know-how" and appropriate software to deal with contractors' claims on a scientific basis—or such professionals face the consequences of another *John Barker Construction* and *London Portland Hotels* type call on their Professional Indemnity policy. Indeed, why should employers expect any lesser degree of expertise from their appointed consultants, whether on an inclusive or on an optional fee basis?

5.8 THE IMPORTANCE OF RECORDS

We have already seen how important it is to keep a record of how the agreed Contract Sum came into being in order to show the tender base line, if ever put to proof in a claim situation, and how useful it can be to demonstrate that when site conditions permitted it was actually possible to achieve the productivity factor required to service that Contract Sum.

We have already seen in respect of weather and claimed loss of productivity that site conditions as experienced can be a law unto themselves. It is therefore necessary to set up a daily log from day 1 recording the weather pattern each day, but highlighting any heavy rain, high winds, the daily temperature at the start and end of the day and any exceptional variations, and in winter making a note of any unusual wind chill factor or site conditions inhibiting normal work. However, it is in respect of labour that it is so important that properly detailed and accurate records be kept, irrespective of any possible anticipated claim.

In the property world it is often said that the three most important aspects of any individual property are location, location, and location. So it is with the construction world when you need to make a claim—records, records and records. You simply can never have enough details of site labour hours, where the labour was deployed on a daily basis, whether the other side had been put on notice that such labour was working unproductively due to unforeseen constraints and whether they were working on a recorded time basis.

With the normal practice of sub-contracting, notably labour-only sub-contracting placed on a lump sum or targeted basis, there is in theory no need to keep site labour records, i.e. names of each operative, what time they presented themselves for work each day and at what time they individually left site. However, when you need to construct a Loss and Expense claim based on enforced loss of productivity, this is the very information you will need to rely on.

Weekends are a case in point. Usually the contractor or sub-contractor has only a skeleton staff on site until mid-day on Saturday and no presence then until Monday morning. Who can then speak for the number of men on site and the actual hours worked on Saturday afternoon or Sundays, let alone the work actually achieved?

The key to proving labour records is of course getting the employer's representative or the main contractor to sign them off as a true record. Often they will be wary of doing so, but so long as you can show when they were submitted, the fact that they had the records shortly after the event, and did not object to them, will be good evidence.

Thus any specialist sub-contractor who does not operate a strict time recording system as a matter of standard practice across all projects is leaving himself badly exposed on two fronts—from the operatives themselves, and from the main contractor when it comes to any dispute.

5.9 COUNTING THE COST

As in all things to do with good Claims practice, attention to detail is everything. For instance what is a day? It might be a calendar day, a working day (which in itself needs to be defined) or a statutory day for the purpose of the HGCR Act 1996—see Chapter 9 for further details; but do be clear in setting up the contract as to what is meant by a "day" for the purpose of contract obligations, etc. Likewise what is the accepted working week or working day for the purpose of productivity calculations?

As previously explained it is necessary when analysing any alleged loss of money or time and then presenting a claim submission to be able to define original and actual labour resources in truly meaningful terms.

As such it is not helpful in the first instance to attempt to quantify labour losses on value alone. All sorts of factors can invalidate the comparison so it should be done first of all on a pure time basis—and once the productivity loss has been established this can be translated to a monetary value.

Equally it is necessary to be careful to compare like with like, in how time is measured. Often "rule of thumb" industry productivity factors are expressed as "per day" or "per week", but as no two jobs are necessarily similar regarding available working hours, and as winter working hours availability will be less than in the summer months, all such productivity "norms" must be assumed to relate to a five-day week of eight hours per day, i.e. an across all projects, round the year, average 40-hour week for productivity calculation purposes.

Thus, given a Bill of Quantities, it should be possible to establish the notional total man weeks allowed in any tender, subject to the detail of the tender build-up as previously discussed. The actual site hours expended, net of non-productive overtime, need in the first instance to be totalled each week on a straight recorded hours worked basis. This must include any late working Monday to Friday, including both Saturday and Sunday working if allowed, but subject to independent verification of arrival and departure times by the contractor's management, and preferably also by the employer's site staff. The total recorded hours worked are then divided by the agreed working week, e.g. 40 hours to give an equivalent Man Weeks total.

The independent verification of out of hours working is important—on one of the author's expert witness instructions 14 hours a day were being claimed by the electricians on a large, high quality refurbishment project. The gate record showed them all signed out, usually as a group, sometime after 9 p.m., which with meal breaks meant they would have had to have been on site and working by 6 a.m.! In fact 8.30 a.m. was the effective start time.

Not only was the basic mathematics patently wrong, but site progress was deplorable. So we borrowed the employer's site security video tapes. These soon revealed the scam: six of the eight electricians regularly left site, without checking out, between 4 p.m. and 5 p.m. and then the other two would then work through until about 9 p.m. checking out and handing in all eight passes! Needless to say the gateman had been suitably rewarded!

Whilst labour is always going to be the most costly head of loss, materials and plant records must also be carefully kept, and checked if investigating a claim. This is a particular problem on overseas contracts where sometimes it is necessary to run your own spot checks; the author has trailed Type V cement lorries in southern Iran and ice bowsers in Riyadh, and in both cases has found that someone in the contractor's organisation was quietly supplying his local friends at the expense of our project.

Summarising therefore, all labour, material and plant costs should be recorded against the discrete project code number, with material and plant invoices confirming the site delivery address. All costs should then be posted once a week to the project cost ledger, so that at any point in time it is possible to factually show the rate of spend on the project, and at the end to be able to show, on an "open book" basis, the total recorded costs, including site salaries, before the addition of indirect costs such as Head Office Overheads.

5.10 OVERHEADS AND PROFIT

In any business undertaking, and particularly in the construction industry, there is a basic assumption of entitlement to profit in return for undertaking risk and meeting one's contractual obligations—and also to recover Overhead costs, without which the project could not have been organised and performed.

So if the project has been delayed and disrupted due to any of the qualifying events set out in the contract conditions, and an Extension of Time has been granted, it then becomes a question of how to reimburse the main contractor, or the sub-contractor as the case might be, for the diminished contribution received through the original contract sum for Overheads and Profit.

There is then a requirement, as established in *Peak Construction (Liverpool) Ltd* v. *McKinney Foundations Ltd* (1971), that a party claiming to have been delayed and caused loss by another party should be able to reasonably show that but for the problems on the site in question they could have gainfully deployed the locked-up labour, plant and management resources elsewhere. As one can never actually prove what might have been, this has to be determined on a balance of probabilities—usually a pattern of trading to demonstrate the dip in turnover during the currency of the project, and a profitable period of trading either side of the dispute.

Assuming this first criterion can be safely negotiated it then comes down to how to reasonably quantify the loss, and here it is most helpful if the tender has been structured to show a separate figure, expressed in lump sum or percentage terms, for Overheads and Profit. If this has been done there is every chance that the claim can, by common acceptance, be assessed on a formula basis—the only question being which of three formulae?

Originally the preferred formula was the "Hudson" formula, which works as follows:

R = Overhead and Profit Recovery (Value)
T = Tendered Overhead and Profit (Percentage of Costs)
CS = Contract Sum (Weeks)
CP = Contract Period (Weeks)
PoD = Period of Delay (Weeks)

the calculation then is:

$$R = T \times \frac{CS}{CP} \times PoD$$

There are however two problems with this approach. Firstly it requires the tender to show a monetary figure or percentage for Overheads and Profit, in the absence of which a retrospective tender analysis would be highly dubious evidence, and secondly, the evidential point above, it is necessary to show that the business is capable of achieving the stated level of Overheads and Profit.

When tendering one starts with tangibles, i.e. the scope of work shown or scheduled. One then has to assess risks, e.g. a tight programme, and for some risks one can make reasoned guesses, but there are always those incidental problems which beset most projects. Where does one price these intangible risks? As likely as not, wrapped up as "Overheads and Profit"— and at the end of the project they hit the Cost Ledger.

It is therefore usual to look for recovery of time-based Overheads and Profit on the "Emden" formula, where instead of taking the percentage declared in the tender for Overheads and Profit, one substitutes the level of Overheads and Profit from the audited accounts, preferably for the preceding three years of trading. The calculation is therefore:

Where A = The audited Overheads and Profit level

$$R = A \times \frac{CS}{CP} \times PoD$$

The preference for "Emden" was endorsed in the case of *J.F. Finegan Ltd* v. *Sheffield City Council* (1988) where the judge very confusingly stated "I infinitely prefer the 'Hudson' formula ...", but evidently meant to say the "Emden" formula, as he went on to say "... that is to say, overheads and profit percentage based on a fair annual average, multiplied by the contract sum and the period of delay in weeks, divided by the contract period".

In another case, heard as an appeal from the award of an arbitrator, the main contractor Claimant in *Norwest Holst Ltd* v. *CWS Ltd* (1998) sought to contend that the Respondent sub-contractor was not entitled to recover Overheads via the "Emden" formula, and the judge summarised the basic ground rules:

— The loss claimed must be shown to be factual.
— The delay must be shown to have prevented other contracts being taken on, or the company accounts must show a clear shortfall in recovery in the relevant period.
— There must be no element of double recovery via partial Overheads recovery through increased measured work value.
— Other work must be shown to have been available on the open market, and it must be shown that the resources could not be released from the project in question.

The judge backed the arbitrator and upheld the application of the "Emden" formula, but in another case the decision went the other way.

In *City Axis Ltd* v. *Daniel P. Jackson* (1998) the Defendant houseowner was held to have delayed the Claimant contractor, but the latter was evidently unable to satisfy the judge that, but for the 37-week delay in renovating Mr Jackson's house, he could have taken on other work, that he could not release the management resource, and there was no downturn in the market which might have been a contributory factor in the damage done to the Claimant's business.

The third formula, rarely used, is the "Eichleay" formula, taken from an American case of the same name. In this approach under-recovery of Overheads and Profit is calculated based on the actual spend as certified, in relation to the contract programme, and taking the audited level of Overheads and Profit as in "Emden". The calculation is therefore:

Where FA = The Final Certified spend, including variations,

$$R = A \times \frac{FA}{CP} \times PoD$$

Assuming the Final Account is greater than the Contract Sum, the recovery of Overheads and Profit using the "Eichleay", rather than the "Emden" formula, will be the greater value. If there have been no authorised delays, then arguably it has not taken additional Head Office management resources to organise the increased value, and so it would probably be more accurate to use "Emden". Conversely, if time has been extended, so will have Head Office management costs, and accordingly a case could be made for "Eichleay".

Whether or not the computer age will cause the next Defendant to a Loss and Expense claim to contend that the Claimant should have properly recorded his additional management time electronically remains to be seen—and if that happens and is upheld, then it will leave just the "*profit*" element to be adduced from the historic company accounts.

5.11 THE COST OF CLAIMS PREPARATION

It is a generally accepted principle that an injured party is put back in the position he would have been in but for the default of the other party, and an extension of this principle is that a successful party in litigation is recompensed by way of a costs award for the reasonable cost of having to pursue his contractual or common law rights.

The cost of preparing a detailed claim is no different, in that if the claim is accepted or proven then it follows that but for the default of the Defendant these costs would not need to have been incurred in the first place by the Claimant. Accordingly it is arbitrary whether they should be a Head of Claim in their own right, or whether they get added in to the legal costs, and go for assessment at the end of the day. Given that some claims do get settled by negotiation, adjudication or mediation, without involving the lawyers too heavily, the author's preference is to make them a Head of Claim, and then they are more likely to figure in any settlement negotiations.

Alternatively, under the new Civil Procedure Rules, as dealt with in detail in Chapter 11, it is required that any settlement distinguishes between accepted damages and costs. In the event of settlement it is also generally accepted that the Party accepting settlement of his claim is reimbursed all his costs up to the date of settlement. Quantum experts are therefore advised to take their solicitor's instructions early in the case preparation, including whether other technical experts' costs should also be included in the Claim submission.

Whichever approach is taken, it is important that one's time taken in claims preparation work be recorded accurately and contemporaneously— much like solicitors recording their time, as this will be persuasive evidence should your time be challenged by the other side or if the matter goes for assessment.

5.12 INTEREST AND FINANCE CHARGES

In practical terms in the construction industry "Interest" and "Finance Charges" are synonymous, but in law there is a distinction which goes back to when Queen Victoria still had a few years to reign and the concept that there was something untoward about interest—a dictionary definition being "a premium paid on the use of money". Evidently it had been public policy for some time that interest was not recoverable at common law, so the thinking was that if public policy was to be changed and interest made recoverable as a right, it was for Parliament to pass a Bill accordingly.

This question came before the Courts in *London Chatham and Dover Railway* v. *South Eastern Railway* (1893) where the Plaintiff sued for payment of a debt and interest, as the debt had not been paid by the agreed date. It was held that interest was not payable since it was contrary to statute law, and was also disallowed as a head of damage claimed on the basis of wrongful retention of the debt.

Even interest on judgment debts was deemed objectionable until public policy was eventually changed by the Law Reform (Miscellaneous Provisions) Act 1934, following which the courts were given discretion as to whether on the facts of each case they should award simple interest on damages as between the date of cause of action and date of judgment.

Time moved on, but it was not until well after the Second World War that the commercial reality of funding a business was at last recognised in respect of the law and the construction industry. The position was then clarified in *F.G. Minter Ltd* (alias Drake & Scull, name borrowing from the main contractor) v. *Welsh Health Technical Services Organisation* (1981) where the Claimant included "Finance Charges" as a head of claim, and ran the legal argument that such costs were a "direct loss and/or expense" within the meaning of the contract, relying on the first limb of *Hadley* v. *Baxendale* (1854), i.e. that in the context of the modern construction industry, if cash flow is wrongfully interrupted and the Claimant consequently incurs bank charges pending dispute resolution, then such charges can be seen to flow naturally from the originating breach.

Any claim should use the phrase "Finance Charges" rather than "Interest" and when notified should make it clear that the costs will continue to accrue until settled by agreement or by judgment. In practice contractors do not have individual bank accounts for individual projects so no statement of interest will be available. It is therefore neccessary to create a project-specific calculation. As the bank will have taken interest every quarter it is now accepted that such calculations can be on the basis of compound interest, not simple, with the actual rate of interest being at whatever percentage above base that has been agreed between the Claimant and his bank manager.

A few contractors, particularly in the specialist field, do not depend upon bank borrowing, but the same principles can be argued on the basis of opportunity (to lend money/invest on the open market) that has been denied by having to lock up the capital needed to finance the temporary shortfall in income from the "guilty" Defendant. However there must be some doubt whether such a claim would be held to be within the legal understanding of "direct loss and/or expense".

CHAPTER 6

KEY ELEMENTS OF PROFESSIONAL NEGLIGENCE CLAIMS

6.1 PROFESSIONAL INDEMNITY INSURANCE AND PROOF OF COVER

The great majority of construction clients are laymen in professional terms, requiring new build or refurbishment of old buildings to further their business interests, or on a domestic level to expand their personal lifestyles. Whatever the cost, a building contract possibly represents the biggest single investment they have yet made in their life and more often than not they have borrowed heavily to achieve their objective. As such, they can find the whole design, procurement, build-out and final account process thoroughly traumatic, and are reliant on professional advice to steer them through the various pitfalls. If they have got thus far without a major cost or time overrun they have done well, and having finished with the contractor the last thing they then expect is for defects to appear in the building. Unfortunately defects are an inherent part of the building process, particularly where lowest price and shortest time have been the dominant criteria of the employer's brief.

In a survey carried out in the late 1990s it was found that of the defects discovered during the first ten years of a building's life only 35% were discovered in the contractual Defects Liability Period—thus on average an alarming 65% remain to manifest themselves once the building has been handed over and supposedly fully snagged. Such defects could be minor, nuisance value items, or they could well be significant errors of design, or construction requiring substantial remedial works which could well adversely affect the income stream of the new investment.

At worst, defects can blight the property and lead to the insolvency of the developer, e.g. the old Pordage & Sons fruit and vegetable depot site on the corner of Hills Road and Brooklands Avenue in Cambridge; this large office block development has never been occupied and has now stood empty and overgrown for years. This project subsequently made case law as *Alfred McAlpine* v. *Panatown* (1998), as referred to in Chapter 2 in connection with a technical "No loss" defence.

Central to the problem of financial recovery is the fact that the aggrieved employer, faced with defects, is not to know until intrusive investigations have been carried out who to point the finger at—Architect? Engineer? Contractor? On the basis that the Contractor built it and it has failed, the Contractor has to be the first port of call, in theory; but when one is setting up a contract tender enquiry one has to provide for all eventualities when acting for the employer, i.e. there can be no certainty that the contractor will be still trading several years later, nor can there be any certainty that the cause of the problem will be found to be simply a construction error.

There is also the consideration that in most construction arrangements, excluding design and build projects, the professionals engaged by the employer to design the building have also been engaged to supervise the workmanship and specification compliance; so from the employer's point of view it is seemingly an each way bet, either the designer got it wrong, or he should have spotted the construction error and had it corrected. Unfortunately the law does not see it in such black and white terms and draws the line on the facts of each case as to what a reasonably competent supervisor might be excused for not spotting during the course of the works, in which case the employer is left with the contractor as the only source of financial recompense.

So, when setting up a contract and appointing the professional team, the matter of Professional Indemnity Insurance cover will be high on the list— and because your client's very livelihood could depend upon it there is no substitute for being very demanding if the selected professionals really want the commission. From each professional's point of view the annual premium for P.I. cover is a very large part of his overheads, paid up front irrespective of whether he has actually any fees coming in. Further, most professional institutions require their members to carry a certain level of minimum cover, but this does not mean to say that the individual you have in mind has so complied, so each member of the proposed professional team must expect to be required to submit written confirmation from their current insurer of the following:

— Policy number
— Class of business covered
— Maximum value of cover for any one claim without limitation by aggregate of claims made in the year
— Renewal date
— Any special conditions attached to the policy.

Ideally one should see a copy of the policy and know the claims record of the individual—often excesses have been imposed and as such the full recovery value could be at risk. However, these are sensitive areas so usually such further information is politely refused.

Assuming defects then appear some time after final completion, as in the survey referred to, the employer will put the various members of the old design team on notice of possible claim, as well as notifying the contractor, if he is still in business. The design professionals will then notify their current insurer as soon as they know of any potential liability, however remote and however strenuously they feel like protesting their innocence— but the current insurer may well not be the same P.I. insurer that was declared at the outset of the project since all P.I. Claims fall to be met on a "Claims made" basis, i.e. when discovered, not when the alleged negligent act may have been committed.

Because the underlying cause of the defect is as yet unknown and because the current practice of professional appointments is based on joint and several liability for defects, this process initially catches the innocent with the guilty, thus causing each consultant and his insurer to reach for their own solicitor, and each solicitor to reach for an expert, all with the hidden agenda of proving it was someone else's fault!

This theoretical hunt for the guilty can often become focused on whoever is left in the frame with a known and current P.I. policy—even pulling in Project Monitors if necessary, or even the original solicitors if it can be shown that a defect in the contractual arrangements has allowed the true guilty party to escape the consequences of his negligence. As such, proof of current P.I. cover is a key factor in determining whether to commence a recovery action against any particular individual or practice, and naturally there is a reluctance for insurers to allow their insured to reveal details of policy cover for fear of being targeted, especially when it was someone else's problem.

However, from the employer's point of view, he needs to be able to recover damages from someone, but if full details of current P.I. cover are not revealed on request—most professionals being careful to ringfence their personal assets, especially if they are not prepared to pay P.I. premiums—it can be a considerable risk to proceed against a potentially worthless party. But help is available for the employer seeking retribution for defects: there are certain agencies, allied to the accountancy profession, who are now able to offer an enquiry service into the P.I. status of any professional individual or practice for a reasonable fee.

6.2 INSURER'S RIGHT TO VOID COVER

It is a fundamental principle of insurance law that both parties act in good faith, particularly where one party (the insurer) is entirely reliant on the information given by the other party (the insured) in assessing the risk and offering cover for a risk assessed price. This principle does not stop with the original insurance bargain and many policies require the insured to keep the insurer informed of any material change in circumstance, known only to the insured, which could affect the risk assessment. Professional Indemnity Insurance policies are no exception, the conditions attaching to the policy usually being widely drawn as to what might constitute a material change in circumstance.

As such the insured Consultant must be very careful to contact his broker or insurance company at the first sign of trouble on a project where rightly or wrongly the finger might be pointed at him. This applies equally to Consultants practising as sole traders, the same as it applies to individuals acting under the P.I. insurance umbrella of a large practice.

In a large practice all fee earners should be required to sign an annual declaration that they either know of no matter which could possibly give rise to a call on the firm's policy, or alternatively that there might be a possible problem—except of course that any such possible problem should be notified on first knowledge, rather than on the annual prompt. Sensibly, this precautionary notification is then reviewed periodically and either withdrawn or promoted to formal notification status.

The Insurer's right if not so notified is to cancel the policy, i.e. to void the Claim. This has serious implications for all concerned, not least the party relying on the Consultant's Insurer's payout to fund the remedial works and pay the inevitable legal expenses of having had to pursue the Consultant in the first place. However, the good news is that this right is very, very rarely invoked in respect of Professional Indemnity Insurance— the author has never heard of such an instance in over 30 years' experience of the construction industry.

6.3 THE DUTIES OF THE CONSTRUCTION PROFESSIONAL

There are of course many types of professional consultants involved in the construction industry and a wide variety of specialist skills they purport to provide. The common denominator is that they all owe a duty of care to anyone to whom they sell their services, and if things go wrong then damages remain to be assessed in accordance with the two limbs of *Hadley* v. *Baxendale* (1854), namely:

— Damages to be "... such as may fairly and reasonably be considered naturally, i.e. according to the usual course of things, from such breach of contract itself ..."; or

— ". . . for such as may reasonably be supposed to have been in the contemplation of both parties at the time they made the contract, as the probable result of the breach of it".

In short Rule 1 is that damages must flow naturally from the breach and Rule 2 is that the loss must be reasonably foreseeable.

Unfortunately for some consultants the principle of duty of care has on occasions even been applied to negligent free advice, but there would have to be exceptional circumstances such as in *Hedley Byrne* v. *Heller & Partners* (1963). However, the usual problem area is not in respect of negligent design work, as this is reasonably identifiable against accepted standards and good practice, but in respect of alleged negligent supervision of building works—defects having been discovered.

The basic position is to be found in an extract from the judgment in *East Ham Corporation* v. *Bernard Sunley & Sons Ltd* (1966). In this case the judge stated:

> "As is well known the Architect is not permanently on site but appears at intervals, it may be of a week or a fortnight, and he has, of course, to inspect the progress of the works. When he arrives on the site there may be very many important matters with which he has to deal ... He may in such circumstances think he knows the builder sufficiently well and can rely upon him to carry out a good job; that it is more important that he should deal with urgent matters on the site than that he should make a minute inspection on the site to see that the builder is complying with the specifications laid down ... It by no means follows that, in failing to discover a defect which a reasonable examination would have disclosed, in fact the Architect was necessarily thereby in breach of his duty to the building owner so as to be liable in an action for negligence. It may well be that the omission of the Architect to find a defect was due to no more than an error of judgement, or was a deliberately calculated risk which, in all the circumstances of the case, was reasonable and proper."

With due respect to the judge, the construction world is now very different from the gentlemanly days of 1966—mainly due to the proliferation of sub-contracting at all levels of the industry—and a higher level of attention to specification compliance is probably now required from the Architect or Contract Administrator.

Much will of course depend upon the terms of the professional appointment and the particular duties required, but in principle if the employer is paying fees for a professional consultant to reasonably ensure that the builder actually complies with the drawings and specification, then if the builder defaults there must, in principle at least, be a right to recovery against the appointed Consultant.

The required quality of professional advice is all a question of degree and reasonableness when judged against current standards, as we shall see later in this Chapter, but in the meantime an interesting case on the issue of workmanship and the level of supervision required was *The Department of National Heritage* v. *Steenson Varming Mulcahy & Others* (1998). This case was all about the "buildability" of "lid-down" cable and trunking installation—measured by the proverbial mile, in the New British Library—another project on which the author had a very small part many years ago, when the original scheme was still on the Architect's drawing board in Cambridge.

The problem was that in drawing the miles of cable through the trunking much damage had been done—snagging and stripping the cable installation on sharp edges and causing faults all over the system. The question for the court was therefore who should pay for the remedial works and the very considerable associated costs?

The fact was that this project stage had been let under a Construction Management arrangement and when this serious and virtually inaccessible defect arose a call was made on the project insurers, who paid out £8.4m and then under their rights of subrogation wanted their money back from whoever might be found to be the guilty party. So the insurers sued in the name of the Government client, alleging that the design by Defendants was inherently "unbuildable". Further, the insurers relied on the wording of the consultancy agreement, wherein the Defendants undertook to "make site visits of inspection to ensure that the works are being properly supervised and executed in accordance with the design and specifications and otherwise to safeguard good engineering practice".

Game, set and match to the employer one might think—but each case depends on its very own facts. In this case the evidence was that:

— The Defendant had specifically warned of the need for a high standard of workmanship, and the Construction Manager had supported the Defendant in this respect at the time of Works Package placement.
— The Defendant's appointment allowed the Construction Manager to require the Defendant to appoint site supervision staff, but such an option had not been exercised.
— The Construction Manager had parallel obligations to supervise and co-ordinate the works.

Accordingly the judge held that the Defendant consultant was not guilty on the charge of negligence, on the basis that:

— The damage arose right inside the installation where even with the closest of periodic inspection it would not necessarily have been evident—the consultant not being required to have the equivalent skill and attention to detail as a site agent installing the work.

— Making visits to ensure that the works were executed in accordance with the specification fell short of being required to guarantee the workmanship of the Works Package Contractor.

Nevertheless it must have been a close run thing given the express wording of the consultancy agreement; and was only presumably defended by insurers acting on behalf of the consultant on the basis of having joined in the installation contractor, i.e. if the consultant had been found liable to the employer, he could have expected a substantial contribution from the party actually responsible for not having exercised due care in pulling the cables through the ducting in the first place.

However, the real moral of the story is, if acting for the employer, you must be absolutely clear that you require your appointed consultant to:

— specify designs which are essentially buildable;
— identify any areas or aspects of the installation requiring particular attention by the contractor;
— be responsible himself for ensuring that difficult areas are fully supervised and spot checked during, rather than at the end of the installation; or
— to recommend if and when full-time site supervision is required.

Unsurprisingly the standard forms of contract are non-specific as to where the duty to supervise ends, and of course the standard forms of consultancy appointment are woollier still, being drafted to protect their own members.

The Architect often acts as lead consultant both pre-contract and post-contract on matters other than design and supervision, and here again he can be in the firing line for the mistakes of others. In *Gable House Estates* v. *The Halpern Partnership and Bovis Construction Ltd* (1995) very confused and inaccurate advice on the available lettable area was provided to the Plaintiff developer by the Defendant Architect, and also direct by his consultant Quantity Surveyor, on a proposed refurbishment scheme, and based on this advice the developer proceeded with the scheme. When the scheme was found to be 2,000 sq. ft. short in lettable area this altered the viability of the scheme and the Plaintiff developer sued for £32.5m— several times the project value.

The Architect was duly held liable for the flawed advice, although it was primarily the Quantity Surveyor who was at fault. The judge found that if at the design stage there was any doubt as to the final lettable area that could be achieved, after the demands of the Building Regulations and Means of Escape had been satisfied, then the Architect had a clear duty to warn the Plaintiff that the advised areas on which the income stream was based might change, and this he had failed to do.

Then when dealing with final account matters there is a duty on the Architect (or quantity surveyor or engineer or construction manager) to act fairly, and not to take a hard-nosed contractual stance. In *Berrnhard's Rugby Landscape* v. *Stockley Park Consortium No. 2* (1998) the construction manager arbitrarily dismissed the contractor's account, calling for further details. The judge disagreed and found that even if the contractor's submission was not entirely complete there was an obligation to deal with those elements on which there was sufficient information and to detail his objection to the remainder.

Finally in this section, what about the duties of quantity surveyors? Apart from some ancient case law in which quantity surveyors featured they appear to have escaped the attention of the courts in recent years. However, we know from cases previously mentioned—*Aggad* v. *Marshall-Andrew* and *Gable House Estates* v. *Halpern*—that the sins of quantity surveyors are sometimes the underlying cause of a dispute between other parties. However, as we shall see when discussing professional duties under Design and Build, unless they step out of their usual area of expertise and offer their services as Employer's Agents, generally speaking quantity surveyors are not a high risk profession from P.I. insurers' point of view.

6.4 THE STANDARD OF PROOF REQUIRED FOR PROFESSIONAL NEGLIGENCE CLAIMS

Quite rightly the level of proof required to find a professional man guilty of negligence has to be fairly high, given that in any walk of life some practitioners will be more expert than others. The question is: where to draw the line?

Firstly of course, following the long-established twin principles of *Hadley* v. *Baxendale* (1854)—see section 6.3—it has to be established that:

— the Claimant relied on the advice given; and
— that in so doing he incurred demonstrable losses which flowed directly from the advice;
— and that such losses could have been reasonably foreseen had such defective advice been contemplated.

It then comes down to the detail of the advice or professional service complained of, and how that is to be measured against acceptable standards.

In a case against a Quantity Surveyor for Professional Negligence the author had prepared a detailed Expert's Report, approved by both leading and junior Counsel, when for various reasons it was necessary to change the leading Counsel, with just two weeks to go before trial. The new QC, not then known as a construction silk, obviously saw the tactics of our client's case very differently. As we went through my Report he wanted *Whitehouse* v. *Jordan* (1981) quoted on every page.

In this unfortunate medical case a forceps delivery had gone wrong, resulting in severe brain damage to the baby, and the parents were awarded £100,000 damages in the High Court, but lost on appeal and lost again in the House of Lords. The central issue was Lord Denning's statement as the appeal judge that "We must say, and say firmly, that, in a professional man an error of judgement is not negligent."

Quite how one could reasonably relate a medical negligence case of a surgeon taking a life or death decision in very difficult circumstances to that of a quantity surveyor simply not bothering to do any sort of a job, and so incurring only financial loss for the employer, did not impress the author. When the author respectfully suggested that if the Expert's Report was to be rewritten to plead the case, then maybe Counsel and Expert should switch fees, there was a predictable sense of humour failure, followed by an apology from Counsel. My Report survived in its then form, and the case was settled by the quantity surveyor's insurers 10 days later for over £2m including costs. Not a bad result considering we had started as second favourites, defending a very modest fee claim, but soon found the counterclaim potential.

Contrary to Counsel's opinion in the author's quantity surveying case, the generally accepted definition of professional negligence is that to be found in another medical negligence case, *Bolam* v. *Friern Barnet Hospital Management Committee* (1957), where the judge stated that "The test is the standard of the ordinary skilled man exercising and professing to have that special skill. It is well established law that it is sufficient if he exercises the ordinary skill of an ordinary competent man exercising that particular art."

The question then arises as to whether the lay client is required to make allowance in his reliance on professional advice for the relative age and experience of the professional offering that advice, i.e. would you not expect better quality advice from a 55-year-old equity partner as compared with a 25-year-old employee? In practice you may well make such an allowance, but the law imposes no duty on you to do so. In *Andrew Master Homes Ltd.* v. *Cruikshank and Fairweather* (1980) it was found that "The degree of knowledge and care to be expected is thus seen to be that degree possessed by a notionally and duly qualified person practising that profession. The test is, therefore, if I may put it that way, an objective test referable to the notional member of the profession and not a subjective test referable to the particular professional man employed."

6.5 EMPLOYER'S AGENTS' DUTIES IN DESIGN AND BUILD

The choice of the term "Employer's Agent" by the JCT drafting committee in preparing the original Standard Form of Contract With Contractors Design 1981 was very deliberate—and distinguishes this form of procurement from the more traditional, fully employer designed, contract represented by JCT SFBC 1980/1998, where the Architect, although employed by the building owner, nevertheless has the duty to act impartially as between employer and contractor in administering the contract.

Quite specifically, under JCT WCD 98 the Employer's Agent is the employer's representative and not a third party certifier. His legal duties are owed to the employer, and no one else, and his role can be summarised as the technical ears, eyes and mouth of the employer.

The fact that under a Design and Build contract it is the contractor, and not the employer's design team, who is responsible for developing and finalising the executed design inevitably creates all kinds of scenarios when problems arise—and often the employer is left badly exposed either by the contractual arrangement, or by the confused liabilities arising. This is regularly the case where, as often happens in practice, the contract is set up on the basis that after the notional design and tender stage the whole design team will then be novated to the successful tenderer, in the belief that such a move will guarantee continuity of design concepts and delivery of required standards. The theory is fine, but reality is harshly different. Very few contractors, whether on JCT SFBC 98 or WCD 98 will do other than their minimal best, as after all they are in business to maximise the shareholders' profits and keep their jobs/earn their personal bonuses.

Just imagine you are the Architect destined to be novated—you need the fees so have reluctantly agreed to the novation agreement. There are five contractors on the tender list, two of whom you consider to be "rogues". Sod's law being what it is, one of the two submits the lowest tender, and try as you might you cannot find legitimate grounds to persuade your present, and possibly long-standing client, that his is not the "best value" tender.

The evil day comes and all of a sudden you are transferred to "the opposition". You are probably regarded as just as big a misfit as you indeed perceive yourself to be, attending your first in-house meeting in the contractor's offices. It quickly becomes apparent that a trusted staff engineer will be making all the design decisions and selecting all materials, and that you are there solely to watch the contractor's back on such matters as Building Regulations, Means of Escape and deleterious materials while at the same time putting your own P.I. policy on the line for your new employer. In the meantime your consultancy agreement is still being prepared in Head Office, and without a signed contract you feel distinctly nervous.

So what are your professional duties? In short they are whatever the contractor says they are, unless of course these details have been wisely prescribed as part of the tender requirement, and more often than not the tender conditions and subsequent novation agreement are silent or at best vague.

In the meantime, the employer has had to appoint someone else in your place as his right hand man, and as the Employer's Agent under the contract. Again, more often than not that person tends to be the original quantity surveyor, for whom there is no place under a novation agreement, so almost by default a consultant has been appointed with no design skill or formal training in architectural or engineering site supervision. This is a recipe for disaster—as we shall see.

Alternatively, should you be the non-novated quantity surveyor offered the appointment to act as Employer's Agent—don't be tempted, not unless you have the necessary technical team of architectural or building surveying advice right behind you, supported by structural engineers and services engineers.

Assuming however that you have managed not to be novated and are now appointed as Employer's Agent under the contract, what are your duties? These can be summarised as:

— To act generally on behalf of the employer in respect of the obligations ascribed to the employer under the contract, except in respect of making payments.
— To receive, comment upon and monitor the contractor's programme.
— To receive, comment upon and return the contractor's "For Construction" drawings.
— To issue "Change Order" instructions only as necessary to the contractor and to operate a system for recording pre-agreement, if required, as to cost and time.
— To inspect the works as necessary to ensure compliance with the "Employer's Requirements" and "Contractor's Proposals", together with the design development drawings.
— To agree payments due each month and on Final Account, and to sign the project off in terms of accepted completion.
— Generally, to safeguard the employer's interests and in particular to ensure that all statutory requirements and consents are obtained.

The reader will notice that all the above are passive duties. This does not mean they are not onerous, but it demonstrates the whole concept of design and build—it is the contractor that must lead the project in all respects, and the Employer's Agent is in the role of super-checker, rather than instigator.

As such any Employer's Agent who accepts his appointment without ensuring that the Supplementary Provisions, Conditions S1 to S7 of the JCT WCD 98, or that an equivalent pre-agreement of cost and time clause is in place, is at risk. Quite probably he is guilty of professional negligence even before the project has started on site in not opting-in these eminently sensible provisions, unless of course the employer has decided otherwise, after due warning. Similarly, solicitors who set up a Design and Build contract on behalf of an employer or funder without opting-in such pre-agreement requirements, without which "Change Orders" do not qualify for adjustment of the Contract Sum or the Completion Date, are putting their P.I. policies on the line.

Likewise, the Employer's Agent who proceeds with the aforesaid pre-agreement requirements contractually in place and then fails to enforce them deserves all that is coming to him when the project overruns either in time or cost—usually both. Such incompetent Employer's Agents do exist—as the author found when called upon to audit a £4m College of Further Education project being administered by the recently privatised Architect's Department of the Local Authority. Suffice it to say their negligence left the College with a Final Account claim of circa £7m.

There is of course no third party certifier under the JCT WCD 98 contract, so it is particularly important from the employer's point of view that the Employer's Agent puts a strictly controlled payment application receipt and approval system in place in order to comply with the requirements of the HGCR Act 1996. Under the original detailed provisions (subject to promised review) large sums of money have been ordered to be paid by adjudicators—without enquiry into the merits or otherwise of the monies claimed where the paying party is in technical default of the statutory payment provisions. Such decisions of adjudicators, given under "The Scheme" provisions, have been robustly and swiftly enforced by the courts.

The provisions of the Housing Grants, Construction and Regeneration Act 1996 (HGCR Act) are dealt with in detail in Chapter 9, but the implications for Architects, Employer's Agents, Engineers, etc are clear: miss a date by one "day" and your client could be having to write a large, and potentially unjustified, cheque in favour of the contractor. As sure as night follows day, you will then have a call on your P.I. policy and however the issue is eventually resolved it is likely to hit your premium at next renewal, as well as increase your excess.

As we shall see in Chapter 9, the statutory definition of a "day" is tricky—some Bank Holidays count and some don't! In any event certain contractors are past masters at knowing when to present a payment application, and then using, or some would say abusing, the legal process when not paid within the contractual or statutory time scale.

An example of this was Christmas 1995. The same Design and Build contract for a Further Education College as referred to above was halfway through with the contractor beginning to struggle, and there was the odd reference in Minutes of Meetings to a possible claim. On 23 December, the last working day before the college shut down at mid-day for two weeks holiday, the contractor sent a lad with a payment application to an outpost of the same college, and obtained a signed receipt for the unopened package timed at 11.58 a.m. Inside the envelope was the usual monthly works in progress build-up totalling circa £300,000, plus a bulky statement of claim for circa £2m.

When the college Principal returned to work on 8 January the first letter opened was from the contractor's solicitor giving notice that as no payment or notice of objection had been received within 10 days as required by the contract, i.e. by 2 January, all work on the site would cease on 9 January unless a cheque was produced by close of play on 8 January for £2.3m. Further, that an Application for Summary Judgment would be commenced within 28 days if the claim could not be settled to the contractor's satisfaction!

Particular attention therefore needs to be paid by both solicitors and Employer's Agents to the detail and the dates of payment arrangements on contracts where application is to be made direct by Party B to Party A, rather than through an intermediary—allowing for the non-allowable Bank Holidays and for the irregularities of how Christmas and New Year's Day fall each day. In this respect it may also be appropriate to prescribe for the 13 Jewish holy days each year, as seen in many of the Canary Wharf contract arrangements.

However, the bottom line is that as a representative of the employer there is simply no alternative to getting the detailed payment provisions correct at the outset of the project, or you may well have stored up a problem which will strain relations between yourself and your client, if the contractor enforces his rights!

Finally the most likely area for exposure as Employer's Agent under a Design and Build contract is if you undertake duties beyond your own professional calling, without recognising the gap in your personal expertise and plugging that gap by sub-contracting the duty. This is an all too familiar scenario on Design and Build projects, where the design team is novated to the contractor, and someone then has to validate the building on behalf of the employer.

The leading case in this respect is *George Fischer Holding Ltd* v. *Davis Langdon and Everest* (1994)—in fact a "Turnkey" Design and Build project; when major defects became apparent, the Design and Build contractor decided to cease trading. Left behind to sort out the problems were one angry employer and one quantity surveying practice, who had taken on the role of Employer's Agent. The principal defect was a thoroughly leaking flat roof over the new production area and part of the administrative offices, the Defendant having recommended the selection of the single span, minimal fall proprietary roof in preference to a more traditional flat roof on the basis of cost and time. Fine maybe as professional advice from a quantity surveyor, but not so fine as professional advice from an Employer's Agent concerned with fitness for purpose, buildability and freedom from future defects.

At the trial the Defendant's principal witness of fact admitted that he had not inspected the roof construction in the course of erection as he considered the access ladders were unsafe! Unfortunately, Counsel also proceeded to have tantamount to an argument with the judge, which was reported verbatim in the judgment. Seemingly also the judge was so unimpressed with certain evidence concerning the Claimant's need for early certification of Practical Completion, that this aspect (on which the Defendant partly relied) did not feature in the judgment.

At the root of the allegations of professional negligence were the twin issues of duty to warn and duty to pay particular attention by way of supervision to what should have been known to be critical areas of workmanship. Unfortunately for the Defendant and his insurers, the Defendant had been particularly foolish in returning the Performance Bond to the bondsman (presumably without taking written legal advice), on the basis that having issued the Practical Completion Certificate (because the employer had insisted on taking partial possession) the Bond said it was to be returned to the Bondsman—yet the roof had leaked like the proverbial sieve almost from day 1 after installation.

The judge was accordingly forthright in his judgment, finding that the errant quantity surveyor had failed to discharge his duties as Employer's Agent. According to the judge the Employer's Agent had a duty to:

— appraise and advise on the suitability of the contractor's design proposals at tender stage;
— approve and comment upon the contractor's pre-start on site design development drawings—an express duty in this case;
— approve the contractor's post-contract design development drawings—held to be an implied term;
— watch the works in progress for specification and workmanship compliance, paying particular attention to high risk areas;
— bring in specialist advice where expertise required is beyond in-house skill base;

— properly certify Practical Completion—patent defects and the contractor not having vacated the works being key criteria in this case, irrespective of partial occupation by the employer;

— warn the employer of the commercial consequences of issuing Practical Completion when patent defects are known to exist, with particular reference to the release of retention monies and return of the Performance Bond.

If therefore you are setting up a Design and Build contract and propose appointing a quantity surveying practice to act as Employer's Agent after novation of the original design team, just ask to see the scope of their P.I. insurance cover. Also, ask who will be approving the contractor's design development drawings and inspecting the works on site for specification compliance and workmanship. The chances are that given the pressure on fees they think they can do it themselves, but can they?

6.6 PROJECT MANAGERS AND PROJECT MONITORS

The same comments about quantity surveyors acting beyond their particular areas of expertise apply equally to Project Managers and Project Monitors. On the basis of "Who guards the guards?" if the prisoner escapes, the responsibility passes up the line, and so it is with defects. As in the *George Fischer Holding Ltd* case financial liability can readily fall, not on the company responsible for the faulty workmanship, which was the direct cause of the damage and business interruption, but on the company who offered themselves as the ensurer of the performance of the guilty contractor or consultant.

As such, and on the principle established in the British Library case, referred to earlier in this chapter, the inspectors cannot be expected to have the same level of expertise as those installing the difficult work, but they are expected to know where the risks lie and to put particular measures in place to ensure that everything that can reasonably be done by way of supervision is so done—but short of actually guaranteeing a defects free installation.

So in the case of Project Managers, and with Project Monitors acting on behalf of funders, they have to make doubly sure that all those with executive authority on the contract are performing correctly. If, when defects arise, the consultant first in line is no more, or if it transpires he has no or inadequate P.I. insurance cover, then the Project Manager or Project Monitor may have to step into the breach and put his own P.I. policy on the line.

As already identified, the need to protect the employer's position as regards dealing with the contractor's payment applications is an obvious area of exposure for Project Managers, but even more critical is the need to make doubly sure that all Bonds, Warranties and P.I. policies are in place. Just such an issue came up in *Pozzolanic Lytag Ltd* v. *Brian Hobson Associates* (1998) where the Defendants had been engaged by the Plaintiffs to act as Project Managers for a pulverised fuel ash storage silo. Unfortunately when the dome collapsed it was discovered that the Design and Build contractor had inadequate insurance cover, as in fact required by Clause 21A.1 of JCT WCD 81. Seemingly the Project Manager had made initial checks on the cover held by the contractor and had merely advised the employer that it was deficient, but had then taken no further action to ensure that the deficiency was made good or that the employer himself had actioned the matter. As such he was held to have fallen short of the professional standards required of a Project Manager.

There is also trouble in store for Project Managers in respect of the HGCR Act 1996 and the fact that all consultancy appointments related to a qualifying construction contract are caught by the statutory requirements. The employer cannot be assumed to be knowledgeable on such matters, although some are, so it falls to the Project Manager to hold the employer's hand in dealing with fee payment applications.

Firstly the individual consultancy appointments must comply with the payment provisions of the Act, or the back-up statutory "Scheme for Construction Contracts" will apply—just the same as it will apply to contracts for the actual building works if the signed contract does not comply with the essential provisions of the HGCR Act 1996. This means that the employer will need to be specifically advised as to when to expect fee applications from each consultant, the strict timetable for dealing with them, and the requirement for the two notices required under the Act— albeit it is only the Withholding Notice that is critical.

The effect of this is that the Project Manager is, by default, now landed with arduous responsibilities that he simply did not have, unless specifically agreed before 1 May 1998 when the HGCR Act came into force. If a consultant's application for fees is not acceptable to the employer for any reason, but no Withholding Notice has been issued by the employer, there is no reason why, if he so wished, he could not invoke section 111 and call for adjudication. The chances are that he would be awarded those fees in full, simply as a matter of statutory default.

Assuming it is at the end of the project, the unhappy employer will then have no opportunity to set off the perceived overpayment from the next fee billing, so will have to litigate or arbitrate to get those fees back. Alternatively he may well point the finger at the Project Manager and invite a contribution—unless of course the Project Manager fancies a claim on his P.I. policy, and the inevitable hike in his policy excess.

This new duty for Project Managers is in line with the requirement for Project Managers to effectively manage the professional team and also specifically to report to the employer any concerns as to non-performance of any other team member: *Chesham Properties* v. *Bucknall Austin* (1996). Whether this "whistle-blowing" duty would apply to all consultants in a team of equal status, i.e. where there is no designated Project Manager or official lead consultant, remains to be seen—but if the industry should go that far it will, in the author's opinion, be one big step too far.

Given the additional duties falling on the Project Manager as a result of the HGCR Act 1996 in administering consultants' fee applications there is no reason why there should not be a separate fee, chargeable for this service—and for taking the risk of getting it wrong. Alternatively it could be expressly excluded in the Project Manager's fee proposal.

6.7 LIMITATION OF LIABILITY

In Chapter 3 we looked at the question of limitation in respect of the legal time barring of actions, but there is also the question of Architects and other professionals seeking to limit their exposure to design liability—either by "risk dumping" on others, i.e. sub-contracting, or by express provision in their terms of appointment.

Dealing with "risk dumping" first, if contractors can limit liability by sub-contracting why can't consultants do likewise? Such a proposition was put to the test in the case of *Cliffe (Holdings) Ltd* v. *Parkman Buck Ltd* (1996) where under a Design and Build contract a structural engineer sub-contracted the architectural elements to an Architect who then so performed as to cause economic loss to the contractor. The contractor therefore commenced proceedings on two fronts: firstly against the engineer based on the contract between contractor and engineer, and secondly against the Architect, alleging a duty of care in tort. The Architect of course sought to rely on the fact that there was no contract between himself and the contractor, and claimed that given his contract with the engineer there could be no parallel liability direct to the contractor.

Unfortunately the court didn't agree and whilst the engineer was held liable for the defective architectural design work, so was the Architect—and it was the latter who had to pay for most of the damages awarded. Seemingly, the court followed the principle established in a non-building case *Henderson* v. *Merrett Syndicates Ltd* (1994) where it was held that a professional consultant "voluntarily assumes responsibility" if he knowingly gives advice that he knows will be passed to a third party and that in all probability will then be relied on by the third party.

As to the second proposition that an Architect, or other professional, may seek to limit his liability by express provision in his terms of appointment—this was tested in another case *Moores* v. *Yakeley Associates* (1998). Now it so happens that in the author's previous existence as a young quantity surveyor in Cambridge I knew the Architect in this case, who has since gone on to be one of the leading lights in the Royal Institute of British Architects.

Apparently, the Defendant Architect had secured a commission at the height of the mid-1990s recession to design a bungalow, estimated to cost circa £250,000, and had entered into contract on exchange of letters wherein terms were proposed and not dissented from by the Claimant. These directly referred to the Architect's Standard Form of Agreement 1992 (SFA/92). Clause 6.2 provided for the limit of liability to be stated and, although the Defendant held P.I. insurance cover for £500,000 on an each and every claim basis, £250,000 was proposed in his letter referring to this clause.

What went wrong we are not told, but evidently £250,000 was insufficient and the Plaintiff house owner thought he could do better than the express term he had agreed, with the benefit of legal advice. He therefore proceeded to go after the Architect's full P.I. cover, again on legal advice, claiming on the basis of the Unfair Contract Terms Act 1977.

Maybe the employer would have been better advised to sue his lawyers, as the judge was not impressed with the claim and gave judgment for the errant Architect. The determining issues were as follows:

— The relative bargaining position of the parties—the Defendant needing the Claimant rather than vice versa, given the acute shortage of work for consultants at the time the contract was entered into for the architectural services.
— The level of fees in relation to the agreed limit—£20,000 v. £250,000.
— The fact that the employer had agreed that if £250,000 was about right for total rebuilding costs then a limit of £250,000 was "fair enough".
— The fact that the Plaintiff had taken and had relied on professional advice before appointing the Defendant.

So here again we see potential exposure for Project Managers and other professionals, not least solicitors, who are in a position pre-contract to make sure that the employer's position is fully secured. However, whilst there is a temptation to go for over-kill, the imposition of excessively high levels of P.I. cover, or Bond cover, when dealing with specialist sub-contractors, is in no one's interests and could well be met with a defence based on the Unfair Contract Terms Act 1997.

6.8 CONTRIBUTION PROCEEDINGS

Under the Civil Liability (Contribution Act) 1978 a Defendant may join in a third party by way of "Part 20" proceedings, subject to the limitation of two years from the date of judgment or settlement of the original action. Thus the question of apportionment of blame and therefore contribution proceedings has arisen in a succession of fire loss cases involving Tesco or Sainsburys supermarkets, which got burnt out by fire in Chichester, Maidenhead, and Maidstone respectively in the early 1990s—and but for the prompt action of the fire brigade would also have happened in Salisbury.

In the last mentioned fire loss, the case came to court as *P & O Developments* v. *British Gas Nominees* (1995) (unreported as it settled after one morning in court), the author being the quantum expert for the Plaintiff who was suing for the balance of the Development Agreement, but defending a major counterclaim following a major fire. This had gutted half the multiple unit shopping centre, but only singed Sainsburys. Below us in the counterclaim action were the usual string of second, third, fourth etc defendants including the builder, all the design consultants and their various sub-consultants. In fact there were in all 17 defendants.

The evidence as regards the origin and then the spread of fire was fascinating, and as the Salisbury fire pre-dated the three similar fires listed above one really does have to question why Sainsburys and Tesco did not heed the evidence arising from Salisbury and inspect their fire walls and fire barriers in the other locations.

At Salisbury the major fire loss would ironically not have happened but for a recent amendment to the Building Regulations requiring eaves to be ventilated! It so happened that the metal bearings failed in an extractor fan set in the rear wall of a fruit and vegetable store, causing friction in two different metals. Fumes from these were highly combustible and permeated the roof space before the red hot metal set fire to the timber surround which then fell out into the carton storage yard—full of cardboard and timber crates after Saturday trading—situated right under the eaves ventilation grille! In no time the fire, which would normally have burnt itself out in the yard, re-entered the roof space over the store and crossed the half-hour fire wall into the main shop.

The development had been built with Sainsburys as the secured corner tenant and all the rest as speculative smaller units available as single or multiple units. Thus the external walls and roof were built first, and when the units were let, the fire division walls were added in, according to the number of units taken by each tenant. Central to the issue of the excessive speed with which the fire had spread was the fact that the Architect had gone for a light-weight timber truss roof held together with metal plates and the standard catalogue detail of fire stopping at the top of two-hour fire division walls. As enquiry showed this could only realistically be achieved if the wall was built before the roof, not the other way round.

The fire broke out at about 11.30 p.m. and the local brigade were there within minutes, complete with professional video camera man. The resulting footage was compelling evidence—each roof space adjacent to the seat of fire would gradually glow brighter and brighter and explode, as the flames found the gases which preceded them. In less than 30 seconds each roof would fall in as the metal truss plates melted—long before the fire consumed the timber trusses—and so the fire progressed around the development, reaching the three-storey part where flats were situated over the shop units. Fortuitously nobody was killed or injured but 12 units were burnt out and most of the others, including the flats, severely damaged, before the fire brigade got it under control.

Luckily the fire brigade had the foresight to tear down the covered way connecting Sainsburys to the development. When the forensic building surveying work got under way it was soon discovered that the fire barriers were very inadequately constructed and that if the fire had crossed into Sainsburys the two-hour fire division walls would not have saved it, and the store would have been burnt out in less than 10 minutes.

So the writs soon flew, the Tenants looking to the Landlord, the Plaintiff, for major losses including business interruption, and the Plaintiff naturally passing all claims through to the Developer, our client. The question was therefore: was it a design failure, i.e. an improper use of a standard fire stopping detail, given the sequence of construction activities, or a failure to use proper standards of workmanship, and should the detail have been condemned given a proper level of supervision by the Architect?

Essentially our client, the first Defendant, had no defence, but was seeking contributions from the Contractor and the Architect in whatever proportions the judge decided, and then they were seeking contributions from sub-contractors and sub-consultants respectively. For our part we were contending that the claimed rebuild costs had been allowed to run on virtually an open cheque basis, so we produced an Expert's Report, agreed with both the contractor's and Architect's quantum experts, cutting the remedial costs by 47% of that claimed.

The Plaintiff could have had little confidence in his quantity surveyor as surprisingly he accepted our quantum Report on day 1 in court—so the case was adjourned whilst all the other Defendants then sorted out the remaining 53% liability amongst themselves and their various insurers, without troubling the judge.

In the Chichester fire, *Sainsburys Plc* v. *Broadway Malyan & Ernest Green Partnership Ltd* (1998), the Architect sought to escape liability by Contribution proceedings, alleging that the structural engineer had approved the fire division wall detail. The detail included structural steel on which the engineer had previously commented, and also showed fire encasement of the steelwork which was not shown originally. When no further objection was raised by the engineer, the Architect issued the drawing for construction and subsequently claimed to have assumed that the engineer had approved and accepted responsibility for the fire encasement detail. Not so said the judge—so establishing the important principle that the mere issue of drawings by the Architect to the design team for comment is insufficient to relieve the Architect of design responsibility.

The Maidenhead fire, *Tesco Stores Ltd* v. *Norman Hitchcox Partnership* (1998), seems to have been a disaster waiting to happen. For some strange reason the Defendant Architect had been engaged by the developer and builder (The Ward Group) to design *but not to supervise* the shell development of multiple units (like Salisbury) and separately Tesco had engaged the Defendant to both design and supervise the major store.

A fire started in the general shopping area and then spread to Tesco, which was gutted. Wards settled with Tesco and two other Plaintiffs and then in Contribution proceedings in Tesco's name sued the Architect for the loss arising due to the failure of the structure to arrest the rapid spread of fire. However, on this occasion the decision went in favour of the Architect—on the basis that it was not possible to show that anything the Architect had done, or failed to do, had been the cause of the rapid spread of fire. Clearly there was the possibility that it was the workmanship of the contractor that may have been the principal cause, and as the Architect had not been appointed to supervise the constructor of the small shop units where the fire originated, then the developer/builder (Wards) failed to recover the damages paid out in the three settlements.

Apart from the obvious desirability of not splitting the design and supervision functions, the important point for an employer is that because it is never easy to prove a single cause of a major building failure it is necessary that all consultants forming the employer's project team be engaged on a joint and several liability basis. Consultancy practices, like contractors, can and do go bankrupt or otherwise cease to trade.

This does of course lead to injustices—particularly where the main culprit has escaped the net by voluntarily ceasing to trade—and is an area of the law that is under review following the Latham Report. Hopefully we shall see a system of capped liability related to the proportion of the contract value involving each discipline in due course—and an easier method of determining who should pay what when things go wrong than expensive Contribution proceedings in court.

CHAPTER 7

PROBLEM AREAS

7.1 NO CONTRACT?

As discussed in the Introduction in Chapter 1, all too often in the past much time and substantial costs were wasted by parties to a dispute and their solicitors attempting to persuade the other that a contract either existed or didn't exist—simply for tactical advantage to determine whether arbitration or litigation should be the real battleground. To those of us non-lawyers involved with a particular case as experts or witnesses of fact this appeared at the time to be good sport, but in reality we would have preferred to get on with the job whichever forum was to be eventually decided.

The almost inevitable arguments as to which bit of paper was actually the offer (or counter-offer) and whether there had ever been an unequivocal acceptance, were largely just spoiling tactics. When clearly there had always been an intention to create a legally binding relationship, with consideration evidenced by way of payments claimed and made each month, such legal niceties seemed academic when one went on site and saw piling rigs banging away and heard steelworkers using language only steelworkers use. Common sense dictated that a contract was in full swing whatever the paperwork deficiencies and whatever respective lawyers might have argued. More often than not there would be some form of Letter of Intent—and this in itself could be grounds for dispute, with the paying party now conveniently finding an alternative meaning to what both parties had previously considered to be perfectly clear and binding.

Not infrequently, after works had commenced on site based on exchange of telephone calls, faxes, letters and meetings, the main contractor would have subsequently issued a formal sub-contract document for the sub-contractor to sign and return. When a payment dispute arose it was surprising how often the trusting sub-contractor had simply signed and returned the main contractor's formal sub-contract without realising that some essential terms on which his accepted tender had been based had been altered. Equally it was the exception rather than the rule if the main contractor had then signed both copies and returned one to the sub-contractor. Of course the sub-contractor who spotted the main contractor's little game and referred the formal sub-contract back without signing it was in a stronger legal position, but it gave the main contractor a perfect excuse, as if further excuse were needed, for reducing or delaying payment for the on-going work.

Now that we have the right to statutory adjudication under the HGCR Act 1996 these "No contract" disputes should be flushed out early in the project—hopefully there will not be too many adjudicators who accept their appointment, only to decide there was no contract after all, thus disqualifying themselves in the process!

In my view, if two parties have been trading for weeks or months, A paying B for work done against evidential paperwork as to the bargain reached, a contract must exist. The terms and conditions may not be entirely clear, but performance and acknowledgement of that performance prior to the dispute evidences that a bargain was struck, in principle. If asked as an adjudicator to find that, for want of a signature or some other defect, a contract had not come into being the author would be in some difficulty to so find. It may be that in the circumstances it would be necessary to imply certain terms to give business efficacy to the transaction, or to make commercial sense of any evident nonsenses, but this would have to be within the framework of the essential bargain evidently struck.

Whether such an implied term constituted a "condition" as opposed to a "warranty" might then be arguable, the former, if breached, giving the aggrieved party the right to repudiate the contract, as well as to claim damages. The distinction between the two can be a close call and is best defined by the case of *Trollope & Colls Ltd* v. *North West Metropolitan Regional Hospital Board* (1973) where it was decided that where the missing term was necessary, rather than just helpful, to give business efficacy to the defective contract then it was a "condition".

When disputes arise as to the terms of a contract, usually the aggrieved party will not have felt strong enough legally to have repudiated the contract, so will have soldiered on under protest. In these circumstances the distinction is academic and the key issue becomes: What is the correct basis of payment? At adjusted contract rates? At contract rates with a separate sum for Loss and Expense? Or conceivably on "*quantum meruit*"?

A typical "No Contract" dispute came to court in *VHE Construction Ltd* v. *Alfred McAlpine Construction Ltd* (1997) where the main contractor first entered into negotiations on 4 January 1993. Work began on site just three days later as negotiations continued as to the contract terms—such negotiations continuing for six months. The issues for the court were twofold:

— Had a contract been formed between the parties, and if so, when?

— Can the court hear evidence as to what was said in negotiations to determine whether a contract had come into being?

The judge held that, whilst it was contrary to legal principle to take into account what was said during negotiations in determining the terms of the contract, it was permissible to do so to decide whether or not a contract had been formed in the first place. On the facts of the case it was further held that a contract had come into existence in early March 1993, as evidenced by the conduct of the parties, and that the negotiations since that date constituted a disagreement as to the details of the contract.

7.2 LETTERS OF INTENT

Letters of Intent are frequently used as an expedient means of getting an early start under way whilst the detailed contract documentation is prepared and then put in place, so extinguishing the Letter of Intent.

Typically Party A instructs Party B to make an early start and undertakes that *if* Party B does so perform then he will receive performance by Party A, either at the contract rates as and when the contract is finalised, or by way of payment of reasonable proven cost should negotiations fail. Hence the concept of "If Contracts".

Sometimes the contract works continue, but the follow-up documentation never does get put in place, and then arguments break out before it can be agreed. The question for the lawyers is then: is there a binding contract, based on the Letter of Intent, and if the project is now abandoned, who owes who what? In other words, it is vital to make clear provision in a Letter of Intent as to what is to happen in any eventuality.

In *Turriff Construction Ltd* v. *Regalia Knitting Mills Ltd* (1971) it had been held that if "... such a letter is no more than the expression in writing of a party's present intention to enter into a contract at a future date, save in exceptional circumstances, it can have no binding effect". This is because an agreement to negotiate or an agreement to agree at some future date is not recognised in law.

In *Monk Construction Ltd* v. *Norwich Union Life Assurance Society* (1992) it was held that a Letter of Intent could have three possible results:

— An ordinary executory contract—each party assuming reciprocal obligations.
— An "If" contract.
— No contract—in which case the law imposes an obligation on the party that made the request to pay a reasonable sum for the work done.

The mere marking of a letter to the proposed contractor at top right of "Letter of Intent" may well be insufficient. To be effective the generally accepted practice in this area now requires:

— The scope of the work currently authorised to be clearly defined and the intended form of contract stated.
— The method of interim payment to be stated, together with any value or time limit on the expiry of which no further work is to be carried out.
— A statement as to whether agreed costs, or reasonable recorded costs are to apply.
— Agreement as to whether the Letter of Intent is a binding contract in its own right or not.
— Clarity as to what is to replace the Letter of Intent, and the procedure for formally extinguishing the Letter of Intent.
— Agreement that once the formal contract is in place it will apply retrospectively and supersede the Letter of Intent.
— A statement as to who will administer the contract *pro tem*.
— A statement of the key matters yet to be agreed, if any, before a formal contract can be agreed.
— Confirmation that VAT will apply.
— Provision for a dispute resolution procedure, if you do not wish "The Scheme" provisions of the HGCR Act 1996 and litigation to apply.

Apart from these ten guiding principles, Letters of Intent should also consider any specific exclusions or special conditions applicable to the project in question.

Equally, Letters of Intent should not:

— attempt to set out all the terms of the contract;
— be regarded as a substitute for a formal contract.

The other thing to remember is to make sure that the Letter of Intent is actually agreed between the parties, and the best way of achieving this is to supervise the joint signature of the Letter of Intent, both parties then taking a copy for safe keeping.

Case law is littered with actions concerning Letters of Intent—which should be warning in itself. Inevitably each case is dependent on the particular facts, so it is difficult to establish any certain ground rules, but one recent case taken in conjunction with an older case gives an overview of the legal principles involved.

In *British Steel Corporation* v. *Cleveland Bridge & Engineering Co. Ltd* (1984) a dispute arose about the manufacture and supply of some special bearings for a multistorey building of futuristic design in Saudi Arabia. The

Plaintiff, acting on the Defendant's Letter of Intent, proceeded to manufacture and deliver most of the steel bearings whilst negotiations continued as to essential terms of the contract. The Letter of Intent was not replaced by a formal contract and when things went wrong on the project it was a question of interpreting the Letter of Intent.

At the subsequent trial it was decided that in certain circumstances a contract may arise where work is carried out in response to a Letter of Intent—a "quasi-contract", entitling the supplier of services to reasonable remuneration. The decided criteria were that either the Letter of Intent:

— was the basis of an ordinary contract, where each party assumed reciprocal obligations; or that
— it was a unilateral contract, whereby the Letter of Intent amounted to a standing offer, which would result in a binding contract if acted upon.

However, on the facts of the case in *British Steel* it was clear that although both parties intended to enter into a formal contract, in fact they had been unable to agree fundamental terms, so it followed that no contract had been formed. Consequently the Defendant was ordered to pay the Plaintiff on a *quantum meruit* basis.

More recently, in *Mitsui Babcock* v. *John Brown* (1996) it was decided that there was "... no reason in principle why two parties should not enter into a binding agreement, even though they have agreed that some proposed terms should be the subject of further discussion and later agreement".

Then, another judge in *Hall & Tawse South Ltd* v. *Ivory Gate Ltd* (1998) gave the following opinion:

— "A unilateral assurance intended to have contractual effect if acted upon, whereby reasonable expenditure reasonably incurred in reliance upon such a letter will be reimbursed."
— "Such a letter places no obligation on the recipient to act upon it, and there is usually no obligation to continue with the work ... the recipient being free to stop work at any time."
— "The effect of such a letter is to promise reasonable reimbursement if the recipient does act."

Having decided that no contract existed, but work had been done in good faith, the judge then decided there was nothing wrong in allowing the quantum of that work to be valued in accordance with the failed contract payment mechanism.

The concept of "If" contracts, which were further exemplified by the case of *Stent Foundations Ltd* v. *Tarmac Construction (Contracts) Ltd* (1999)—formerly Wimpey Management Contracting Ltd who had been engaged by a developer in Docklands for a major project. Wimpey intended to place the Piling Works Package with Stent, but as the details of the Management Contract between the developer and Wimpey needed time to be finally agreed Stent accepted a Letter of Intent from the developer. This was on the basis that the Letter of Intent would be extinguished by a formal Works Contract placed by Wimpey, as and when Wimpey closed negotiations with the developer.

However, the developer went into receivership before the contract with Wimpey was signed. Stent had little option but to go against Wimpey (by now Tarmac), having completed the Piling Works, claiming circa £300,000, but the court was having none of it, finding no evidence to suggest that Wimpey/Tarmac had assumed responsibility under the developer's Letter of Intent.

So it is what the Letter of Intent says that matters and whether there is sufficient certainty as to what the subsequent contract might have said had it ever been signed by both parties. Perhaps the perfect Letter of Intent (in legal terms), yet the most commercially naive, was that relied on in *Galliard Homes Ltd* v. *J. Jarvis & Sons Ltd* (1999). Galliard entered into negotiations with Jarvis to fit-out some flats which Galliard had built intending to award the contract on the basis of JCT 80. Their Letter of Intent said in terms that no contract came into existence until replaced by the signed JCT 80—and in so doing Galliard cut their own throat. Negotiations broke down amid confusion about the basis of a provisionally agreed price, so Jarvis said something along the lines: "Thank you very much—we have had enough. No contract (as per your Letter of Intent). Here is the bill to date, we are off." The court had little difficulty in finding for Jarvis, ordering payment on the basis of *quantum meruit*, firstly on the express wording of the Galliard Letter of Intent, and secondly on the basis of fundamental uncertainty of intended contract.

Thus letters of Intent are often essential to secure a prompt start, but need the most careful drafting. As Galliard Homes found to their cost, they can all too easily be a hostage to fortune!

7.3 WHAT IS A "VARIATION"?

Each standard or bespoke form of construction contract will have a form of words attempting to address this question, but bearing in mind that all such contracts are essentially written by the procurer of the service to be paid for, it is hardly surprising that the contract definitions are usually economically worded.

Some attempted definitions are of course prescriptive, i.e. "You will do anything I tell you to do, or is shown on drawings issued to you by my

Architect, and there will be no change in price or time unless I have previously agreed the extra money and time." Such a unilateral definition can work, either by mutual reasonableness or by the contractor taking an equally robust attitude—"If you want me to do that, you will agree my price and my additional time before I will even order the materials."

Mutual reasonableness cannot be relied on so there has to be a "Third Party Umpire" to whom either party can apply for an immediate decision, if such pre-agreement of cost and time contract requirements are to work effectively, e.g. the optional Supplementary Provisions, Clauses S.1 to S.7 of the old JCT WCD 81 contract which led the way for similar optional provisions in JCT SFBC 98.

In fact the mere existence of a "Third Party Umpire", formally given statutory status by the HGCR Act 1996 as the adjudicator and available to tell either party that they have been acting unreasonably, would appear to have had a salutary effect on the behaviour of contract administrators and parties generally. As such, this trend should see pre-agreement of variations in respect of both cost and time become the "norm". The statutory provision of the right of either party to call for an adjudicator should also take care of the old stumbling block of what was a "Variation", and what was a mere clarification or confirmation of detail, e.g. drawing issues.

Looking at the question from the supplier of services point of view, anything which costs unforeseen money or slows productivity down is a change in the basis on which the accepted price, and agreed time, was assessed. In principle therefore it is a "Variation", but this may well not fit with the contract definition. Changes in scope, quantity or quality of instructed work should be a matter of fact, and therefore capable of sensible agreement. However where most "Variation" disputes originate is in the circumstances in which the originally specified work can be carried out as and when the site is ready.

The usual scenario is that preceding trades are running late, that their work has not been fully completed and checked by the main contractor, and yet you are instructed to start your work—working over, under or around the late running trade. The fact that the contractor gave you an indicative programme at time of tender showing a defined period for your works, with your work shown in solid bar form, starting only when others had finished, cascading from one area to the next, then apparently counts for nothing when you claim that the method of your working has been varied, e.g. you have been directed on an ad hoc, weekly basis where you may work. The contractor simply points to a clause in the sub-contract saying that "Continuity of working cannot be guaranteed". What then?

Until recently there was no specific case law on this point other than the generally accepted concept that Party A must not hinder Party B in the execution of his work, and that Party A must do all in his power to enable

Party B to proceed efficiently, e.g. by the issue of drawings at the proper time. Then came a case in the Scottish High Court, *Scottish Power Plc* v. *Kvaerner Construction Regions Ltd* (1999), where it was held *inter alia* that:

— Having required the sub-contractor Claimant to complete his works in 24 weeks to suit the main contractor Defendant's programme, and the Defendant having stipulated that no guarantee of continuous working could be given ...
— The works programme having been substantially delayed and disrupted by preceding trades, so hindering the Claimant in the execution of his contractual obligation to the Defendant ...
— The Defendant was nevertheless entitled to require the Claimant to comply with the varied programme requirements, including interrupted working, without being entitled to financial recompense.

This would appear to be rough justice and at time of writing is the subject of an appeal. If upheld, however, many a pending Loss and Expense claim will fail and sub-contractors will have to get much smarter in tying down the contract conditions.

Certainly, if the author was called on to decide as an adjudicator what a no guarantee of continuity of working clause meant alongside a given timescale my decision and reasoning would be as follows:

— It is an implied term that in seeking a tender the enquirer has sought your "Best Price", balancing the scope of work described and the available time.
— It is to be assumed that the enquirer has taken the benefit of your "Best Price" and that he has in turn built it into his own "Best Price" in tendering to his client.
— That in specifying "no continuity of working guaranteed" the enquirer is merely protecting his position as against possible determination, but that if the works have to be temporarily suspended, then an adjustment of price is required, i.e. an act of prevention is a Variation.

Hopefully we shall be wiser after the appeal is heard, but it is a pivotal argument in most claims and the sooner there is a defining case in the London TCC the better.

Whether or not a change in working arrangement can be claimed as a "Variation", as opposed to an act of obstruction and therefore a breach of an implied term giving rise to a claim in damages for loss and expense, will depend on how narrow the contractual definition of a "Variation" is.

In *Strachan & Henshaw* v. *Stein Industrie (UK) Ltd and GEC Alsthom Ltd* (1998) a power station was to be built and it was agreed before contract that the Plaintiff's labour force would have clocking in and messing facilities close to the work site. Post contract it was decided to relocate these facilities outside the site perimeter, thus involving considerable lost time in the operatives walking to toilets and canteen facilities. The Plaintiff made a claim, a major head of claim being the alleged "Variation" involved in this change in site facilities.

The Defendant then pointed to the definition in the standard form of contract which limited a "Variation" to "Any alteration of the Works whether by way of addition, modification or omission." The "Works" were defined as "All plant to be provided and work to be done by the Contractor under the Contract." As such, the arbitrator had disallowed the claim as outside the definition of a "Variation". Leave to appeal was given, but it did not avail the Plaintiff as he lost again!

Thus it all comes down to how to plead the alleged wrongdoing with particular reference to the contract provisions. However, even if that hurdle is successfully negotiated, proving causation and quantifying the directly attributable loss can be the really difficult area—as previously discussed in Chapter 4.

7.4 WHEN IS "QUANTUM MERUIT" ALLOWABLE?

In a situation where there has been a total change of working conditions resulting in the typical mixture of delayed and partial access, hand-to-mouth instructions, loss of productivity and then a mad panic to get the project completed, it is totally unrealistic to pretend to be able to attribute the overall financial loss to individual events or causes. All one has as hard evidence of loss is the company Cost Ledger showing a substantial overspend before any contribution to Head Office overheads and profit. Similarly, if one has started on a project working under a Letter of Intent, but then the project is stopped, is not the Cost Ledger equivalent to "reasonable expenditure reasonably incurred"?

Quantum meruit (often referred to as QM, i.e. as much as has been earned), and *quantum valebat* (as much as it is worth) are legal concepts most frequently used to give restitution where it is found no contract exists. In practice they are often accepted as being proved by recorded costs, but claimed costs are unlikely to be accepted if there is some other comparable. The application of QM is accordingly usually limited to single issue disputes of short duration—typically contracts commenced against Letters of Intent and then abandoned when final contract negotiations break down.

For those longer running contracts, where a dispute breaks out and then the alleged contract terms are found to be so inherently defective as to lead to a "No Contract" finding, the principle of reasonable reimbursement usually applies. This will most likely be based on the Cost Ledger, but disallowing non-essential items and usually making a notional allowance for the inefficiencies which even the best run contractor will have to carry in his Profit and Loss Account.

Successful claims for reimbursement on a QM basis are few and far apart. *British Steel Corporation Ltd* v. *Cleveland Bridge and Engineering Co. Ltd* (1984), referred to above in connection with Letters of Intent, and *Peter Lind & Co. Ltd* v. *Mersey Docks & Harbour Board* (1972), where alternative tenders were sought for the construction of a freight terminal, but where it was unclear which tender had been accepted, leading to abandonment of the partly built works, are rare examples.

What is clear is that, whilst reasonable proven costs are the most likely basis of reimbursement, the concept of actual worth both to the provider and to the receiver of the partly delivered service cannot be ignored, albeit they are inevitably substantially different. However, where there is a properly concluded contract, reimbursement on a QM basis will not be likely to get past first post, however extreme the breaches made out by the Claimant.

7.5 SUSPENSION, DETERMINATION AND REPUDIATION

These three legal concepts are complex areas of law, covering the breakdown in previously agreed contractual arrangements, and providing for different remedies, so are best left to lawyers as evidenced in the case of *Leung* v. *Leung* (1998). This was a Design and Build case where seemingly two members of the same family fell out over the quality of the work and ended up in the Court of Appeal—the Plaintiff builder having been thrown off site by the Defendant Employer, who counterclaimed for £21,000 for employing a replacement contractor, as against the Plaintiff's claim for unpaid variations (value unknown).

Now it is an invariable rule that the smaller the value is, the more troublesome the case is, and further, that if there is a quasi-incestuous relationship between the two disputants, anything can happen. In this case the judge at first instance decided that the contract had been wrongfully repudiated by Leung, the Employer, but still awarded Leung, the Defendant, £7,500 on his counterclaim. Whether the Plaintiff succeeded in part on his final account claim is not related in the commentary, not being relevant to the question of law.

Unsurprisingly, Leung the Plaintiff appealed, but unhappily lost again— no doubt with a total costs bill out of all proportion to the values pleaded.

However, the legally interesting point is the two different reasons given by two Appeal Court judges for rejecting the Plaintiff's case:

— One judge stated that once a Party has repudiated he is barred from bringing an action on a contract, unless he is himself sued on the same contract. He is then entitled to defend and bring a counterclaim.

— A second judge reasoned differently, saying that if a Party is in breach of the contract he relies on, i.e. wrongful determination as in this case, he cannot claim damages arising from his breach, but he is entitled to a credit for the cost of making good the other Party's separate breach, i.e. £7,500 worth of defects.

It is therefore dangerous, as an aggrieved party, to lead with your chin, when to do so will probably invite a counterclaim—as indeed the quantity surveyors referred to in Chapter 6 did, claiming some £50,000 in alleged unpaid fees and ending up with P.I. insurers writing a cheque for circa £2m.

The only mitigation in those particular circumstances was that the quantity surveyors had so over-estimated the E.P.C. (Estimate of Prime Cost) on a refurbishment Management Contract that they simply had no idea that they were being negligent—the Management Contractor having every reason to allow the Works Package costs to run up unchallenged! As such, the quantity surveyors could possibly be excused for not having seen the employer's counterclaim coming when they issued proceedings against their longstanding client. Perhaps they were also lulled into a false sense of security by the fact that on several major overseas commissions, placed by the same client through his related companies or connections, there was a cosy 10% fee kick-back arrangement! But that is another story.

It also hazardous to try to play the "repudiation" card alleging that the other party has done so by his conduct, and that therefore your party's subsequent default was entirely justified, e.g. suspending the works—a pleading seemingly beloved of a certain school of one time quantity surveyors pretending to be lawyers. It follows that if you are wrong on your opening premise, then you are tantamount to putting your client's neck in the legal noose. Not very clever! As a Claims Consultant one must therefore be pragmatic, and if a contract has come to grief so be it. Leave it to the lawyers to do their bit and focus on where the money claim—or the time claim—really lies.

As regards suspension of the works, happily the law on the right to suspend is now coming out of the closet—thanks to the HGCR Act 1996 and the Fair Payment Provisions therein, but it has some way to go. Most standard forms of contract now follow the HGCR Act 1996 and make their own provisions for when a contractor or sub-contractor may suspend in relation to non-payment, and in particular: What if a sub-contractor suspends due to payment default of the main contractor, as he is entitled to do, and how does this affect the position as between the employer and the main contractor? No doubt we shall see some future case law in this area.

However, when you are a sub-contractor on site with your weekly payroll and suppliers to pay yet insufficient money coming in each month because you are simply not being allowed to proceed efficiently, what do you do? Continue down the slippery slope or make a stand, having first found a good Claims Consultant? Obviously you need to identify an alleged default under the contract, e.g. on-going acts of prevention by the main contractor, and to put the other side on notice of claim.

You might then care to look at *J.M. Hill & Sons Ltd* v. *London Borough of Camden* (1980), which neatly covers both the last scenario as well as the point made above of the dangers of alleging repudiation by the other side, only to find it is yourself who repudiated in the eyes of the law! In this case there must have been an unusual relationship between employer and contractor—until the big falling out—as although the standard form of contract payment terms were 14 days from the date of the Architect's Certificate, there was a separate agreement, honoured in practice for several successive months, that payment would be made more or less by return to assist the contractor's cash flow.

On 15 March 1979 the next Certificate was issued, but when payment was not immediately forthcoming the Plaintiff reduced his labour force to a skeleton team a week later. Words evidently followed, the Defendant Local Authority alleging failure to proceed diligently, repudiatory breach, etc. The payment was contractually due on or before 29 March and on 2 April the Plaintiff contractor gave written notice to the Defendant that unless paid within seven days he would terminate his employment. On 10 April the Plaintiff was as good as his word, serving written notice of termination and abandoning the site.

The Defendant then ordered the Plaintiff to return to site by 13 April, or it would treat the contract as at an end due to the Plaintiff's alleged default and repudiation, and continued to withhold the certified payment as against the losses yet to be incurred in reorganising the project. The court had little difficulty in finding for the Plaintiff—holding that the reduction of site staff was at worst a minor breach and fell well short of the alleged repudiatory breach.

Another Local Authority also got it badly wrong in *Bedfordshire County Council* v. *Fitzpatrick Contractors* (1998). In that case the Plaintiff tried during the course of a contract to make time of the essence and then terminated the contract when the Defendant contractor failed to accelerate. On the facts it was found that insufficient time had been allowed for the Defendant to effect the required increase in rate of progress and consequently it was the Plaintiff who had wrongfully repudiated.

So the message has to be: find a better and factual breach if you can, rather than rely on the law to excuse your own behaviour. Claim repudiation or wrongful suspension at your peril!

7.6 SHOULD MANAGEMENT CONTRACTORS ACTUALLY MANAGE?

When the first version of the old JCT Management Contractor WCD 87 first came out it was rightly perceived by contractors as a low risk contract—and a licence to print money, providing they didn't kill the goose that laid the golden egg. As far as contractors were concerned, they took their management fee usually on a percentage of final price basis, with Preliminaries paid for on a running cost basis, irrespective of their own performance.

This was of course not good news for employers, and comes about due to the so called "Relief" provisions whereby, after the contractor has tried and failed to manage the project, the consequences as well as the costs of proceeding against a defaulting Works Package Contractor in arbitration or litigation simply get added to the employer's monthly bill.

The operative Clauses 3.21 to 3.22 are the same in both JCT WCD 87 and 98. In respect of the Management Contractor's duties and obligations they provide as follows:

3.21.1.1 A duty to manage the project and obtain damages in respect of default by Works Package Contractors on behalf of the employer.

3.21.1.2 A duty to secure satisfactory completion of the contract, including the employment of a replacement Works Package Contractor, as necessary.

3.21.1.3 A duty to deal with any counterclaim from the defaulting Works Package Contractor and claims arising from other Works Package Contractors.

3.21.1.3 The right to set off from the defaulting Works Package Contractor monies paid or due to be paid in respect of dependent claims from other Works Package Contractors, as well as own costs.

3.21.2.1 The right to payment by the employer of all costs incurred, subject to consent in principle, of recovery proceedings taken against the defaulting Works Package Contractor.

3.21.2.2 A stay of imposition of Liquidated and Ascertained Damages.

> 3.21.2.3 A duty to credit the employer with all default costs as successfully recovered from the defaulting Works Package Contractor.
>
> 3.22.1 A duty to inform the Architect directly a claim against the Management Contractor is made by a Works Package Contractor.
>
> 3.22.2 A duty, subject to any instruction of the Architect, to settle or defend the claim from the Works Package Contractor; and
>
> 3.22.3 The right to reimbursement of the above settlement or defence costs, but "... only to the extent, and not further or otherwise, that the obligation to pay such amounts has been incurred other than by reason of any breach of contract or negligence of the Management Contractor in discharging his obligations under this contract." But subject to
>
> 3.22.3 The key exclusion that "This limitation on reimbursement to the Management Contractor shall not, however, apply to breaches of contract to which Clause 3.21 applies which shall be governed by that Clause."

From the employer's point of view, if he appoints a contractor under JCT SFBC 98 he gets his project managed for a fixed lump sum and little exposure to non-performing sub-contractors. On the other hand, under JCT WCD 98, when things go wrong inevitably more site staff are required, all being paid for on a time basis, and he finds himself fully exposed to additional cost and time if a key Works Package Contractor is allowed to disrupt the whole project.

Someone has to take responsibility for planning and co-ordinating the complex and often conflicting requirements of specialist trades, e.g. construction sequencing, design development, client changes, etc—and if someone offers his services as a "Management Contractor" the man in the street isn't going to be impressed by JCT WCD 98 Clause 3.22.3.

Some construction lawyers have taken Clause 3.22 by the scruff of the neck and turned it round to make the Management Contractor equally responsible, as under JCT SFBC 98, for delivering the completed project—hence the concept of the "soft" standard WCD 98 version, and the "hard" Clause 3.22 amended version.

Then along came the case of *Copthorne Hotel (Newcastle) Ltd* v. *Arup Associates and Others* (1996). Seemingly a key Works Package Contractor had failed to perform before going insolvent, the evidence being that the Management Contractor could and should have been far more proactive in site planning and co-ordination of the various trades. He sought to pass the consequences of the project disarray onto the employer under the relief provision of Clause 3.22.3, but the judge disagreed, finding that the

Management Contractor could not escape the consequences of his earlier non-management on the technicality of the insolvency of the Works Package Contractor, i.e. Management Contractors have a basic obligation to manage.

Seemingly, therefore, commercial reality has been read into the "fudge" of JCT WCD 98 Clause 3.22.3 and hopefully the drafting committee will be required to reconvene. Certainty of meaning is all that is required, so why not an amendment offering an optional provision—best endeavours only by the Management Contractor (Soft) or express duty to manage (Hard)?

If this were done, maybe we would see the renaissance of Management Contracting as a more popular form of procurement—and the reduction in preference for Design and Build, which all too often is chosen by default, being perceived by employers as the least risky form of procurement, backed by a standard form of contract.

7.7 EFFECT OF FINAL CERTIFICATE AND LATENT DEFECTS

This is another area of the law where it is easy to be confused as to what the generally accepted standard forms of contract apparently say and what they actually mean. In the good old days of virtually all building, as opposed to civil engineering, contracts being let on JCT SFBC 1963, when the contractor applied for Practical Completion a defects list was prepared, and the items were cleared as soon as practicable. Six or 12 months later the Final Certificate would be issued, whereby the Architect certified that the contractor had discharged all his duties under the contract and in particular that all materials and workmanship expressly reserved in the contract as to be to the Architect's approval and satisfaction had been so accepted. The final moiety of retention would then be released.

Then along came JCT SFBC 1980 with various changes, but the understanding as to the effect of the Final Certificate and the need to notify written objection if either party disagreed with the Architect's verdict within 28 days remained intact until challenge was made in 1992.

In *Colbart* v. *Kumar* (1992) the Official Referee decided, on a JCT Standard Intermediate Form of Building Contract, that we had all been getting it wrong for several years, and that all matters were "inherently" for the Architect's approval. Accordingly the Final Certificate really was final as regards the contractor's obligations under the contract.

In *Crown Estate Commissioners* v. *John Mowlem & Co. Ltd* (1994) the Court of Appeal decided that Clause 30(9) in JCT SFBC 80 was no different, which sent the JCT into a flat spin and they hurriedly issued an Amendment, making only matters expressly reserved for the Architect's approval subject to finality under the Final Certificate.

Further clarification was then provided by *Oxford University Fixed Assets Ltd* v. *Architect Design Partnership/Tarmac Construction (Contracts) Ltd* (formerly Wimpey Construction Ltd) (1999) where it was held as a preliminary issue that the issue of the Final Certificate acted as an evidential bar to the Architect being able to join in the contractor in contribution proceedings, the Architect having been sued for failure to ensure that defective blockwork in the Pharmacology Block walls had been properly repaired before issuing the Final Certificate, i.e. being a specifically noted and significant defect it clearly was a matter for the Architect's considered approval—and as a matter of fact he still hadn't got it right. In a very robust judgment addressing the commercial realities of Final Certificates the judge found that the Final Certificate "merely operates to express the state of affairs at the date of its issue and not to provide conclusive evidence that the works had always been 'perfect'".

Thus, accrued rights between employer and contractor remain in place on issue of the Final Certificate, i.e. liability for latent defects remains until discharged by rectification, by payment of damages, or by expiry of time. Latent defects are regrettably a real risk—as identified by the 1990s' survey referred to at the beginning of Chapter 6.

7.8 "PARTNERING" AND "BEST VALUE" PROCUREMENT

Whilst the "call for change" in how we collectively make the construction industry more efficient is long overdue and welcome, it amazes the author that people seem to think they can reinvent the wheel by such panaceas as "Boot" schemes (Build, Own, Operate, Transfer—back to end user) or "Partnering"—or, in respect of mega infrastructure or defence projects, the latest politically correct title, "Prime Contracting". Undoubtedly there is a place for such sophisticated and complex procurement arrangements in high value infrastructure and public authority projects, but these concepts do not relate to the great majority of construction projects where finance is available by conventional borrowing.

Proponents of "Partnering" will point to the benefits of limited lists of proven suppliers and sub-contractors, but one only has to see how supposed blue chip clients such as British Airports Authority treat their consultants, or Marks & Spencer treat their suppliers, to realise the dangers of consultants becoming beholden to the client.

In any event there is nothing new in partnering—only that someone thought of the tag, and dressed it up. In reality the better organised employers and main contractors have quietly been operating informal and low key partnering systems for several years. Equally some sub-contractors and suppliers have in the past developed partnering a step too far and set up "rings", and certain Local Authorities have developed "incestuous" relationships with their own Direct Works Departments—all supposedly in the name of "best value". The cynics will say partnering has a short shelf life and that after a while it is difficult to demonstrate "best value", as against the open and wider market.

At least with competitive tendering—beloved of Public Works procurement for so long—there is transparency and accountability, whereas with partnering or negotiated tendering based on perceived "best value" there is every opportunity of hidden agendas and corruption.

Then there are "Mission Statements" and "Total Quality Management". In practice these are pure hype, making those in the cosy inner cabinet of a project feel comfortable and presenting an appearance of credibility to the outside world, and funders in particular. The problem is that the everyday risks of the construction industry don't go away. When the project runs late, and the Air Show date or Shopping Centre opening date is cast in stone, the risk is simply passed down the supply chain and dumped on the sub-contractors, who find themselves funding the project involuntarily.

"Partnering" came to the attention of the courts in *Birse Construction Ltd* v. *St David Ltd* (1999) where a partnering charter had been signed between employer and contractor at the outset of the project in June 1997, mutually undertaking "to produce an exceptional quality development within the agreed time frame, at least cost, enhancing our reputations through mutual co-operation and trust". The development in question was some fancy apartments overlooking Cardiff Bay, work being commenced against a Letter of Intent.

Now the problem was that Birse, for whatever reason, refused to sign the formal contract, and after starting the work and applying to be paid on *quantum meruit* abandoned the site when not so paid. And so the matter came to court, there being no signed contract and the partnering charter expressly stating that it was to be "non-binding".

The judge, however, was equal to the task and found that although there was "... clearly no distinct offer and acceptance since the parties were converging by stages ..." the parties had contracted on the basis of the JCT terms since "... people who have agreed to proceed on the basis of mutual co-operation and trust, are hardly likely at the same time to adopt a rigid attitude to the formation of a contract." Helpfully the judge added, referring to the partnering charter, "... the terms of that document, though clearly not legally binding, are important for they were clearly intended to provide the standards by which the parties were to conduct themselves and against which their conduct and attitudes were to be measured."

Perhaps the last word on "Partnering" should rightfully belong to a Director of Scottish Power, who when asked of his experience of partnering with the contractor on a major water project in Southern England is reputed to have replied "like synchronised swimming with sharks". It happens that the contractor in question was the same contractor as in the Cardiff Bay divorce case!

"Best Value" or "Quality v. Price" was one of Sir Michael Latham's themes in his Report, and the subject of a separate Working Party afterwards. Unfortunately the government then seemed to go overboard and decreed that "best value" should be the cornerstone of public procurement, relegating "lowest price" to a distant second place, and seemingly instructing all Local Authorities to adopt the same policy.

No sooner had they done this than along came *Harmon* v. *The Commissioners of the House of Commons* (1999). In this case it was found that the employer, who of all employers should have led by example and been entirely above suspicion, had placed a very valuable specialist cladding contract with a specially formed British-led Joint Venture company rather than the Claimant, an American company, who were £2.4m cheaper in £34m, i.e. a 7% difference. Various allegations were made by the Claimant, who subsequently went into receivership, including:

— That the Claimant had not been fairly or equally treated in the tender process.
— That the Agency, the Parliamentary Works Directorate (PWD), and the main contractor, Laing Management Ltd, had conspired to operate a "Buy British" policy, contrary to EC law and contrary to their own tender invitation.
— That Laing Management Ltd tried to bully the Claimant into dropping its threatened legal action by threatening legal action of their own on two other projects.

The judge was scathing in his judgment, finding that:

— "There was cogent evidence of misconduct on the part of one senior public official, a civil servant in the Parliamentary Works Directorate", which made the House of Commons collectively guilty of misfeasance in public office.
— The guilty civil servant in the PWD "... gave no satisfactory explanation for not telling Harmon the true reasons for his decision and why they were not awarded the contract ..."— having been commissioned to build the mock-up façade for over £200,000.
— The judge went on to describe the PWD's Project Manager's evidence as "incredible", "disingenuous", "profoundly disquieting".

— Then it was Laing's Project Manager's turn. According to the judge he "... successfully conveyed the impression of a Teflon man, which may account for his position within Laing Management, as otherwise he did not display a grasp of the project." Not a good commendation for one's CV!

Whether or not any aspect of this landmark case on "best value" will reach the Court of Appeal remains to be seen, but the present score in favour of the Receiver of Harmon is:

— Tender Costs: £420,000.
— Loss of Profit: circa £5 million.
— Legal Costs: circa £2 million.

One of the clear messages arising is that "best value" procurement must be transparent—and this can only be achieved if the criteria by which the tenders are to be assessed, and maybe the lowest tender being declined, are stated as part of the tender enquiry. It may also be that, as a matter of public policy on public sector projects, all tenders over a certain value are awarded by a three-man Tender Adjudication Panel—with the third man being a project outsider.

7.9 IMPARTIALITY OF CERTIFIER

It is generally accepted, although not written down, that a certifier appointed under a construction contract between an employer and contractor has a duty to act impartially, albeit it is the employer who pays his fees. This principle was then confirmed in the previously mentioned case of *John Barker Construction Ltd* v. *London Portman Hotels Ltd* (1996). Apart from the central issue of how the Architect should have gone about assessing the Extension of Time due to the Contractor, the judge was also required to confirm in relation to Clause 25 the basis of the certifier's duty to both parties. In the judge's opinion the certifier was bound to act both fairly and lawfully.

However, the great majority of construction contracts are at sub-contractor and sub-sub-contractor level, with no appointed third party certifier. In these contracts it is the paying party who decides what he should pay, and until the introduction of the HGCR Act 1996, they effectively acted as judges in their own court and there was very little the aggrieved, short-paid, party could do about it.

Then along came two cases which helped to define proper practice and to balance up the relative bargaining position of the two parties in such a situation—albeit the solicitor in the first case was very pleasantly surprised not to come second. However, that particular decision has been criticised in subsequent judgments.

The first case, *Balfour Beatty Ltd* v. *Docklands Light Railway Ltd* (1996), was unusual in that although it was let on the ICE 5th Edition standard form of contract, the employer had deleted the "Engineer" as the contract administrator and substituted his own in-house representative. He had also deleted the standard arbitration clause. A delay and disruption claim arose, and the "Employer's Representative" refused to certify more than £3 million.

Here the central issue was whether, in the absence of a third party certifier and the absence of an arbitration clause, the aggrieved contractor could ask the court to open up and review the "Employer's Representative's" decision, given the proximity of the individual to the employer. Clearly the contractor should have envisaged when entering into the contract that decisions given in due course by the unusually appointed certifier might be unfavourable—the judge duly deciding, in the circumstances of effective self-certification by the employer, that so long as the certifier acted honestly, fairly and reasonably in exercising his power under the contract, then the contractor could have no complaint.

In the second case, *Rosehaugh Stanhope* v. *Redpath Dorman Long Ltd* (1990), as already referred to in Chapter 4, the court was very clear, the judge stating that a party acting as self-certifier was not entitled to:

— rely on his own position in a disputed liability situation;
— deny payment of substantial sums by way of claimed but unproven set-off when by so doing the other party might well be forced into insolvency;
— assume to himself a greater power than even a court can in an Application for Summary Judgment where an arguable defence is raised.

Now that the fair payment and statutory right to adjudication provisions of the HGCR Act 1996 are biting, arbitrary under-certification by the paying party will hopefully become a thing of the past, and experience is already indicating that the mere threat of a third party professional possibly being called in is in itself imposing a better approach by all concerned, not least engineers called upon for a re-decision.

7.10 DAMAGES AND ASCERTAINMENT

The payment of damages is the most common form of redress where one party to a construction contract agrees that he has, or is found to have, caused a financial loss to the other party by some default, and following long-established principle an award of damages is intended, so far as possible, to put the injured party back in his original position prior to the breach of contract.

It follows that the quantum of any damages must be ascertained on as factual a basis as possible, and in particular that the damages be directly attributable to the breach, i.e. that they do not sweep up other losses which would equate to a "windfall" gain. The onus is therefore on the Claimant to reasonably account for the losses and to show how they flowed from the breach, but this is rarely an easy and unchallengeable exercise—as already discussed in Chapter 4.

There will be various degrees of certainty ranging from one-off direct costs obviously attributable to the breach, and indirect costs such as diminished contribution to Head Office Overheads if a project is delayed but the contract value remains essentially the same. Other claimed consequences of the breach may well fail the reasonable foreseeability test of *Hadley* v. *Baxendale* (1854). As ever, each case must be assessed on its own facts, so it is not possible to say where the line will be drawn in respect of consequential costs.

There are also the two limitation rules in respect of direct costs:

— Damages recoverable for breach of contract can never exceed the contract value—*British Sugar* v. *NEI Power Projects Ltd* (1997).
— The injured party can never recover more than it would have cost the transgressor to have made good the default, e.g. defective work, had he been given the opportunity to do so—*Pearce & High Ltd* v. *Baxter* (1999).

Most standard forms of building contract legislate for the eventuality of the contractor not finishing on the required and agreed completion date by way of stated weekly or monthly rates, known as Liquidated and Ascertained Damages (LADs), e.g. £5,000 per week. In practice this area is fraught with difficulties. Firstly the level of LADs must be a genuine pre-estimate of what the employer's loss might be—either by reference to an auditable income stream or by reference to the open market cost of taking alternative accommodation. If not, they are deemed to be a penalty and therefore unenforceable—and many projects do not so comply.

Particular projects throw up particular problems, e.g. a refurbishment contract over 26 months for a Hall of Residence in one of the older Cambridge Colleges for 30 undergraduates, where it is necessary to pre-book town digs and sign rental agreements for 12 months. So on the basis that the project had to be completed by the start of the University year in October, the College solicitors decided that the contract LADs should be 30 × £300 × 12 months, i.e. £108,000 for any delay over one month up to 12 months.

The only trouble was that because of the historic nature of the building and some unexpected problems, Extensions of Time of four months had to be granted, so overtaking the basis on which the figure had been calculated, but which might have been correct. The College then had no basis for recovering any LADs for the two months further overrun, having had no option but to take 30 town lodgings in any event on annual leases.

This highlights the reverse of the coin in respect of prescribing LADs. It is done as a mutual benefit to both employer and contractor, giving a sensible and pre-agreed figure for culpable delay on the part of the contractor, if applicable at the end of the project. The alternative would be endless and unmanageable disputes as to the losses allegedly caused.

It follows that any non-culpable delay, outside the control and contractual responsibility of the contractor, must be dealt with fairly and objectively by the Architect or Contract Administrator and failure to grant Extensions of Time when due will deny the employer the right to recover LADs.

The other main problem area with LADs occurs at the other end of the construction supply chain. All too often main contractors will in the sub-contract documentation pass down the full head contract LADs provision, i.e. the same £5,000 per week as our example above. Now the theory is fine: any non-performance of the sub-contract could in its own right cause the main contract to overrun, and so give the employer the right to deduct LADs from monies otherwise due to the main contractor.

However, in reality this passing down of the 100% LADs value may be iniquitous, as was held in the case of *Ballast Wiltshire Plc* v. *Thomas Barnes & Sons Ltd* (1998). Seemingly the sub-contract only involved part of the project, and as such the non-completion of these areas did not prevent partial handover of the remainder by the Claimant to the employer. Also on the facts of this case the Claimant's actual loss was circa £150,000, whereas £2m was being levied by way of set-off. Accordingly the LADs were held to be a penalty and were therefore unenforceable, as indeed they probably would be if it was found that they were being held against more than one sub-contractor or if other trades could by programme analysis be shown to be in even greater delay, independent of the trade against which they were being deducted.

So we return to where we started in this section: the ascertainment of damages claimed under the contract as loss and expense, usually on the basis of disruption or imposed delay denying the Claimant of allegedly being able to earn the planned return from his labour resource as tendered. If one is defending such a claim the favourite tactic is to reach for a dictionary and find the most favourable definition of "ascertain". The usually quoted definitions are "to make certain", "to make sure or find out by examination", "to establish", and "to determine with certainty".

However, to do this will merely prolong the dispute and rack up fees, whereas the approach likely to be taken by courts and arbitrators is less rigid, i.e. the common law burden of proof on the balance of probability, provided a genuine effort has been made to deal with the more factual aspects first. This approach will almost certainly be the "norm" under the new Civil Procedure Rules, given the overriding objective of accessible justice and proportionality of cost in obtaining it as against the level of damages in issue.

The final word on "ascertainment" is probably that before taking an entrenched position any certifier, whether acting in the appointed third party umpire role, or acting on own account, would do well to reflect on two matters:

— The decision in *Rosehaugh Stanhope* v. *Redpath Dorman Long* (1990) wherein it was held that Bovis, acting as Construction Manager, could not act as judge and jury in their own court—see Section 4.6 and Section 5.9.
— The fact that if he acts unreasonably he may well force the other side to call in an adjudicator, who may very well find that he has acted unreasonably and order the employer or his own company to pay the disputed amount immediately, complete with statutory interest at 8% above MLR, and costs.

If the certifier is too high-handed in dealing with the contractor's interim payment application, or in denying an Extension of Time application, he runs a real risk of exposing the employer to having to pay the disputed monies, as decided by the Adjudicator, out to the contractor—the employer probably not being at all happy, especially if the underlying cause is the late release of requested design information.

The contractor, as opposed to the employer under the old scheme of things, is now in the "box" seat, as it is the employer who must now start any recovery proceedings in arbitration or litigation for the disputed money (or time) and who, as Claimant, will have the burden of proof, not to mention the need to fund both the unsuccessful Adjudication and the subsequent action.

The same situation pertains as between contractor and sub-contractor, where previously the former effectively decided how much he felt like paying and when. Now he must be reasonable and play by the rules in administering the sub-contract, or possibly find himself on the wrong end of an adjudication decision, and therefore having to face the risks of being the Claimant, as opposed to the Defendant, in a future recovery action.

7.11 RETENTION FUNDS AND BONDS

The basic premise of Retention Funds is sound in that:

— only compliant work qualifies for interim payment; and
— the 3% to 5% retention is withheld as against the fact that inevitably some of that work, paid for in good faith, will on most jobs require snagging, and there can be no guarantee that the contractor will be able or willing to do so at Practical Completion.

So far so good, but problems arise concerning the legal ownership of the retention monies and how they are, or should be, released on Practical Completion, which in itself can be a difficult area, as discussed in the final section of this Chapter.

As regards ownership of the retention funds they are of course due to the contractor for work done, if at the end of the day no fault is found with that work; and at employer/contractor level in the supply chain there is rarely a problem for the simple reason that generally speaking employers don't go into receivership during a building contract.

The problem comes lower down the supply chain, i.e. at contractor/sub-contractor level, or at the next level down. It is all too tempting for a cash-strapped main contractor to conveniently forget that he is holding money against various sub-contractors and to use that as working capital. It is therefore bad news day when one of those sub-contractors knocks on the site cabin door and wants a bit of paper signed to the effect that his small part of the overall works is complete and beautiful. That sub-contractor wants his own Certificate of Practical Completion, which in turn will entitle him to release of half of the sub-contract Retention Fund now, and release of the remaining half six or 12 months later.

This gives the main contractor an instant headache. Not only will he have to find working capital to fund the retention release, but in six or 12 months that sub-contractor will be fully paid up whereas the main contractor may well not have offered the total project to the employer for hand-over, so will still be fully exposed to any defective work that may be identified on Practical Completion inspection, including that carried out by the paid-up sub-contractor.

Often, main contractors try to define Practical Completion for all trades as the total project Completion Date, and so kill two birds with one stone—locking in the maintenance liability and retaining the sub-contract Retention Fund till the last possible moment, in effect operating "Pay-when-Paid". This gives the sub-contractor not only a liquidity problem, but a very real risk exposure that maybe the contractor will not still be in business as and when the sub-contractor can actually demand final payment.

Most standard forms of contract now require the party withholding retention to put the monies in a Trust Fund Account, in favour of the other party—to safeguard the insolvency risk. If this is not done the Receiver of the insolvent employer or main contractor will not distinguish between current assets and the monies truly the property of the party who has completed but only been paid 97%. Unfortunately few employers, and even fewer main contractors comply, and until the introduction of the HGCR Act 1996 those sub-contractors who asked to have their retention monies placed in a Trust Fund were usually ignored.

However, now that adjudication is working and is proving itself a very cost effective and quick way of airing contractual grievances it is to be anticipated that we shall see adjudicators called in to resolve disputes concerning:

— The placement of retention monies into Trust Funds.
— The failure to release retention monies to sub-contractors in relation to the completion of the sub-contract works.

So we come to Bonds—unquestionably the biggest waste of money in the construction industry. As suggested in Chapter 3 most projects are in effect double bonded—the contractor giving the employer a bond for the total contract value, and then each sub-contractor being required to give a separate bond on the sub-contract value. If there is further sub-contracting, then quite possibly there will be yet further duplication of bond cover.

The reality is even worse. Bonds don't work, and in fact can never work, unless there is very particular and clear wording which covers the situation when the bond needs to be called. To understand the reasons for this it is necessary to go back a few years.

Basically there are two types of Bond:

— "On-Demand" Bonds—lacking any terms defining in what circumstances the guarantor of a sub-contractor could be called upon to pay the main contractor, or the guarantor of the main contractor could be called upon to pay the employer. In short they could be called vexatiously and it was amazing that anyone in their right mind ever agreed to provide one. Quite rightly these have fallen into virtual disuse in favour of ...
— "Performance" Bonds—callable on the defined default of the party providing the Bond, and required as the best way of dealing with the risk of the sudden insolvency of any link in the contract supply chain effectively stopping the project.

The main difficulty was the archaic wording traditionally used in the formal bond wording, and for many years it was assumed that the holder of a "Performance" Bond provided by the guarantor of a party who then went into receivership could proceed to engage an alternative contractor, and, subject to making a claim for "the net established and ascertained damages" based on quotations and estimates, could then collect on the Bond.

The turning point came with *Trafalgar House Construction (Regions) Ltd* v. *General Surety & Guarantee Co. Ltd* (1994) where on a leisure centre project in Maidstone the groundworks sub-contractor went into receivership. The main contractor Claimant then called the Bond based on the assessed additional costs involved, but was unsuccessful, the court holding that:

— The Bond wording amounted to an "On-demand" Bond—to the general surprise of all concerned in the Bond industry!
— The Bond bound the sub-contractor, or in his place the Defendant surety, to pay damages up to the written value, but that obligation was discharged if there was performance by the surety of the sub-contractor's obligations, i.e. the surety had the option of appointing his own replacement sub-contractor, whether acceptable or not to the main contractor, employer, Architect or Engineer.

This radical decision has led to Bondsmen generally forming alliances with certain tame general contracting companies, who do little else than "fire-salvage" work and over whom the main contractor can have little effective control.

Then along came another case where the Bond provider relied on the following wording: "... the Guarantor shall ... satisfy and discharge the damages sustained by the Employer as established and ascertained pursuant to and in accordance with the provisions of or by reference to the Contract or as agreed between the Employer and the Contractor." He took the stance that, yes he would pay, but only when the total Final Account had been settled and all additional costs were factual rather than estimated. This was a major financial embarrassment to the cash-strapped employer, who then found enough money to bring an action against the Bondsman—but lost.

Then, in *Paddington Churches Housing Association Ltd* v. *Technical & General Guarantee Company Ltd* (1999) it was held that:

— The Bondsman had no liability until the insolvent contractor's liabilities crystallised—and that this, by virtue of the words "net" and "ascertained", could only be on completion of the Final Account.
— Such account could only be taken with due regard to the JCT WCD 81 contract and Clause 27.6 in particular.

So in two successive cases the courts took away the very reason most employers wanted a Bond in the first place, and also the main contractors' essential defence against being themselves left holding the contractual baby if one of their sub-contractors failed and called in the Receiver. In other words the Bond money will not be immediately available, as originally assumed, and separate further funds will be needed to keep the project flowing. Now Bondsmen are not benevolent societies, they are hard businessmen who, with the deep pockets of insurers behind them, can well afford to litigate and pay the top rates.

In over 30 years experience of the industry the author has only been party to the successful calling of a Bond on two occasions—and neither was a straightforward call following insolvency. The first was in respect of a non-performing dredger in the Persian Gulf, owned by a Greek lady, married to an Iranian, on a major dry dock project for the Iranian Navy. Twice we tried to call the Bond and twice we were refused permission by our client, the Iranian Navy. Then one day the Shah sacked his Prime Minister of 17 years—the ex-Prime Minister and the Iranian husband of the lady dredger owner having been best friends at school! Within the week we had the Bond money in the bank and had mobilised a much larger Dutch dredger, which in due course put us back on programme!

The second Bond call was in respect of a Development Agreement between a developer and a middle-England small town football club playing in the Isthmian league, where the football club were to get cash, a total new ground and improved facilities on the outskirts of the town in return for vacating their town centre site, which was eminently suitable for a major supermarket. Unfortunately the developer caught a cold on a London scheme and called in the Receiver, followed into Receivership very shortly by his tame contractor whose offices and yard just happened to back onto said town centre football ground. Very fortuitously, in an amendment to the original Development Agreement the provincial solicitors had advised their football club clients to secure their interest with a 100% Development Bond.

So there was the football club, with their planned development dead in the water, their existing ground owned by the Receiver, and under notice of expulsion from the League if they did not bring their ground up to Taylor Report standard within 18 months. The only asset they now had was a piece of paper in the safe, headed "Bond", so enter the author, stage left, acting for the Receiver, and of both the developer and the signed up contractor. The Bondsman played hard to get, essentially trying to build the new ground much cheaper than the written Bond value, but after certain representations by yours truly to the Planning Authorities was forced to use the original plans and the original contractor, now sold to one of the original directors.

Eighteen months later we saw the scheme completed, at a cost including finance just inside the Bond value, and the football club was presented with a cheque in front of the insurance industry press in the Lloyd's building—only for the Bondsman to lean across after the photographs and take the cheque back to supposedly have a spelling mistake in the name of the payee corrected. Two days later, and only after threat of a writ was the money then paid by telegraphic transfer.

For Bonds to work as intended to guard primarily against the risk of insolvency they need to be "Performance" Bonds specifically worded to spell out the circumstances which define "default", including who will be the independent arbiter of "default". They could also usefully provide for:

— A 75% immediate payout, with the balance to be ascertained on Final Account.
— A main contract provision that all sub-contract Bond values should be pro rata in value to the proportion that the sub-contract value bears to the overall project value.

The latter provision is necessary to stop the practice of some main contractors of passing down the full Bond value, or a disproportionately high Bond value, in sub-contract enquiries. Not only does this inflate the premium paid, and is passed back as a cost to the project, but the Bondsman may well take security with the sub-contractor's bank as a condition of Bond cover, thus reducing the available overdraft facility on which to run the business.

In the opinion of the author there is a place in our industry for simply worded Bonds covering insolvency, advance payments (usual practice in overseas contracting), and possibly retention monies. Whether insurers and Bondsmen will offer such specifically limited and better defined cover must however be doubtful.

One such Bond, written specifically for insolvency protection, is that issued with the ICE Standard Form of Engineering Contract 7th Edition. Headed "Default Bond" it is triggered by the contractor being expelled from site, i.e. a scenario which could occur in extreme cases of non-performance, but one more usually associated with insolvency. A copy of this form of "Default Bond" is included at Appendix B.

Another of the recommendations of the Latham Report was that Retention Bonds might in due course be the preferred method of guarding against the non-performance of the contractor. Accordingly, some specialist contractor trade organisations are trying to force the issue by way of getting their members only to tender if Retention Bonds will be acceptable. Unfortunately there is no reliable information as yet to show that there are clear benefits in changing the old cash retention system—and it is the employers and their solicitors who dictate contract conditions in the first place, not specialist sub-contractors.

7.12 PRACTICAL COMPLETION

On any project, Practical Completion is a defining moment when important obligations on the part of the contractor are deemed to be at an end, and the employer takes possession, together with the duty to insure in his own name. However, in law, Practical Completion is one of the most difficult terms to define. For the Contract Administrator it is probably the most onerous of his tasks, as so much depends upon *when* in the opinion of the Contract Administrator the contractor *should* have finished, and *when* he *did* actually finish. Often the project will be phased, and will provide for Partial Possession, with defined Completion Dates and Liquidated and Ascertained Damages expressed by phases of the project.

The essence of Practical Completion is that the contractor moves out and the employer moves in, subject to any notified defects being made good by the contractor at the convenience of the employer. However there are defects—and defects. Some are incidental and can be made good with little disturbance to the employer; other defects are more fundamental and will be disruptive to the employer's privacy or business. There are also usually some items of incomplete work which by agreement are to be done when the contractor returns to site to attend to the defects, commonly referred to as snagging. The problem then comes in objectively deciding, independently of employer pressure, what is an incidental defect and what is in fact a non-compliance issue. If it is in the latter category then Practical Completion has not been achieved and the Architect, Engineer, Employer's Agent, or Contract Administrator who certifies Practical Completion does so at his, and his P.I. insurer's peril.

Likewise Project Managers and Project Auditors, although they have no line responsibility in the certification process, need to be very clear that it is agreed in advance with the certifier as to what will be the necessary criteria against which Practical Completion will be judged, and in particular what test certificates of key materials and installations are prerequisites.

Recent case law on Practical Completion is patchy, but it starts with *J. Jarvis & Sons* v. *Westminster Corporation* (1970) where the judge described the Defects Liability Period as "... provided in order to enable defects not apparent at the date of practical completion to be remedied. If they had been then apparent, no such certificate would have been issued." He considered "Practical Completion" to mean "... completion for all practical purposes, that is to say for the purposes of allowing the employers to take possession of the works and use them as intended. If completion in clause 21 meant completion down to the last detail, however trivial and unimportant, then clause 22 would be a penalty clause and as such unenforceable."

This seemingly resolute definition came to be challenged in *H.W. Neville (Sunblest)* v. *William Press* (1981) and the judge gave particular consideration to the real meaning of Practical Completion. He duly stated that "I think that the word 'practical' ... gave the Architect a discretion to certify that William Press had fulfilled its obligation ... where very minor de minimis work had not been carried out, but if there were any patent defects in what William Press had done the architect could not have given a certificate of practical completion." In other words "completion" was when the contractor completed and the employer moved in, subject to a realistic view being taken of listed defects.

Ten years later the same judge was called upon to consider the meaning of "completion" where Practical Completion had been granted and then some two months later the contractor called in the Receiver, who then sued the employer for over £500,000 in respect of the usual disputed Final Account and Claim issues, but was met with a defence and a counter-claim contending substantial set-off costs as allegedly paid to a replacement contractor.

In *Emson Eastern Ltd* v. *EME Developments Ltd* (1991), heard as a Preliminary Issue, the Receiver relied on Clause 17 of JCT SFBC 1980 and the judge's earlier interpretation of "completion" as above, whereas the Defendant employer relied on Clause 27.4.1: "The employer may employ and pay other persons to carry out and complete the Works and he or they may enter upon the Works ..."; and Clause 27.4.4 "... after completion of the Works under Clause 27.4.1 the Employer shall not be bound by any provisions of this contract to make any further payment to the Contractor, but upon such completion ... the Architect shall certify the amount of expenses properly incurred by the Employer and the amount of any direct loss and/or damage caused to the Employer by the determination."

The then editor-in-chief of *Building Law Reports*, now a judge himself in the Technology and Construction Court disagreed with this decision, saying "Surely 'completion' in Clause 27.4.1 refers to the rectification of defective works in the defects liability period? Such work could be extensive as a result of latent defects." And "It makes no sense at all that the employer should have to pay a contractor—still less a contractor who may be worthless and who will be unable to repay the money."

With due respect this cannot be right. Firstly, latent defects if they are to occur are unlikely to do so in the few months remaining of the Defects

Liability Period as against the next 10 years or so, besides which the employer's contractual remedy in the remaining period of the contract is the retention fund—not to arbitrarily set off against defects which don't presently exist and which may never exist.

In any event Clause 27.4.1 says it all "... enter upon the Works ...". Only during the live construction period does the contractor have this right—not after Practical Completion when he only enters as an invited visitor; i.e. in the context of Clause 27 "completion" must be the same as "Practical Completion" as referred to in Clause 17.

The contract also refers at Condition 1.3 to the "Date for Possession", "Date for Completion" and "Defects Liability Period"—all to run consecutively, not with the last two running concurrently, so for various reasons this author at least believes the judge in *Emson Eastern* got it spot on.

Some years later the author found himself enjoying a cup of tea in a seminar break and got into conversation with the judge—not about "completion" but about the seminar subject: conflicting terms and conditions. The judge was very clear: one Saturday morning he had had found himself with nothing to do, so he picked up the quotation his wife had obtained for a further area of hardwood flooring in their dining room. He didn't think much of two of the printed trading conditions on the back of the quotation so he rang up the firm and spoke to the Managing Director. The MD said he had never seen them—or if he had, he couldn't understand them! So the judge decided there and then that in any future cases the small print on the back of quotations etc was out, unless it could be shown to have been relied on by both parties!

Curiously some years earlier the author had also met the Plaintiff in *Emson Eastern*—trying to sell him consultancy services! Politely he told me he did not have the need to employ claims consultants or expensive solicitors as "I reckon I can negotiate my way out of any situation". Famous last words, as a year later he started a profitable sideline in installing jacuzzi baths and saunas in the rich North Hertfordshire commuter belt. Unfortunately he also developed a whole new meaning to "Practical Completion" undreamt of by the JCT drafting committee or the judge—until one afternoon his then wife caught up with him. Evidently his negotiating skills were found wanting and he needed solicitors big time!— his wife wanting most of his assets. The rest is history, but if it hadn't been for that jacuzzi on that steamy afternoon we would probably have never read about the Plaintiff's subsequent insolvency and the redefinition of "completion" in *Emson Eastern Ltd* v. *E.M.E. Developments Ltd!*

PART TWO: CASE MANAGEMENT

CHAPTER 8

THE LATHAM REPORT

8.1 THE NEED FOR TRUST

In his first Report, published as a deliberately thought-provoking, hopefully ground-breaking discussion document in December 1993, Sir Michael Latham took the twin themes of "Trust" and "Money" as his basic line of enquiry into the ills of the construction industry. Extensive discussions and generally favourable industry comment followed, and in July 1994 Sir Michael's finalised Report, *Constructing the Team*, was published.

Taking therefore the first of Sir Michael's twin themes, "Trust", it is interesting to look back six years and see how the problem was then perceived. In Chapter 10, Sir Michael went to the heart of the matter in saying: "It is absolutely fundamental to trust within the construction industry that participants should be paid for the work which they have undertaken."

It really was unacceptable that at the bottom end of the supply chain small firms, often little bigger than sole traders and providing specialist services, could be expected to:

— bid their best price, often on inadequate information and in an impossibly short time;
— then have to re-bid, often in a Dutch auction;
— be told to be ready to start work on a given date, but then at less than 10 days' notice be told some future date, thus having to find alternative fill-in work at short notice;
— accept complex and unintelligible sub-contract conditions after starting work, often with onerous terms not previously mentioned.
— work in a "free-for-all" scenario on site, because the main contractor has lost control of the construction programme.

As if the above was not bad enough, before the Housing Grants, Construction and Regeneration Act 1996, which was a direct result of the Latham Report and introduced the right of either party to call for adjudication, the supplier of services would have to invoice each month for his money, but then the application would often disappear into a "black hole".

This entirely unregulated payment situation was discussed in detail in Chapter 1, but the bottom line was that the genuine trader was often put under financial pressure, the usual trick being to make an unexplained part payment. In the meantime he would have had to purchase and pay for materials etc. and, if employing labour, would have had to put cash into pay packets each Friday. He would also have had to deal with the Inland Revenue, often paying out before actually earning.

If the party up the supply chain, i.e. another sub-contractor or the main contractor, did not process the application fairly and promptly, this caused real hardship which inevitably translated itself to under-performance on site by way of involuntary material starvation to severe demotivation of the labour force.

Often therefore payments would be:

— paid substantially late;
— partial payments, made without explanation;
— subject to surprise and unjustified set-off claims.

Further, there was no defined payment timetable for sub-contractors. When expected payments failed to materialise from the contractor inevitably promises would be given that payments would follow shortly, but when repeated promises were repeatedly broken any trust that once existed would be a cherished memory only.

This was particularly galling for sub-contractors as from their point of view:

— The contractor would have been put in funds by the employer for the work that the sub-contractor had in fact done, but not been paid for.
— The sub-contractor was expected to give a Performance Bond as against his own non-performance, and, most gallingly, against his own potential insolvency when it was entirely within the gift of the contractor as to when to pay and so keep him out of insolvency.
— There was no reciprocal security as against the insolvency of the employer or of the main contractor.

Perhaps the most public example of the injustice that can arise when occasionally an employer goes bankrupt was the Carlton Gate case, which eventually came to court as *John Mowlem Construction Ltd* v. *Eagle Star Insurance Company & Others* (1995).

Now it so happens that the author might bear some minimal responsibility for all the grief, and huge legal fees, that were eventually involved in that most unfortunate of projects—which might never have happened, but for a game of cards! I had just bid a tricky "4 Spades" in an alcoholic, but fiercely competitive, game of bridge with our friends—the husband then being a senior Mowlem Construction engineer. His wife was taking an undue length of time to make her eventual and resentful "No bid", sensing quite rightly that she had been conned out of a perfectly safe game in "3 No Trumps". Bored with his wife's delay the husband asked out of the blue: "Jeremy, what is Management Contracting all about?" Our "talking shop" then annoyed his wife even more, who promptly spat her "No bid" through clenched teeth. So we finished our game and over a bottle of whisky I explained all I then knew about Management Contracting.

The next month Mowlem Management Contracting Ltd was born and my friend was appointed Construction Director. All went well at first, but one day he mentioned some major job in West London which he had bid for and won, but where the Developer was not now paying his bills on time. In consequence, Mowlems were having a hard time keeping the Works Package Contractors happy. The inevitable happened and the Developer folded, but a rescue package was put together by a lead funder and a special purpose vehicle (SPV) company was formed to build the job out. Matters on site did not improve, and Claims proliferated so Mowlem commenced arbitration, not so much on their own behalf as on behalf of the many underpaid sub-contractors.

Worse was to follow: the arbitrator found substantially for Mowlem, so almost before the ink was dry on the Award the SPV wound itself up, leaving the many sub-contractors still unpaid. The fact that Mowlems then made certain allegations of collusion against the SPV and certain members of the design team is history, but by all accounts it was a close run thing. Certainly it left a very bad smell in the industry.

Now there can't be many projects where the specialist sub-contractors have suffered the slings and arrows of the employer going bust twice; the Carlton Gate case simply emphasises that trust can only work if underpinned by fallback contract conditions, which when the chips are down *actually work both ways*, i.e. up the supply chain as well as down the supply chain.

Accordingly, Sir Michael Latham came out very strongly in his Report that employers should be required to set up Trust Funds, putting money aside on short-term deposit to secure the future funding of the project. Such funds would be controlled by independent Trustees, such that in the event of employer insolvency, as in the Carlton Gate situation, the Receiver would not be able to seize the money rightly due to the sub-contractors for work properly carried out.

8.2 THE NEED FOR CASH FLOW

The nonsense is of course that in an insolvency situation on a large project, if the employer has a Receiver appointed by its bank, this is likely to set off a string of sub-contractor insolvencies. Given the limited number of main lending banks, the bank in question can then find itself bankrupting its own other perfectly good, but struggling customers, further down the supply chain.

Judges other than the late Lord Denning are of course on record as having pronounced on the importance of cash flow in the construction industry, but it is probably the Denning judgment in *Dawnays* v. *F.G. Minter Ltd* (1971), quoted in Chapter 3, that is generally recognised as the most telling judicial commentary on the subject.

Of course the construction industry does have provision for interim payments, but in the pre-Latham days the cash flow problem on a badly managed project could assume major proportions for the man at the bottom of the supply chain, and many an otherwise profitable specialist company was forced into receivership just because of payment abuse further up the supply chain. The reality of being an unpaid, or under-paid sub-contractor, is that it then requires a major financial investment to pursue the original money—with all the attendant risks that that involves, so depleting the liquidity of the business even further.

In the past this has been compounded by the wholly inconsistent behaviour of some banks. Whilst there must be a lending policy with clear terms and penalties for repayment default, it serves no useful purpose, other than to keep Receivers and their lawyers gainfully employed, if a sub-contractor can agree a facility one month with a particular manager, only for that manager to go sick or be replaced the next month by some newly promoted youngster anxious to impress his superiors, who then calls in all unsecured loans at a week's notice.

An appalling example of such myopic management happened to a client of the author's during the course of an adjudication. At issue was the contractor's failure to issue a Withholding Notice under the "Scheme" provisions (see Chapter 9) and it was a virtual formality that the adjudicator would be ordering circa £100,000 to be paid forthwith—until the new 30+ manager arrived at the Claimant's bank. An existing £60,000 facility was required to be secured within a week against my client sub-contractor's house, and quite rightly his wife, advised by her solicitor, refused to sign. Under threat of having the VAT and some recently issued trade supplier cheques stopped, my client felt so pressured he considered he had no alternative but to strike a deal with the main contractor—accepting circa £65,000 for an immediate cheque. The day my client got the contractor's cheque, I received the adjudicator's decision awarding my client £97,800. So effectively the new bank manager had cost his customer almost £40,000 after fees, i.e. nearly 70% of the facility. Needless to say, my client changed his bank very shortly afterwards.

It is thus one thing to be able to show a strong balance sheet and a solid business plan, but it is quite another to maintain an even level of borrowing over the year and keep bank managers happy. Cash flow really does matter in the construction industry where certain major costs, e.g. wages, have to be paid out several weeks before they can be converted to earned income, even if paid promptly, so it is vital that late payers are hit hard until they learn to play by the rules.

Most contractors survived in the past by operating a policy of "Pay-when-Paid" and this could have worked if operated on a 48-hour minimum delay basis. Unfortunately most contractors then added up to 30 days into the equation, effectively "stealing" other people's money and reducing their own borrowings. Quite rightly "Pay-when-Paid" is now banned by section 113(1) of the HGCRA, repeated at Part II, Para. 11 of the "Scheme for Construction Contracts".

A final salutary fact is that, over the last 10 years, 80% of companies (all industries) declared insolvent have actually been trading profitably, if viewed on an annual basis—so perhaps Sir Michael Latham might usefully be commissioned to pronounce on good practice in the banking industry next!

8.3 THE IMPORTANCE OF SPECIALIST SUB-CONTRACTORS

It may appear to readers of this book that the author is championing the cause of sub-contractors at the expense of main contractors. If so I plead guilty to the first part of the charge, but not guilty to the second part. It is a fact of construction industry development that buildings have had to become more complex over recent years, with an increasing emphasis on the performance of the building needing to serve the end user function.

Whilst the design development process can only start on the Architect's drawing board, the final realisation is often dependent on what is technically achievable, and more often than not this comes down to specialist products and systems. Such products and systems naturally have to be guaranteed as to their performance over a given number of years, so the construction industry has seen over the last 15 years a huge spawning of specialist contractors, often acting as high value sub-contractors. Thus long gone are the days when main contractors carried all trades and brought in specialists only when the job was likely to be too big or difficult for them. The emphasis now is on design input from the specialist and pre-fabrication off-site.

Inevitably the rise of sub-contracting has seen a proliferation of paperwork, especially legal documentation attempting to delegate design development yet tie in all the obligations of the main contractor to the employer. In its crudest form this is no more than risk dumping, but if the design or performance specification of the building demands it, it is very much in the employer's interests that a specialist takes responsibility for the work.

This sub-division of responsibilities is, however, no substitute for single point responsibility in the first instance. If the Architect adopts a proprietary system he should not disclaim it when it goes wrong and likewise the contractor should always be first in line when the employer needs to recover remedial works costs. Given the increasing dependence of any project on specialist sub-contractors it follows that such firms need at the same time to be contractually locked into the project, but also looked after in terms of prompt payment and helped, not hindered, when site problems threaten to cause loss and expense all round. It is therefore very much in the employer's interest that specialist sub-contractors are recognised for their particular skills as modern-day tradesmen, and for the added value they bring to projects. This demands mutual respect and trust—fair payment being an essential ingredient.

8.4 THE PRINCIPLE OF ADJUDICATION

Adjudication is not new to the construction industry, but the Latham Report certainly raised the profile and general awareness of adjudication as a real "hands-on" method of dispute resolution.

As previously described in Chapter 3 the great majority of contracts which go together to make up any one project have no "Third Party Umpire" to certify money, time and quality—the three regular battlegrounds—as between parties who fail to agree and then lock horns with one another, usually adding new allegations and counter-allegations the longer the dispute remains unresolved. This is of course entirely unhealthy, not only for the disputants themselves, but inevitably for the various third parties whose own positions are affected by the subject matter of the dispute. It is therefore in everyone's interests, not least the employer's interest, that any dispute is resolved as soon as it arises by a cost-effective prescribed process administered by an appropriately qualified neutral expert.

"Why have a dispute in the first place?" I hear you ask. "Why not get all the contract conditions so balanced that all will be sweetness and light for ever more?" Well, anyone who can honestly propound such pious notions had better get real—and fast. The construction industry on site is a raw and rough world and when it moves indoors it is little better: bargains have to be struck and when someone steps out of line the fur can fly. The knack is having the proverbial boxing ring and the Queensberry rules all prepared, with the referee a telephone call away. Most matters can be resolved there and then if only caught soon enough and after an initial bloody nose or two the parties know better than to pick an avoidable fight again, particularly if it is going to cost real money to get revenge, or a different decision, after losing the first fisticuffs.

However, certain matters do run deeper, particularly where the underlying cause is the non-performance of a third party—the classic examples being late release of information by the design team, or the failure of the main contractor to manage the site and co-ordinate the activities of the various specialist sub-contractors. Such matters can well have insurance implications and substantial monies can rest on the result of any final decision, so complicated and high value disputes cannot necessarily be fairly determined in a "one-off, quick fix". For serious disputes there has to be the safety valve of a two-stage procedure.

Sir Michael duly pronounced on adjudication, finding that pre-pricing of variations would cut out one layer of disputes and that "Both main contractors and sub-contractors have pressed hard for such a system to be standard procedure for dispute resolution." Accordingly, in his "Recommendations 26.1–26.5 Adjudication" Sir Michael's principal proposals were:

— No restrictions on issues capable of being referred, either under the main contract or under dependent sub-contracts.
— Adjudicators' awards to be implemented immediately.
— Trustee Stakeholder accounts to be used if both parties so agree (unlikely!), or if the adjudicator so directs.
— No right to arbitration or litigation on the same issues until after Practical Completion.
— The right of immediate access to the courts if an adjudicator's award is not complied with.
— Training for adjudicators and a Code of Practice to be published in due course.

As we shall see in Chapter 9, Sir Michael's efforts did not fall on stony ground and thanks to industry acclamation and all-party support the political will was found to translate *Constructing the Team* into statutory legislation without emasculating the key ideas, albeit some "Recommendations" did not survive.

8.5 THE ALLOCATION OF DESIGN RISK

The allocation of design risk must start with the employer. In Chapter 3 of his Report at "Recommendation 2: Guide for Clients on Briefing" Sir Michael says: "It should also be part of the contractual process that the client should approve the design brief by 'signing it off'." Moving on, Sir Michael then highlights, in Chapter 4 of his Report, seven aspects of design management which he sees as "crucial for the success of the project", *inter alia*:

— The appointment of a lead manager.
— Clear definition of design responsibilities in the design of building services, Electrical and Mechanical, as between consultants and specialist engineering contractors.
— The implementation of Co-ordinated Project Information (CPI).

It is particularly interesting to reflect on what Sir Michael had to say on this last aspect of design management, now six years ago. "CPI is a technique which should have become normal practice years ago. In conjunction with the preparation of a full matrix of documents, its use should be made part of the conditions of engagement of all designers. If, as a result of the client's own instructions or through some problem on the part of the design team, the design drawings and specifications are not fully complete, and provisional sums are used, the consultants must make the client aware of the risks of incomplete design .... ."

With due respect to Sir Michael, this is hardly rocket science and does not address the reality of modern construction procurement as illustrated in "Table 2: Contract Options" of the Report. Perhaps Sir Michael had in mind just one such option: Lump Sum tendering based on Bills of Quantities. Maybe Sir Michael should then have inserted two provisos:

— The dangers of changes of mind by the client: that instructed Variations should be limited in number—and preferably pre-agreed in both cost and time.
— That C.P.I. will count for nothing if it is not carried right through the post-contract period, covering drawing issues, approvals of sub-contractors shop drawings, and, most important of all, the sequencing and co-ordination of rival services drawings competing for limited spaces and routeing, e.g. ceiling voids.

Computers and fast-developing IT know-how enable large projects, open for construction activities for say 10 hours a day, to be serviced 24 hours a day by design teams located on different (and cheaper cost base) continents, so the world has moved on in the last six years, but back in the

UK so-called Construction Managers still don't deliver the goods where it matters—on site.

The problem for clients, and particularly for main contractors, including Construction Managers and Management Contractors, whose principal responsibility is to co-ordinate site activities, is that CPI sets up an audit trail—for all to see. When things start going off-line there is no hiding place: the information is in the project domain, including that of the specialist sub-contractors, as indeed it should be. The problem is that delays are expensive and blame can now be factually attributed to where it truly belongs! All of a sudden, all the pre-contract sales talk about CPI is forgotten and project "Mission Statements" are made to look very foolish by the realities of what has actually happened on site. Typically the CPI system becomes one-way traffic, with the specialist sub-contractors still expected, on pain of contractual default notices, to contribute their design input information against tight deadlines—but then getting nothing meaningful back by return.

In the last six years since the Latham Report the author has acted for specialist sub-contractors on two high-profile projects, where on both projects well known Project Managers were paid large fees. However, when the bullets started flying on site it was the specialist sub-contractors who dug deep, mostly without financial reward, and got both projects open on time, with the CPI systems having been found wanting when it really mattered.

Theory is fine, but actually delivering a complex project, rather than hiding behind alleged design risk issues and dumping all risks on the smallest in the supply chain, is the real skill, possessed by few. However, the good news is that risk dumpers will now have to explain themselves to adjudicators—and unless the contract terms are clear, this author believes they can expect little sympathy. Previously risk dumpers only got away with it because impoverished sub-contractors could not afford, or risk, arbitration or litigation. Now they can get a "first-fix" decision and quite possibly a substantial payment for an investment of less than £10,000.

THE HOUSING GRANTS, CONSTRUCTION AND REGENERATION ACT 1996

9.1 THE CONCEPT AND BASIS OF APPLICATION

Otherwise known in the trade as "Son of Latham", this welcome and long overdue legislation got off to a rocky start. Having won plaudits from both industry and Parliament, the then Conservative government committed itself to enacting, subject to parliamentary time, the principal recommendations of the Latham Report. The then Labour opposition spokesman on Housing went one better—if elected the Labour Party would enact the Latham Report in its entirety.

So the Latham Report got into the hands of the Property Services Agency—a government department in its death throes as it was about to be privatised and sold off! Seemingly the proverbial rats had had the good sense to leave the sinking ship, so the task of translating the Latham Report into draft government legislation fell to one of the few remaining senior staff—apparently a lawyer specialising in microbiology!

The government had also sensibly promised wide public consultation and had set up specifically tasked working parties as also recommended by Sir Michael. The first draft, covering most, but not all, of the Latham recommendations, was welcomed in principle and generated a public response which might be summarised as "Good try—but could do a lot better"—the mail bag from the public being overwhelmingly large. Consequently the final draft was delayed, and the scheduled legislation ran out of parliamentary time before the general election.

The incoming Labour government then made the decision that rather than start again and deal with the totality of the Latham Report, as promised, they would live with the Act as drafted, and with the support of all parties it became law, albeit with a commitment to a formal review once the Act had been proven or otherwise in practice. In the meantime, and very much at the last moment, a group of eminent lawyers had decided to set their face against the whole principle of statutory adjudication in 28 days, identifying most of the potential pitfalls and suggesting that the whole concept of adjudication was doomed to failure. How wrong can one be!

So the big day eventually came and the Housing Grants, Construction and Regeneration Act 1996, complete with the supplementary Scheme for Construction Contracts, enacted by Statutory Instrument 1998 No. 649, was finally released from HMSO. The effective date was set at 1 May 1998, and Sir Michael must have been well pleased.

Unsurprisingly adjudication grabbed the construction press headlines and all sorts of commentators went off at tangents prophesying legal battles ahead. Very few focused on the actual clauses that were to change the payment culture in the industry, i.e. the mandatory Fair Payment requirements of the HGCRA, and the default Scheme provisions.

Most pre-Latham disputes had inevitably been over money, i.e. *who* owed *who*, *what* and *when*, the typical "Mushroom Farm" scenario touched on in Chapter 3, all due to the non-transparent and unregulated interim valuation procedure then in general use, so the basic concept of adjudication was of a quick and cheap "first fix" decision, and payment as ordered, followed by the due process of law in due course if the dispute hadn't disappeared in the meantime—as had been the experience under the old Blue and Green forms of JCT sub-contract set-off adjudications.

So in fact, the real ground-breaking sections have proved to be sections 109 to 113, headed "Payment", and section 114 bringing in statutory default procedures, under the heading "Supplementary provisions", i.e. the Scheme Part II payment rules and timescales apply on a clause by clause basis where any individual section 109 to 113 contract requirement is not provided for.

At the same time under the heading of "Adjudication", HGCRA section 108 lays down various mandatory requirements to be written into every construction contract, as defined by sections 104 to 107, providing for the right of any party to refer a dispute to adjudication for a temporary, but binding decision, pending arbitration, litigation or mutual compromise—with section 114 catching any non-compliant section 108 contract drafting, in which case the Scheme provisions Part I replace the eight essential requirements of section 108 in their totality.

However, before we get into the detail of the provisions it is necessary to state that not all construction projects are subject to the statutory provisions of the HGCRA—the very great majority are, but at either end of the spectrum certain categories of project are exempt. At the top end, the line is drawn at process engineering, section 105(1) and (2) setting out what are intended to be definitive lists of what are deemed to be construction activities. At the bottom end the definition is much clearer: section 106(1)(a) excludes domestic owner-occupier contracts.

It is particularly important not to lose sight of the further definitions in section 104:

— "Arranging for the carrying out of construction operations by others"
— "Providing his own labour, or the labour of others, for the carrying out of construction operations."

Thus, also caught as "Construction Contracts" for the purpose of the HGCRA are:

— All consultancy contracts involving design or project management services, including Planning Supervisor services under the Construction (Design & Management) Regulations 1994.
— Any Labour Agency contract for the supply of operatives and staff.

Presumably, the line has to be drawn somewhere, but what about Recruitment Agencies providing professional staff to professional practices, who in turn "arrange for the carrying out of construction operations"?

Also specifically excluded by virtue of the Construction Contracts (England and Wales) Exclusion Order 1998 are:

— Certain Private Finance Initiative projects.
— Construction-related Finance Agreements such as Bonds and Funding Arrangements.
— Development Agreements which include the onward sale of the freehold or agreement to grant a lease in excess of 12 months, but Tenants' obligations to repair are not excluded.

Then at section 107(1) the HGCRA very sensibly states that "The provisions of this Part apply only where the construction contract is in writing, and any other agreement between the parties as to any matter is effective for the purposes of this Part only if in writing"—where "... this Part ..." refers to Part II of the Act, covering:

— section 104: Construction Contracts
— section 105: Meaning of "Construction Operations"
— section 106: Provisions not applicable to contracts with a residential occupier
— section 107: Provisions applicable only to contracts in writing
— section 108: Right to refer disputes to adjudication
— section 109: Entitlement to stage payments
— section 110: Dates for payment
— section 111: Notice of intention to withhold payment
— section 112: Right to suspend performance for non-payment
— section 113: Prohibition of conditional payment provisions
— section 114: The Scheme for Construction Contracts
— section 115: Service of notices, etc.
— section 116: Reckoning periods of time
— section 117: Crown application.

Having decreed at section 107(1) that the contract needs to be in writing to qualify under the provisions of the HGCRA, there is then a wide definition of what is deemed to be a written contract—plainly conceived to counter the games played pre-Latham by parties who sought to claim "no contract" as a reason for not paying what by all accounts they rightly owed, or those other parties who wished to muddy the waters when it came to having a dispute about a dispute, i.e. Was there or was there not an effective arbitration clause? For these artful dodgers the time is up—and there should now rightly be no hiding place.

Section 107(2) is therefore a crucial part of the new provisions and reads as follows:

"There is an agreement in writing:

(a) if the agreement is made in writing (whether or not it is signed by the parties);

(b) if the agreement is made by exchange of communications in writing, or ...

(c) if the agreement is evidenced in writing."

Section 107(3) to (6) continue in similar vein:

"(3) Where parties agree otherwise than in writing by reference to terms which are in writing, they make an agreement in writing.

(4) An agreement is evidenced in writing if an agreement made otherwise than in writing is recorded by one of the parties, or by a third party, with the authority of the parties to the agreement.

(5) An exchange of written submissions in adjudication proceedings, or in arbitral or legal proceedings in which the existence of an agreement otherwise than in writing is alleged by one party against another party and not denied by the other party in his response, constitutes as between those parties an agreement in writing to the alleged effect.

(6) References in this Part to anything being written or in writing include it being recorded by any means."

A very valiant attempt, but one can just see the arguments coming if the money at issue justifies the cost of arguing that somehow the alleged contract escaped the above definition—with the attendant risk of losing, and having to pick up both sides' costs.

Section 107(2)(a) could be very tricky—an alleged agreement in written form, but unsigned. Typically there will be no doubt that some form of agreement was relied on in good faith by each party, but the devil is in the detail and there could be lack of certainty, if not different versions of essential terms. Would that be a "contract in writing"? In the meantime can an adjudicator safely enter upon the dispute, despite one party contending that as there is no "contract in writing" he is not empowered by the HGCRA?

Sections 107(3) and (4), "Where parties agree otherwise than in writing ..." and "An agreement is evidenced in writing if an agreement made otherwise than in writing is recorded by one of the parties ...", really do stretch the imagination and fly in the face of the first principles of contract law, i.e. the basic rules of offer and acceptance.

Hopefully challenges on these vagaries will be few and far between, as generally speaking it is only parties with bad cases who take bad points, and so far adjudicators have been encouraged to proceed irrespective of challenges to their jurisdiction. More on jurisdiction problems, arising so far, appears later in this Chapter.

9.2 THE FAIR PAYMENT PROVISIONS

As already stated, sections 109 to 113 are the core sections of the HGCRA, i.e. the long overdue regulation of Cash Flow in the construction industry, without which the adjudication provisions of section 108 would have been of very limited application. In particular, the introduction at section 112 of the statutory right for an unpaid party, after due notice, to suspend work and leave site is most welcome—subject to it not prejudicing an innocent third party's position.

So now we have a strict two-stage payment regime, laid down by statute at sections 109 to 111 of the HGCRA, which allow the party drafting the contract limited options as regards payment procedures and timing—with compulsory provisions under the Scheme, which apply on an individual basis if the contract provisions are deficient.

At this point it is necessary to turn to the very back of the Scheme para. 12 Interpretation to understand when a "construction contract" is, or isn't, a "relevant construction contract"—the rather tortuous definition essentially being those contracts exceeding 45 days, as this then determines the back-up Scheme provisions, where they are needed. Having done this the *optional HGCRA stage or interim payment provisions* and the back-up compulsory Scheme provisions for "relevant construction contracts" can be summarised as follows:

Section 109(2): Option of stating whether scheduled lump sum or stage payments are required, and when they are to become due, such as:

— by instalments, e.g. defined amounts and dates;
— by stage payments, e.g. defined milestones such as roof-on, or value attributed floor areas;
— by periodic payments, e.g. monthly;

the fallback Scheme provision, if the option is not exercised, being Periodic with "Relevant Periods" of 28 days duration—see para. 12.

Section 110(1): Option of providing an adequate mechanism for agreeing the amount and actual timing of any payments, specifically:

— assessing the payment due and when it is due, i.e. the amount due and when it *becomes* payable, defined as the Due Date for Payment;
— determining a Final Date for Payment in relation to the Due Date for Payment, as above;

the fallback Scheme provisions under section 110(3) being:

— *Valuation method as Part II, para. 2.*
— *Due Date for Payment being seven days from the end of the Relevant Period in question, or the date of the payee's claim, if later—see Part II, para. 4.*
— *Final Date for Payment being 17 days thereafter—see Part II, para. 8(2).*

Section 110(2): A non-optional provision, i.e. the Scheme repeats the HGCRA requirement, in the event the contract omits to so provide:

— The party receiving the payment application, shall, no later than five days after the Due Date for Payment, give a notice to the payee, either confirming the payment due, or, if he is not happy to pay the full amount, state the amount that will be paid.
— ***This obligation on the part of the paying party applies even if there is some dispute as to the payee's performance of his obligations, i.e. section 110(2)(a) is the key provision and so establishes "the sum due under the contract".***

Section 111: Option to dictate the prescribed period during which the paying party must set out in reasonable detail and reasoning why any other monies applied for are being withheld from the amount otherwise payable, e.g. contra charges:

— *Counted back from the Final Date for Payment (s. 110 (1)), so allowing a defined number of days following the five-day notice required at section 110(2)—see Appendix C;*

the fallback Scheme provision under section 111(3), if no countback period is stated in the contract, being seven days—Part II, para. 10.

The above are, as stated, the statutory provisions for the administration of interim payments on construction contracts. In respect of final payments the HGCRA makes no provision, yet at the Scheme Part II, paras. 5 and 6 (Relevant and Non-Relevant Contracts) it appears that final payments must now be made within 30 days of completion of the work, or the payee's final invoice, whichever is the later—normally the Final Account when presented.

Given a typical sub-contract with payment governed by the Scheme rules, does this mean that a sub-contractor is entitled to invoice 100% on completion of his specialist works and be paid in full within 30 days of his leaving site, even if the sub-contract makes provision for main contractor's retention? Surely not, but it is certainly arguable if no retention provision is made in the sub-contract.

However, in practice, it is HGCRA section 110, Notice of Intended Payment, subject to section 111, Notice of Intention to Withhold, which are biting—being responsible for many of the early referrals to adjudication, before paying parties woke up to the fact that they were bound by statute. In short, if anyone fails to pay in full without first complying with the strict requirements of sections 110 and 111 they put themselves in statutory default. It follows that if the subsequent Referral Notice is limited to these specific issues, then adjudicators have little option but to award full payment, plus interest, even if the amount claimed includes wholly unproven and disputed Variations or Claim values.

Thus paying parties, having lost adjudications brought on the basis of failure to issue valid Notices under sections 110 and 111 may find themselves having to commence separate adjudications, arbitrations or litigation to recover the disputed Variation and Claim value, but only after having to honour the original adjudication decision, and being parted from the disputed cash.

It is therefore in the detail of the statutory provisions that the key obligations are to be found, so starting with section 110 this reads as follows:

"(1) Every construction contract shall—

(a) provide an adequate mechanism for determining what payments become due under the contract, and when, and

(b) provide for a final date for payment in relation to any sum which becomes due.

The parties are free to agree how long the period is to be between the date on which a sum becomes due and the final date for payment.

(2) Every construction contract shall provide for the giving of notice by a party not later than five days after the date on which a payment becomes due from him under the contract, or would have become due if—

(a) the other party had carried out his obligations under the contract, and

(b) no set-off or abatement was permitted by reference to any sum claimed to be due under one or more other contracts,

specifying the amount (if any) of the payment made or proposed to be made, and the basis on which that amount was calculated.

(3) If or to the extent that a contract does not contain such provision as is mentioned in subsection (1) or (2), the relevant provisions of the Scheme for Construction Contracts apply."

Equally, what does section 111 say in detail as to what a paying party must do to successfully withhold monies from a paying party's payment application? It reads as follows:

"(1) A party to a construction contract may not withhold payment after the final date for payment of a sum due under the contract unless he has given an effective notice of intention to withhold payment. The notice mentioned in section 110(2) may suffice as a notice of intention to withhold payment if it complies with the requirements of this section.

(2) To be effective such notice must specify:

(a) the amount proposed to be withheld and the grounds for withholding payment, or ...

(b) if there is more than one ground, each ground and the amount attributable to it, ...

(c) ... and must be given not later than the prescribed period before the final date for payment."

It should be stressed that the author is of the "robust school" of Adjudicators, i.e. the HGCRA provisions as drafted leave a lot to be desired as to interpretation of what Parliament actually thought they were approving.

Thus the "robust school" believe that, if a party invoices the other, section 110 does not allow the paying party to remain silent—we believe that if he does remain silent the amount applied *de facto* becomes the amount due under the contract. Section 111 is then applicable only to genuine set-offs, not arguments about value of work or defects. Thus A (section 110) less B (section 111) determines C, the amount payable.

Other adjudicators and legal commentators are not so sure that section 110 is sufficiently strongly worded as to allow this interpretation. So, until we have a test case on this particular issue, the jury remains out at time of going to press (June 2000).

However, in commercial reality rather than legal niceties, in the event of non-payment and no effective Notices the immediate concern is cash flow, i.e. company liquidity, so despite the right to suspend provisions at HGCRA section 112, the most effective course of action is for the non-paid party to apply for the appointment of an adjudicator and swiftly follow the application with the formal Referral Notice—limited to the single issue of statutory default under sections 110 and 111. One should also ask the adjudicator to order the payment of his fees, and all your costs of the adjudication, by your opponent—on the basis that your award as to the sums due under the contract is not diluted by any split costs award. There is apparently nothing to stop the non-paid party also exercising his right to suspend the works now provided by HGCRA section 112, provided the prescribed notice procedure is observed.

If this is done as part of the Referral Notice this puts the Defendant Party in a very difficult position in terms of site management. Can he risk a potential delay of 28 days, or more, or would it not be prudent to pay up this month and make sure he issues the proper Notices next month?

In detail, in section 112 the HGCRA provisions on the non-paid party's right to suspend read as follows:

"(1) Where a sum due under a construction contract is not paid in full by the final date for payment and no effective notice to withhold payment has been given, the person to whom the sum is due has the right ... to suspend performance of his obligations under the contract to the party by whom payment ought to have been made ('the party in default').

(2) The right may not be exercised without first giving to the party in default at least seven days' notice of intention to suspend performance, stating the ground or grounds on which it is intended to suspend performance.

(3) The right to suspend performance ceases when the party in default makes payment in full of the amount due.

(4) Any period during which performance is suspended in pursuance of the right conferred by this section shall be disregarded in computing for the purposes of any contractual time limit the time taken, by the party exercising the right or by a third party, to complete any work directly or indirectly affected by the exercise of this right. Where the contractual time limit is set by reference to a date rather than a period, the date shall be adjusted accordingly".

The above provision is deceptively logical and simply stated, but in practice things aren't so simple. Firstly one can't just pull labour off one job, relocate them to another, and then re-re-locate them back to the original site immediately the "party in default" eventually pays up. Secondly, a "third party" presumably means following trades, so the potential for satellite disputes concerning knock-on delays and attendant costs is ominous—the employer in the meantime being the totally innocent party.

It has to be assumed, therefore, that a main contractor who fails to pay in time as required by the provisions of the HGCRA and still fails to pay within seven days of default notification will get no sympathy from the employer—and will lay himself open to all consequential sub-contractor claims, as well as LADs.

A situation could well arise therefore where a sub-contractor suspends work, leaving site three weeks before an adjudication decision in his favour, or following an adjudication decision in his favour, if payment is still not forthcoming and the sub-contractor goes to court and gets an enforcement order, and by the time he collects his unpaid monies the work has been stopped say by six weeks. The contractor in the meantime commences arbitration on the same issue decided by the adjudicator and the arbitrator reverses the decision.

Whilst the original monies in dispute can be returned, who is liable for the sub-contractor's stand-down and remobilisation costs, third party delay costs and the employer's losses involved in the delay to completion of the contract? The answer is that in the given circumstance, the sub-contractor was perfectly entitled under section 112 to suspend, and equally it was the contractor who acted outside the law in withholding payment. This has to be an anomaly, requiring section 112 to be amended by Parliament to exclude the right to suspend during the currency of an adjudication referral.

In short, the contractor's remedies were to have paid up as ordered and then to have commenced recovery action through arbitration. Equally, if the dispute originated over money, and statutory default in not giving Notices under sections 110 and 111, then the contractor only has himself to blame in not having played by the rules in the first place. The arbitrator's award, reversing the adjudicator's, can only affect the original contractual position—to do otherwise would make HGCRA section 112 unworkable and all other costs must arguably be for the main contractor's account as the "party in default" of the statutory payment requirements.

Finally, in this discussion of the Fair Payment provisions we have the key section 113 outlawing, with one exception, any form of "Pay-when-paid", "Pay-if-paid" etc. This reads:

> "(1) A provision making payment under a construction contract conditional on the payer receiving payment from a third person is ineffective, unless that third person, or any other person payment by whom is under the contract (directly or indirectly) a condition of payment by that third person, is insolvent."

This is followed by technical definitions concerning company and individual insolvency, but in plain English the bottom line is that as the payee you are assured of payment once your invoice has *not* been challenged by a counter notice under section 110, or a valid Notice of Withholding issued under section 111, *unless a party once or more removed up the payment chain from your client has called in a Receiver.*

Thus insolvency is the one circumstance where "Pay-if-paid" is allowed, with downstream parties taking their losses where they lie at the time of the declared insolvency. There is therefore every reason to invoice as regularly as the contract, or the Scheme provisions, allow—and, if not paid promptly, to press for payment using adjudication as a first option.

So, it is essential to understand what a "Day" is according to the HGCR Act 1996, and for this one must turn to section 116, "Reckoning periods of time". This reads:

> "(2) Where an act is required to be done within a specified period after or from a specified date, the period begins immediately after that date."—[I take this to mean that the next day is Day 1.]
>
> "(3) Where the period would include Christmas Day, Good Friday or a day which under the Banking and Financial Dealings Act 1971 is a bank holiday in England and Wales or, as the case may be, in Scotland, that day shall be excluded."

Thus Saturdays and Sundays count as "Days", but New Year's Day, Good Friday, Easter Monday, Spring Bank Holiday, Summer Bank Holiday, Christmas Day and Boxing Day do not count.

What about the May Day Bank Holiday? This ranks as a normal day as it has been introduced since the 1971 Banking Act. So don't get caught short by one day—it could be expensive, as the Defendant found to his cost in the very first adjudicator's decision enforcement case. See *Macob Civil Engineering Ltd* v. *Morrison Construction Ltd* (1999) later in this Chapter.

As mentioned there are also several drafting errors in the current HGCRA and the associated Scheme. In particular the Scheme Part II Payment provisions don't bear close scrutiny:

> "2(1) The amount of any payment by way of instalments or stage or periodic payments in respect of a relevant period shall be the difference between the amount determined in accordance with sub-paragraph (2) and ... (3).
>
> (2) The aggregate of the following amounts—
>
> (a) an amount equal to the value of any work performed in accordance with the relevant construction contract *during the period from the commencement of the contract to the end of the relevant period*, ..." [i.e. the gross cumulative value to date, less ...]
>
> "(3) The aggregate of any sums which have been paid or are due for payment ... *during the period from the commencement of the contract to the end of the relevant period*." [i.e. the gross cumulative value again.]

Unsurprisingly the answer is nought (key words in italics). But, we professionals know what we are about even if the parliamentary draftsman didn't! Maybe the last line of para. 2(3) should have read: "... to the end of the *previous* relevant period." In this connection it is important to note that under the Scheme the definition at para. 12 of "relevant period" is 28 days.

Thus, whilst a sub-contractor may not make a payment application within 28 days of his previous application, *he is perfectly entitled under the Scheme to invoice every four weeks and to be paid every four weeks, whether or not it suits the convenience of the employer's and main contractor's own accounting procedures.*

Most head contracts will now be let on standard contracts or bespoke contracts which comply with the HGCRA sections 109 to 113, providing for monthly (30/31 days) interim payments by the employer. There is therefore a real risk of main contractors being caught by non-back-to-back payment periods with their sub-contractors, and where these are 28 days under the Scheme, of actually having to forward fund the sub-contract works—a concept unheard of under the pre-Latham regime!

Then at para. 2(4) we have a further nonsense:

> "An amount calculated in accordance with this paragraph shall not exceed the difference between:
> (a) the contract price, and ...
> (b) the aggregate of the instalments or stage or periodic payments which have become due."

Now the "Contract Price" as defined at para. 12 means "the entire sum payable under the construction contract in respect of the work".

Any problems with that? Well there might be: firstly, the parliamentary draftsman has carefully distinguished at para. 6 between a "construction contract" and a "relevant construction contract". So when it comes to para. 2 which is it? and have you got one of them, or one of the other? Secondly, it is perfectly obvious that one cannot be required to pay more than the total price, so the situation envisaged by para. 2(4) is a contractual impossibility.

In fact the whole of the Scheme Part II Payment provisions could usefully be restructured, not altered per se, to deal firstly with the minor contracts lasting less than 45 days (non-relevant construction contracts) and then with the "relevant construction contracts" with which we are really concerned. It would also be hugely helpful to find some better terminology to distinguish more clearly between the two categories of "construction contract" at the promised review.

9.3 THE STATUTORY RIGHT TO ADJUDICATION

Complementing the statutory payment provisions of HGCRA sections 109 to 113 is section 108 which lays down strict rules for all construction contracts in respect of the right of any party to refer a dispute to adjudication, mentioned briefly above. To understand the full requirements, and therefore when the fall-back Scheme provisions apply, further explanation is required.

HGCRA sections 108(1) to (5) are the key provisions and read as follows:

"(1) A party to a construction contract has the right to refer a dispute arising under the contract for adjudication under a procedure complying with this section. For this purpose 'dispute' includes any difference.

(2) The contract shall:

(a) Enable a party to give notice at any time of his intention to refer a dispute to adjudication.

(b) Provide a timetable with the object of securing the appointment of the adjudicator and referral of the dispute to him within 7 days of such notice.

(c) Require the adjudicator to reach a decision within 28 days of referral or such longer period as is agreed by the parties after the dispute has been referred.

(d) Allow the adjudicator to extend the period of 28 days by up to 14 days, with the consent of the party by whom the dispute was referred.

(e) Impose a duty on the adjudicator to act impartially.

(f) Enable the adjudicator to take the initiative in ascertaining the facts and the law.

(3) The contract shall provide that the decision of the adjudicator is binding until the dispute is finally determined by legal proceedings, by arbitration ... or by agreement.

(4) The contract shall also provide that the adjudicator is not liable for anything done or omitted in the discharge or purported discharge of his functions as adjudicator unless the act or omission is in bad faith, and that any employee or agent of the adjudicator is similarly protected for liability.

(5) If the contract does not comply with the requirements of subsections (1) to (4), the adjudication provisions of the Scheme for Construction Contracts apply."

If you survive the six specific requirements of HGCRA section 108(2)(a)–(f), and the further two in sections 108(3) and (4), then you have set up a contract, compliant with the *statutory adjudication provisions* of the HGCRA. *But if you have only scored 7 out of 8* your attempted adjudication provisions are all lost and you are bound by HGCRA section 114 and Statutory Instrument 1998 No. 649, alias the Scheme (England and Wales only). *Any necessary adjudication falls to be administered accordingly.*

The Scheme Part I Adjudication notification procedure might usefully be summarised by paragraph references as follows:

1(1) The Referring Party may give written Notice of his intention to refer any dispute arising under the contract to adjudication ...

1(2) "... to every other party to the contract", which begs two immediate questions:

Q.1 At any time, as per section 108(2)(a)? Presumably, yes.

Q.2 Can there be more than two parties to a contract? Unusual to say the least!

1(3) The Notice of Adjudication, i.e. the intention to refer and not to be confused with the formal submission known as the Referral Notice, must then cover the following basic points:

— Names of the parties, and their addresses for the giving of notices.
— The nature and brief description of the dispute.
— Where and when the dispute occurred.
— The nature of the redress sought.

The Scheme, para. 2(1) then provides for how one might get an independent adjudicator appointed, the order of precedence being:

— The parties agreeing on an individual to act as adjudicator.
— Contacting the previously agreed name stated in the contract.
— By application to an Adjudicator Nominating Body (ANB) named in the contract, e.g. the President of the Royal Institution of Chartered Surveyors.
— Failing all else, by application to any of the ANBs.

Whichever method is applicable the Scheme, para. 3 requires the application to be accompanied by a copy of the Notice of Adjudication.

Now the ANB must be fairly fast on its feet, particularly if the request for the appointment of an adjudicator is made other than on a Monday. This is because para. 5.1 requires the ANB to have communicated the name of the appointed adjudicator to the Referring Party within five days of the initial application—and Saturdays and Sundays count as "Days". This means that an application made on Tuesdays onwards effectively has to be made within three or four days, including establishing whether the selected individual is in fact available and willing—para. 2(2) requiring the selected individual to respond within two days of first being approached. However in practice, ANB appointments are done by fax or e-mail and are being achieved within the required timescale.

The Scheme, para. 4 then makes it clear that any adjudicator named in the contract must be "a natural person acting in his personal capacity". Thus for the purpose of the Scheme it is not possible for the employer to nominate a member of his own staff as the adjudicator, or for a company or practice to be named. It is a personal appointment, and should an ANB appoint an individual as adjudicator who has had some dealings on any matter in any way connected with the dispute or has knowledge of one of the parties, the normal rules of conflict and disclosure apply.

As noted above, the Scheme, para. 5(1) then requires the ANB to notify the name of the appointed adjudicator to the Referring Party within five days of the Referring Party's application—strangely the other party does not have to be so informed, but in practice this is usually done. Should the five-day rule not be complied with by the ANB, then the Referring Party is given two options by para. 5(2). The Referring Party may either:

— agree the name of an individual who will act as adjudicator with the other side; or
— request any other listed ANB to nominate an adjudicator.

At this point, one might well ask: What happens to the application fee (typically £200, plus), paid in good faith—is it refundable?

The Scheme, para. 6 then covers the situation where an adjudicator named in the contract is unable or unwilling or simply doesn't respond when called upon to act, e.g. he may be out of the country, providing three sensible options for the Referring Party to pursue.

Thus, one way or another under the Scheme provisions, an adjudicator should be in post within five days of the Referring Party serving a Notice of Adjudication. In practice soundings are taken by the officers of the ANBs by telephone, fax, or e-mail, and the adjudicator's acceptance can be obtained as quickly as the day after the Referring Party posts his application. However, with weekends intervening, but counting as "Days", it only needs one to be out of the office a day or so and the process can get frenetic.

Certainly there is no time for the adjudicator to take a position about his fees, which requires both parties to confirm his charges on a joint and several basis before he will consider himself properly empowered. Adjudicators are there to be pragmatic and robust, so the normal procedure is that the adjudicator simply writes to both parties telling them what his hourly rates are (typically £75–£125 per hour) and making it clear that they are both jointly and severally liable.

Under the Scheme the Referring Party's Notice of Referral sets the basic 28-day time limit for the adjudicator to deliver his decision, subject to the seven-day time limit of para. 7 for the maximum period allowable between the Notice of Adjudication and the Notice of Referral and subject to the extension of time provision at para. 19. So the clock is in fact already running from the Referring Party's Notice of Adjudication, which is served on the other party at the same time as application is made to the ANB or to the adjudicator named in the contract.

Having started the process, the Referring Party has the first action: para. 7 requires him, not later than seven days after having served the Notice of Adjudication, to follow this up with a written Notice of Referral, served on both the adjudicator and the other party(s), setting out:

— His statement of claim.
— Copy of the key contract terms relied on.
— Copies of other documents relied on.

Thereafter it is for the appointed adjudicator to set the timetable for the Defendant Party's submission and the agenda for any further action appropriate to the detail of the dispute.

Whilst the provisions require decisions to be given in 28 days, or longer as allowed by para. 19, there is every reason for adjudicators to give their decisions well within 28 days, e.g. a single-issue adjudication such as statutory default in respect of a failure to issue valid Notices under sections 110 or 111 should be dealt with in days rather than weeks.

The Scheme, para. 8 allows an adjudicator, with the consent of all parties, to handle multi-party disputes, and even cross-contract disputes involving the same parties. In the event that the Defendant Party contends that the current reference is a re-run of a previous dispute already adjudicated, para. 9 requires the newly appointed adjudicator to resign, but in practice matters will have moved on, so usually there are some fresh matters in dispute.

Equally the adjudicator may, if he sees fit, resign at any time without giving any reasons. However, in practice it would be unusual if he didn't explain his resignation, yet at the same time expect the parties to pay his fees, in theory commencing their dispute all over again with a different adjudicator. Even if the skill actually required differs from that envisaged at the time of appointment there is nothing to stop the adjudicator seeking outside advice, providing he has first informed the parties of his intention, and obtained their consent, express or tacit.

Having been appointed, para. 10 expressly precludes either party from objecting to his appointment—unless presumably there is a matter touching on conflicts of interest. However, the adjudicator may be removed on the joint application of both parties, in which case para. 11 secures his fees, unless he has obviously misconducted himself.

Paragraph 12 requires the adjudicator to:

"(a) act impartially ... in accordance with any relevant terms of the contract and ... reach his decision in accordance with the applicable law in relation to the contract, and ...

(c) avoid incurring unnecessary expense."

Subject to any particular adjudication procedure rules prescribed by the contract, the Scheme para. 13 states the basic rules for the conduct of the adjudication, in that the adjudicator shall:

— Take the initiative in establishing the relevant facts and law.
— Decide on the procedure to be followed.
— Call for further documents.
— Call for further statements.
— Decide on the language of the adjudication and the procedure for any necessary translations.
— Meet and question any party to the contract, or their representatives.
— Make visits and inspections, with any necessary third party consent, whether accompanied by the parties or not.
— Obtain technical and legal advice from experts, subject to prior notification of the parties of his proposed course of action.
— Give directions as to the timetable for the adjudication.
— Set deadlines and limitations on length of written or oral submissions.
— Issue further directions.

The Scheme para. 14 then makes it clear that full compliance is required of both parties, but should one party, usually the Defendant Party not co-operate para. 15 allows the adjudicator to:

— Proceed regardless.
— Draw inferences from the non-compliance.
— Proceed on the basis of information properly provided.
— Form a view as to the "weight" to be attributed to any evidence provided late.

The Scheme para. 16 allows either party to take whatever outside advice they need, but if a hearing is directed each party may only have one representative unless the adjudicator allows otherwise.

Paragraph 17 then requires the adjudicator to consider all relevant information put to him by the parties, and that he makes available to the parties all information relied on for his decision. Presumably this refers to situations where, with the prior knowledge of the parties, the adjudicator has himself taken outside advice, e.g. legal opinion.

Paragraph 18 stipulates that if any party submits information with a request for confidentiality, then this will be observed by all concerned.

The all-important provision as to when the parties may expect a decision then comes at para. 19(1). As such the adjudicator is required to reach a decision and deliver that decision to each of the parties:

— within 28 days (or less); or
— within 42 days if the extra 14 days has been agreed to by the Referring Party; or
— within whatever time period has been mutually agreed.

The Scheme para. 19(2) then provides fall-back provisions should the adjudicator fail to perform within the required time frame, essentially allowing either party to apply for the appointment of a new adjudicator and requiring the same documentation to be served afresh, if the new adjudicator so directs.

Finally under the Scheme Part I—Adjudication, we come to the provisions under a sub-heading of "Adjudicator's decision", and "Effects of the decision". These can be summarised thus (para. 20):

— The adjudicator shall decide the matters in dispute (limited to those items put in the Notice of Referral), unless
— the parties agree other matters may be added to the reference, or unless
— the adjudicator deems other matters necessarily relevant to the dispute (another interesting departure from basic legal principles).
— In particular the adjudicator is empowered to "Open up, revise and review any decision taken or any certificate given by any person referred to in the contract unless the contract states that the decision or certificate is final and conclusive." This far-reaching provision could create serious implications for the on-going administration of the contract, although no sensible adjudicator is likely to wish to interfere with existing interim and extension of time certifications without wholly overwhelming evidence of error.
— The adjudicator is then empowered to order a further payment, setting a final date for payment, and to order interest to be paid on the disputed value, now to be paid.

The Scheme para. 21 provides that unless directed otherwise, any decision of the adjudicator shall be effected immediately, whereas para. 23(1) allows the adjudicator to order either party to comply peremptorily with his decision or any part of it.

Para. 22 then stipulates that if requested by either party the adjudicator is required to give reasons for his decision. This, of course, leads to the usual debate: one school of thought says give the minimum of reasons, whereas others say one should set out all issues and responses, and rehearse the arguments, etc. Personally, this author believes in giving reasons in any event, but as an Appendix to the "Decision", and limited to the principal issues. As such three sides of A4 is probably enough, unless it is a major multi-issue dispute.

The Scheme para. 23(2) is *the* crucial provision—the adjudicator's decision is binding on the parties and shall be complied with forthwith, even if one of the parties wishes to subsequently take the dispute to arbitration or litigation. Several "losers" have to date tried to use the courts to avoid paying monies arising on adjudicators' decisions, but have been generally slapped down by the judges, as will be seen in the section of this chapter covering enforcement of decisions.

The Scheme para. 24 is a housekeeping provision to tie in statutory adjudication into section 42 of the Arbitration Act 1996, whereas paras. 25 and 26 also follow arbitration practice. Para. 25 then provides that the adjudicator may set his own fees and expenses, and that unless otherwise directed, such costs shall be payable by the parties on a joint and several liability basis. Finally para. 26 then provides immunity from suit for the adjudicator or any assistants.

This concludes the basic coverage of the provisions in the statutory Scheme for Construction Contracts, Part I—Adjudication, applicable where the contractual arrangements between the parties do not comply with the strict adjudication requirements of the HGCR Act 1996, or conceivably where the parties elect to adopt the Scheme adjudication procedures.

Inevitably there are implications arising, particularly in how contractors will actually manage the typical interim valuation procedure on a large project and minimise their risk of having to explain themselves to an adjudicator if a sub-contractor makes a referral.

During the consultation process some of us suggested that adjudication should not be an *optional* first-stage process—why not make it a compulsory first-stage process, i.e. a mini pre-trial, and why not time-bar it, i.e. to within say three months of the originating cause for complaint? Maybe this would have thrown up operational problems, but now we have the situation under section 108(2)(a) that an aggrieved party may call for adjudication "... at any time ...". Now this could lead to all sorts of mischief, typically reopening an ancient grievance long after everyone thought it was forgotten in the project history, or a party just threatening to reopen old issues in order to exert commercial pressure. It could even be used to undo historic payments made in good faith, where the party now at risk of being ordered to allow a credit has no prospect of recovering the monies involved from a long-since paid sub-contractor. This cannot be equitable and personally I see no good reason for allowing this. Certainly this is one aspect that should be tightened up.

Thus the HGCRA not only was a remarkable piece of legislation in its own right, but was also remarkable in that Parliament decided it was time to take a hand in laying down the rules of proper (payment) behaviour in an industry that patently could not agree to regulate itself.

Whilst therefore in a dispute situation either party has the option to call for adjudication, the critical point is that the party in receipt of a Notice of Adjudication cannot avoid the dispute by hiding behind the law of contract. Any contractual right to go to arbitration or litigation must be put on the back-burner until the statutory, first-stage, dispute resolution process has been completed, and any decision of the adjudicator fully implemented.

So it is the fundamental concept—that the will of Parliament concerning regulation of payment procedures in the construction industry should be upheld via the appointed adjudicators—which is coming through loud and clear in the "appeal" cases so far heard by the courts about enforcement of adjudicators' decisions.

Adjudicators are accepted as fallible, but so long as they get 95% of referrals about right, the HGCRA will only need fine tuning when it comes up for review. The remaining 5% of disputes can of course proceed to a final resolution by the appropriate tribunal as written into the contract, should the aggrieved party feel so inclined.

The above statutory provisions can be most confusing, with optional or mandatory timescales for payment and adjudication actions, depending on whether the principal provisions of the HGCRA, or the back-up provisions of the Scheme apply. Hopefully clarity will be assisted by two flow charts in the Appendices, setting out the Scheme provisions in bold, and the options in italics:

— Appendix C—Flow Chart of the statutory Payment Provisions.
— Appendix D—Flow Chart of the statutory Adjudication Rules.

9.4 THE JCT RESPONSE TO LATHAM

The emergence of the HGCRA caused the JCT drafting committee to go into emergency session. They might well have opted for minimal changes to their various standard forms of contract to make them HGCRA compliant, but very sensibly they took the opportunity to also include some of the further features of the Latham Report, which had been overlooked by the parliamentary draftsman.

Taking the most popular standard form of contract, i.e. JCT SFBC 98 by way of reference, the JCT have accordingly introduced Clause 41(A) which, *inter alia*, covers, or provides that:

— The appointed adjudicator must complete the JCT Standard Agreement for the appointment of an adjudicator.
— The information to be provided to the adjudicator and the timeframe for so doing.

— The adjudicator's powers, including the power to open up and review any previously issued certificate or notice, etc—not just a current certificate.

— Parties' costs—each to pay their own, which could be contentious in cases of statutory default, i.e. failure to serve the required Notices under sections 110 and 111, or blatant contract abuse prior to the referral to adjudication.

— Discretion as to costs of agreed tests, etc and the adjudicator's own fees.

— The decision of the adjudicator is binding until overtaken by agreement between the parties to accept it as final, or by the award of a judge or arbitrator.

In this last respect, the old Clause 41 provision that certain matters could not be arbitrated until after Practical Completion is amended to allow an aggrieved party to make immediate reference to arbitration of any matter decided by an adjudicator, albeit that this may divert key staff from their primary function of getting the project built and handed over.

The new JCT payment rules at Clause 30 closely follow the Scheme provisions, including the key requirement for the employer to issue a Notice of Intended Payment within five days of the issue of the Interim certificate by the Architect. The only real differences from pre-HGCRA practice are that, firstly, Interim certificates need to show the basis of calculation, and secondly that the contractor is formally given the right to commence the process by submitting his detailed payment application, provided he does so no later than the agreed payment certificate date. In this event the Quantity Surveyor or Architect must then issue a certificate and then must also issue a statement identifying any monies disallowed with reasons for so doing.

In the not infrequent event of no payment or only part payment, and no sections 110 and 111 Notices having been issued by the employer to the contractor, the JCT have repeated the HGCRA provisions concerning the right to suspend the works, and then added to them. There is the usual requirement for a seven-day notice alerting the employer to his default, to give him the opportunity to rectify his oversight. Thereafter the contractor may down tools and leave site until fully paid.

As previously noted this is unrealistic: What do you do with the men? Re-deploy them elsewhere and then not be able to bring them back within 24 hours of belated payment by the employer, or send them home on full pay? Realistically the main contractor might reduce the operatives to a skeleton crew, off-loading sub-contract labour and charging the employer on a cost-plus basis until full resumption for at least keeping the site open, plus any claims received and paid to sub-contractors for remobilisation.

Contractually the position is secured by the new JCT provision for suspension in response to non-payment by the employer being both a Relevant Event and a Relevant Matter—Clauses 25.4.18 and 26.2.10—but one can just see the arguments coming, particularly when similar provisions are passed down to sub-contractor level and the suspension of work by one specialist has a knock-on effect on other sub-contractors.

Sensibly one local dispute cannot be allowed to jeopardise the whole project, so it is this author's opinion that in the employer's interests the main contract should reserve the right, after a stated period of time, for the employer to instruct the contractor to pay the sub-contractor and put his case to adjudication, if the unpaid sub-contractor hasn't already done so, i.e. the developer or employer who has commissioned the project must be given effective power to order a resumption of work, whilst the lower-level squabbles are sorted out.

This will be particularly relevant when the Late Payment of Commercial Debts (Interest) Act 1998 becomes fully operational, as an aggrieved sub-contractor who has properly suspended can expect to collect a penal rate of interest from the main contractor, so long as the money remains unpaid—substantially in excess of his overdraft rate. If in the meantime he can relocate his operatives to another project he has every reason *not* to press for payment and accordingly is unlikely to seek adjudication himself, unless hounded by his bank manager to recover the dip in cash flow.

Thus there has to be provision for the employer to resolve any deadlock not of his own making, and for prescribing a period after which suspension by a sub-contractor for reasons of non-payment gives the right for the sub-contractor to determine—leaving the contractor responsible for engaging a replacement sub-contractor and meeting all costs involved.

In addition to the right to suspend work in the event of non-payment, the JCT have at Clause 30.1.1.1 also provided for the contractor's right to interest on late payment by the employer. Currently the rate of interest is set at 5% by the JCT, but this runs contrary to the stated policy of the Late Payment of Commercial Debts (Interest) Act 1998 which deliberately imposes a penal rate of interest on late payers—currently set at 8.75% above the Lending Banks' Base Rate. It remains to be seen whether the JCT will amend accordingly.

Another major change imported by the JCT from the Latham Report into SFBC 98 is at the Sixth Recital and Clause 5.4.1. As part of the contract documentation the parties are required to agree an Information Release Schedule setting out what information the Architect will release during the course of the project and the date of that release. Any default by the Architect in this respect then becomes a "Relevant Event" and a "Relevant Matter"—Clauses 25.4.6.1 and 26.2.1.1. However, the requirement for an Information Release Schedule is not to be confused with the need to make proper provision, on a project by project basis, for the status of the contractor's Construction Programme. Key information release dates should be incorporated in the programme—see Chapter 5 and Appendix E setting out suggested contractual provisions for monitoring project progress against Construction Programmes.

Then at Clause 1.11 the JCT have anticipated the twenty-first century by providing that "Where the Appendix so states, the Supplemental Provisions for EDI annexed to the Conditions will apply." So what is "EDI" you ask—"Electronic Data Interchange" according to the side note. Now turn to the very back page of SFBC 98 and you cannot fail to realise just how quickly both the construction practices and language of today will be history tomorrow!

Taking a leaf out of JCT WCD 81, SFBC 98 also introduces the option of pre-costing of requested Variations at Alternative A in Clause 13.4.1. Some perceive this as yet another onerous duty imposed on the contractor by the employer, but in reality if handled sensibly by both parties it has great mutual benefit: the certainty of how the twin goalposts of final cost and likely completion have been mutually moved, so eliminating at a stroke of the pen, if opted in, the most fruitful area for disputes. As such, any professional adviser, solicitor, surveyor, architect, etc, not forgetting project managers, who does not recommend the adoption of this clause could be in real difficulties, if and when a project overruns in time or cost and a major dispute ensues.

Then taking a lead from international contracting practice, the JCT have at Clause 30 introduced the option of the contractor being paid upfront, as against an agreed Form of Advance Payment Bond—a standard Form of Bond being included as an Appendix with provision for the parties to agree when the payment should be made and how it is to be repaid.

The JCT have then turned their attention to how adjudication and the fair payment rules should be made to work as between main contractors and sub-contractors, so have amended DOM/1 to suit. Unsurprisingly the JCT have replicated most of the SFBC 98 wording very closely, but:

— DOM/1 1980 Edition, Conditions 21 (Payment of Sub-Contractor) and 38 (Settlement of Disputes—bringing in adjudication and the option of litigation, alongside arbitration) have been redrafted to comply with the HGCRA.

— Recognising that at the sub-contractor level there will be no third party certifier, whose action will trigger the monthly interim valuation process, the onus is on the contractor to make the regular assessment of work done and monies due to each sub-contractor, with the sub-contractors being free to submit their draft submissions in the preceding week—Clause 21.4.

In practice it is likely that only the better organised main contractors will grasp the opportunity to operate a regular interim valuation procedure, such that all sub-contractors get paid at the same time. Importantly, key dates for who will submit what to whom need to be set up, such that the main contractor not only receives the employer's cheque, but can actually clear it and convert it to cash before having to pay most of it out again to the various sub-contractors.

The danger is that employer and contractor will have agreed a compliant main contract such as JCT SFBC 98 with relaxed timescales as allowed at section 110, and Condition 30.1.1, e.g. interim valuations every month, which could be every 30/31 days, but the contractor might slip up in placing sub-contracts so these are, for whatever reason, non-compliant with the HGCRA and therefore entitle sub-contractors to payment every 28 days. Once this happens on a project, the contractor's cash flow is likely to be negative from about month 3 and may never really recover.

Very often a main contractor will place a sub-contract on a Letter of Intent and then never replace it with a properly executed sub-contract. In this event the payment system is inevitably going to be governed by the Scheme provisions. Given this scenario, the main contractor is likely to be in a non-back-to-back payment regime and timetable in respect of getting money in from the employer from month 1 or thereabouts.

9.5 HOW TO SELECT YOUR ADJUDICATOR

Before the HGCRA came into operation great concern was expressed as to how in practice adjudicators would come to be appointed and what the quality of adjudicators would be. Bearing in mind that disputes could arise concerning any aspect of a construction contract at any time, including related consultancy appointments, it was thought that the employer should either name the adjudicator up front in the tender enquiry, or preferably name three adjudicators covering different skills—with a further requirement that such nominations be passed down through dependent sub-contracts, to avoid the potential for win-win or lose-lose results arising on adjacent, but unjoined adjudications, down the payment chain. Obviously this could lead to a suspicion of cronyism, with the employer naming his preferred colleagues, or even his in-house colleagues, by company designation or by individual nomination.

A variant of this was to set up the tender enquiry for the head contract on the basis that as part of the tender acceptance procedure the employer and the successful contractor would agree a mutually acceptable adjudicator, or agree a list of three names covering different skills. There was also speculation as to which professions would provide most adjudicators, with one survey suggesting the following odds:

7/2 Quantity Surveyors
5/1 Engineers
6/1 Architects
13/2 Solicitors
7/1 Building Surveyors
9/1 Counsel
10/1 Bar—bar "The Bar".

Given the very tight timescales allowed by the HGCRA and the associated Scheme provisions for getting proceedings under way, it was also a very real concern as to whether the approved Adjudicator Nominating Bodies (ANBs), i.e. mainly recognised construction industry professional organisations, would be able to react quickly enough when requested to appoint. With the effective start date of contracts let after 1 May 1998, it was not surprising that initially there was very little activity, but as the months passed, as sub-contractors slowly woke up to the fact that there was a new dawn, and as the first cases on enforcement hit the headlines, so there was a very sharp take-up of adjudication as a quick and effective dispute resolution process. Happily the ANBs did generally staff up and had workable appointment systems in place shortly after 1 May 1998—and the adjudicators subsequently appointed, with one or two exceptions, proved themselves to be robust, professional and fair. They also proved that the 28-day, plus the optional extra 14 days, deadline for reaching decisions was achievable.

As such, adjudication has been a resounding success already—so much so that apparently that there is only now a trickle of construction cases being submitted to the Technology and Construction Court (TCC) for full trial. If this trend is sustained then it is bad news for arbitrators! At a stroke the principal reason for preferring arbitration to litigation, i.e. the long and unpredictable wait for trial dates, will have been removed.

So what are the statutory options for appointing an adjudicator? Section 108(2)(b) requires the contract "to provide a timetable with the object of securing the appointment of the adjudicator and referral of the dispute to him within 7 days ...", but the HGCRA is otherwise silent as to *how* an adjudicator is selected, i.e. the parties are free to agree to make their own arrangements, as outlined above, which could be interesting if they have failed to agree a name or a procedure before falling out with one another.

In this event one party, relying on the Scheme provisions, might apply to one of the ANBs, but the other party might then challenge the jurisdiction of the appointed adjudicator on the basis that there is actually no default provision in the HGCRA section 108(1)–(4) as presently drafted, letting in the Scheme adjudicator appointment procedure—a fine technical challenge!

However, if a standard form of building contract is being used there should be little chance of failing to specify an appointing procedure, by making the appropriate Appendix provision, but stranger things have happened in the best run organisations. Moreover, the JCT have covered this eventuality by providing the three-way option of the parties either:

— agreeing an adjudicator; or
— naming an appointee in the Appendix; or
— by default leaving it to the RIBA. This might sensibly be amended to the RICS, given the fact that most disputes concern money, not design issues, and also that the RICS, being the most popular ANB, have probably the slickest appointment secretariat.

However, let us assume that, intentionally or by default, the parties are bound under the fall-back Scheme adjudicator appointment procedures, there is then an order of precedence set out in Part I, para. 2.

(1) The parties may agree on an adjudicator; or
    (a) The Referring Party may call upon the person named in the contract as the adjudicator; or
    (b) The Referring Party may apply to the ANB named in the contract, including in the circumstance where a named adjudicator is unable to act, and the contract also provides for a named ANB; or finally
    (c) Where all else fails, the Referring Party is free to apply to any of the approved ANBs.

It should be noted that the statutory provisions lay down no requirements as to who may or may not act as adjudicators, other than at Scheme para. 4 which states that they act in an individual capacity and may not be an employee of one of the parties. However, in practice they are likely to be accredited adjudicators, trained and admitted to one of the ANB panels.

Whether or not one can influence the selection of an adjudicator, i.e. by expressing a preference for a particular skill base, or having the opportunity to name individuals who would not be considered acceptable, will depend upon the individual ANB's application procedure, but once appointed there is no room for either party to object to the adjudicator.

An appointed adjudicator should be upfront in declaring any possible conflict of interest, either actual or of possible perception. Typically the selected adjudicator may professionally know the representative of one of the parties. In this event he should inform the other party as soon as he is appointed, giving him the option to identify any objection before matters proceed. However, if the acquaintance is purely of an occasional professional nature it is unlikely that any exception will be taken.

Finally, a word of warning for Referring Parties applying for the appointment of an adjudicator. It is very easy to start the process, but once started the process demands a tight timescale.

Although the 28-day period for the adjudicator to give his decision runs from the date of the Notice of Referral, i.e. the date the Referring Party submits his statement of case to the adjudicator, with copy to the other side, the date of referral is required by section 108(2)(b) of the HGCRA to be within seven days of issuing the Notice of Intention to Refer, and making application for the appointment of the adjudicator. So the message must be: don't launch your challenge until all necessary information has been assembled and rehearsed, with the Notice of Referral already drafted.

If you time it right, putting in the Notice of Referral the next day, preferably just before a weekend, the Defendant Party really has got his work cut out to assemble and serve a response document in the usual seven days!

9.6 WHOSE RULES TO PLAY BY?

Before the HGCRA came into operation there was much speculation as to how it would all work, and in particular what adjudicators would be allowed to do, or not do, as the case might be. As we have seen, the statutory provisions for the conduct of adjudications, as laid down in the HGCRA and in the supporting Scheme, set out only the basic rules; and within the framework of those rules the provisions give the adjudicator total flexibility, providing he:

- acts impartially—section 108(2)(e) and para. 12(a)
- avoids incurring unnecessary expense—para. 12(b)
- acts within the required timescale—section 108(2) and para. 19(1).

Quite specifically, at section 108(2)(f) and para. 13 he is "to take the initiative in ascertaining the facts and the law necessary to determine the dispute, and shall decide on the procedure to be followed in the adjudication." But there are then no restrictions as to how he should do so. To several legal commentators this was heresy and would undoubtedly lead to all manner of mayhem, with appeals flooding the courts from maverick decisions of adjudicators, who had either been too robust or not robust enough. What was wanted, they and others said, was a prescriptive second tier of rules governing just how an adjudicator would conduct a referral, so that at least all parties knew their obligations and entitlements and there was little scope for procedural anomalies.

So various industry bodies set about putting their heads together as individual committees, not really knowing themselves how the provisions of the HGCRA would work, and in particular not knowing what the take-up for adjudication would be. Some bodies quite properly recognised the need to train and accredit a panel of adjudicators, such that when the time came they could as an approved ANB appoint adjudicators with some degree of confidence that most would conform, and would be seen to be giving fair and understandable decisions within the parameters laid down.

Now it has to be said that the general perception at the outset, particularly amongst lawyers, was that an adjudication should be little more than a quick mini-arbitration, with the adjudicator having to get a tight grip of the timescale, but otherwise keeping his head down and playing by whichever set of secondary rules had been agreed, i.e. the traditional concept of each party adducing its own evidence, being challenged by the other side and then the silent "umpire" putting his finger up, or not, as he alone saw fit.

However, those of us practitioners who had advocated the wider adoption of adjudication as a first-stage dispute resolution process, wanted to see clear blue water between the formality of arbitration and the commercial reality of obtaining common-sense temporary decisions. The concept was that such temporary decisions should be based on pro-active investigation by practitioners, bound only by the contractual framework and generally accepted procedures, with both parties then having the option of burying the proverbial hatchet. Alternatively, the parties might then decide to spend real money in formal arbitration or litigation, but only once the initial decision of the adjudicator had been implemented.

At Appendix F is a brief summary in tabular form of various official bodies' further Rules, i.e. JCT, CIC, ORSA (now TeCSA), CEDR, and ICE, summarising the main areas where adjudicators may find themselves limited in their procedural discretion. This may well be overtaken in due course by the promised government review of the HGCR Act 1996 in action, but when this will materialise, and whether it will be more than a minor edit or major amendment, no one is yet saying. But do we really need these Rules?

Parliament decided that adjudicators should be given wide discretion as to how they went about their task—provided they were quick about it, complying generally with the 28-day provision in order to fit with the usual monthly interim payment provision cycle. This author believes that if neither the HGCRA nor the supporting Scheme say otherwise, and subject to any contract provision, then the adjudicator is free to order whatever practical solution meets the situation. I would however expect an adjudicator, contemplating any unconventional order, to intimate his thinking to both parties and to invite them to address him accordingly, before proceeding. Above all else the adjudicator must be mindful of any irreversible injustice that could arise from his decision.

Sooner or later there will be an adjudication where one party at first instance wins a decision and a substantial award, but it is perfectly obvious on the facts that at a subsequent arbitration the decision might very well go the other way. As some banks seem to have a rather nasty policy of keeping insolvent sub-contractors alive until conveniently there is an influx of funds—when Receivers are conveniently appointed—there is good reason for protecting funds in such marginal decisions. However, a way has to be found of doing this without actually stopping the cash flow down the payment chain.

In the bad old days of adjudication for arbitrary payment set-off under the old JCT SFBC 1963 "Blue" and "Green" Standard Forms of Sub-Contract, Trustee Stakeholder Accounts were a printed option. Unfortunately most adjudicators saw this as a soft option, so the money got denied to both parties—and rightly adjudication fell away into obscurity, locking up the money to the end of the project when arbitration could be commenced. Certainly this author, as an adjudicator under the old JCT 1963 based scheme always gave decisions one way or the other—so the money was kept live. However, just because no such Trustee Stakeholder Account provision appears in the HGCRA, or in the supporting Scheme provisions, is not to say it has no place.

As we have seen in *Bouygues UK Ltd* v. *Dahl Jensen UK Ltd (In Liquidation)* (1999) an adjudicator can get it very wrong. In that case, circa £250,000 was patently awarded to the wrong party. When Bouygues failed to pay, Dahl Jensen promptly won an enforcement order from the court and despite having gone into receivership had to be paid. Dahl Jensen then closed their UK operation and vanished back to Denmark! More on this extraordinary case in section 9.7 below.

So to guard against this very situation, in a dispute concerning technical design issues or workmanship etc, pending a possible appeal from the paying party by way of arbitration or litigation, who would quarrel with me, if, as an adjudicator I ordered:

— payment in favour of the sub-contractor; but
— monies to be placed in a Trust Fund Account, and to be released after three months if no arbitration or litigation commenced in that time;
— in the meantime, the Contractor to pay the sub-contractor interest at Minimum Lending Rate plus 5% to enable the sub-contractor to replace the money locked up in the Trust Fund?

Hopefully, lateral-thinking adjudicators will be able to respect the legal framework of the contract, remain absolutely impartial and still administer justice which fits this commercial world.

For the above reasons I do not believe it is necessary or desirable to lay down restrictive rules as the various industry bodies have done—the will of Parliament giving wide discretion to adjudicators should prevail unless, of course, we adjudicators prove ourselves unworthy of such trust.

It is therefore in my opinion unfortunate, if one is appointed adjudicator to a dispute under a JCT Form of Contract, that one is required to sign up to the JCT Adjudication Procedure Rules. If the resolution scenario is likely to require unconventional action, such as outlined above, there is nothing to stop a robust adjudicator seeking consent from both parties to step outside the prescribed rules. However, such action would be the exception rather than the rule and certainly should not be contemplated if there was any chance of such action prejudicing a third party.

So much for this author's opinions, which inevitably will not be well received in some quarters, but I claim author's prerogative to be deliberately thought provoking! Now for the really interesting section—adjudication problem corner—with apologies in advance, if by the time you, the reader, get to this section some case has been decided which helps to answer the questions posed.

9.7 ADJUDICATION IN PRACTICE—PROBLEM AREAS AND ENFORCEMENT

At time of writing we have seen almost 20 High Court judgments following the unsuccessful party in an adjudication—almost inevitably the Defendant Party—not having paid the successful party as directed by the adjudicator. In response to the successful party's enforcement application, various legal points have been taken asking the judge to set aside the adjudicator's decision, but so far the judges have come out very strongly in favour of adjudicators, including at least the highly questionable decision just mentioned, where the very opposite of justice was apparently done. Despite the insolvency aspect, this matter has now become the first Adjudication case to go to the Court of Appeal (31 July 2000)–with the Appeal Court upholding the TCC enforcement decision. However, what the Appeal Court have done is to order a stay on any payment, presumably no monies have been paid by Bougre's after the enforcement decision. So in a roundabout way, pending insolvency proceedings, justice may yet be done and a manifest error by the Adjudicator corrected.

What has also been surprising is that several adjudications have in fact been mini-trials, i.e. the full range of a typical multi-issue Final Account dispute, including Extension of Time and Defects. Also surprising has been the absence of "ambushes", where the Referring Party prepares a voluminous case, which the other side then has to defend in a very limited period of time.

Having said that, on some projects the sub-contractors have quite deliberately co-ordinated their Notices of Intention to Refer and have pooled information to cause maximum stress and embarrassment to the non-paying main contractor.

On another project the main contractor pulled a stunt of his own, knowing that the sub-contractor was seriously considering adjudication. With one month of work to go, he completely revalued all the works and very arbitrarily disallowed some £200,000 already paid in respect of long since agreed Variations. At the same time he saved the sub-contractor the bother of applying for an adjudicator by applying himself—just before Christmas, in a form of reverse ambush! How does such a stunt sit with HGCRA sections 110 and 111 and the requirement for the paying party to serve Notices *each month* if he wishes to challenge the further monies being claimed? Surely the paying party cannot, six months after clearing an invoice for payment and actually paying the money, be allowed to snatch monies back whenever it suits him?

So how about the proposition that having failed to issue section 110 or 111 Notices one month, the contractor is estopped from changing his mind after one further month, i.e. he is allowed two mistakes, but not three. Surely it was the will of Parliament that there should be certainty of payment down the supply chain and it would be an abuse of the system if contractors adopt the practice of paying on account whilst they need the sub-contractors, but then totally reviewing and arbitrarily reducing values previously agreed, just when the sub-contractors have lost commercial leverage in terms of completing the work.

Certainly the right to suspend will not come into the equation if the work is effectively completed, but what then would an adjudicator do if the sub-contractor sought the remedy of an injunction preventing the contractor taking the benefit of his work (and/or design input) until paid for? Part I section 1(3) of the HGCR Act 1996 requires the Referring Party to state "the nature of the redress which is sought", but is one necessarily limited to remedies provided for under the construction contract? Why not common law remedies?

However I speculate on where this all will lead and in a further year's time we shall all be a lot wiser—with some legal prophets of doom already saying that adjudication will not survive in its present form when European law and the latest EC human rights legislation becomes fully applicable in the UK later this year.

For the present therefore (June 2000), these are the subject areas that have been tested before the courts by unhappy parties trying to overturn adjudicators:

— Jurisdiction of the adjudicator within the HGCR Act 1996 definitions.
— When is a contract a written contract for the purpose of the HGCR Act 1996?
— Whether default in serving the section 111 Notice precludes the adjudicator from considering the merits of the dispute.
— Power of the adjudicator to decide his own jurisdiction.
— Power of the adjudicator to assess the Parties' costs.
— The right to enforcement, given an arbitration clause in the contract.
— The right to enforcement, given an apparent and significant error within a reasoned decision of an adjudicator.
— What if the Claimant fails to state the remedy claimed?
— When is a second adjudication essentially a re-run of a previous adjudication?
— What works constitute a 'Construction Contract'? e.g. Scaffolding or an annual boiler maintainance contract.

The first case to come before the court, *Macob Civil Engineering Ltd* v. *Morrison Construction Ltd* (1999) was remarkable, not just because it was the first case, but because of the issues it raised. Basically it was a Groundworks claim for £302,366 including interest and fees, plus VAT, on a retail development in South Wales. Morrison had tried to write a bespoke contract, compliant with the HGCR Act 1996, providing for an optional period for any Notice of Withholding and, as such, Notice had been properly given. When the money was not paid Macob took advice and contended that the sub-contract did not comply with section 110—Dates for Payment and the requirement for an adequate mechanism including dates etc. If this was correct then the periods laid down in the Scheme for Construction Contracts applied, and accordingly the Notice of Withholding was out of time—the Scheme requiring any such Notice to be served within seven days of the Final Date for Payment. On that basis, Morrison's Notice of Withholding had been served one day too late, leaving Morrison in default when they failed to pay Macob's invoice in full.

The adjudicator had little difficulty in finding that Morrison was in default, albeit by only a matter of one day, and ordered the money to be paid—a common scenario in the old JCT Blue and Green Form set-off adjudications—without looking into the merit or otherwise of the claim, whereupon Morrison seized upon the arbitration clause, served notice on Macob, refused to hand over the money awarded and generally claimed breach of natural justice.

Being mindful of section 9 of the Arbitration Act 1996 Counsel for Macob did not apply for Summary Judgment, but instead went under section 24 of the Scheme, which modifies section 42 of the Arbitration Act, asking the court for:

— a mandatory injunction requiring Morrison to pay the sums awarded by the adjudicator; or
— a declaration that Morrison were bound to pay.

The judge acted very promptly, and set the scene for subsequent "appeals" from the decisions of adjudicators. Firstly he decided that on public policy grounds "The intention of Parliament in enacting the Act was plain. It was to introduce a speedy mechanism for settling disputes in construction cases on a provisional interim basis and requiring the decisions of adjudicators to be enforced pending ... final determination."

As such he dismissed Morrison's contentions that it was entitled to be heard by the adjudicator as to the merits or otherwise of their set-off claim and that accordingly the adjudicator's decision was in breach of the rules of natural justice. The judge agreed with the adjudicator that Morrison were in default, so must pay up *pro tem.*

The judge also dealt with the procedural point of section 9 of the Arbitration Act and refused Morrison's application for a stay of the proceedings under section 9 on the grounds that a dispute as to the validity of the adjudicator's decision, as opposed to the merits of the decision, ought to be so referred. Seemingly the reasoning was that by serving notice of arbitration, immediately after learning of the adjudicator's decision, Morrison had impliedly accepted the procedure under the HGCRA, and had effectively appealed that decision, as was their entitlement. As such, the judge decided that it was open to Macob to have applied for summary judgment after all, to secure the unpaid monies as awarded by the adjudicator, HGCRA section 23(2) stating that "The decision of the adjudicator shall be binding on the parties, and they shall comply with it until the dispute is finally determined by legal proceedings, by arbitration ... or by agreement between the parties."

The second adjudication "appeal" case, *Outwing Construction Ltd* v. *H. Randell & Sons Ltd* (1999), was entirely unremarkable other than that it not only signalled the court's continued support for adjudicators, but also allowed the Civil Procedure Rules (CPR) time limits to be abridged to give speedy enforcement. Randell only paid the £16,000 as ordered by the adjudicator just four hours before the enforcement hearing and Outwing then claimed their costs of preparing the enforcement proceedings. The court helpfully confirmed that enforcement of monetary awards made by adjudicators should be expedited, and not just treated as ordinary debt recovery actions, and awarded Outwing their costs in preparing the enforcement proceedings.

We then had a most unfortunate case where there were no winners—only losers. In *A & D Maintenance Ltd* v. *Pagehurst Construction Ltd* (1999) the sub-contractor, A & D, contended they were being underpaid on a school project, so had reduced their site labour strength, which prompted a row with the contractor, Pagehurst. The contractor then terminated the sub-contractor's employment for failure to proceed etc, although the sub-contractor contended it had by now completed the works. No formal contract had ever been signed and as usual the parties could not agree on what had been the originally intended scope of A & D's work. Was there even a contract, let alone a written contract, for the purposes of the HGCRA?

As if the above wasn't enough, a fire then broke out which undid much of what A & D claimed to have done, and more, so there was a sizeable counterclaim against A & D, who had installed the supposedly defective boiler and so allegedly caused the fire! Just the job for an adjudicator to sort out in 28 days! A & D duly won a decision awarding them over £100,000. When unsurprisingly this was not paid A & D commenced enforcement proceedings and sought Summary Judgment.

Pagehurst had three tiers to their defence, having reserved their position in the original adjudication by participating only under protest. Firstly on the basis that the adjudicator had no jurisdiction in the alleged absence of a written contract, and secondly on the basis that the contract had been determined in any event. The third tier was that the dispute could not be limited to the issues A & D had referred, but must be widened to take in the subsequent events as they allegedly arose from defects on the works in contention.

So what was the court to do with this all too typical tale of woe? In order of the defence, as pleaded, the court found:

1. For A & D on the basis of section 107(5) of the HGCRA, i.e. that during the adjudication A & D had alleged the existence of a written contract and Pagehurst had not opposed this assertion.
2. For A & D on the basis that in arbitration as the arbitration provision survives any alleged termination, citing *Heyman* v. *Darwins* (1942), the judge saw no reason not to apply the same principle to adjudication. Further, in any event section 23(2) of the HGCRA provides for adjudication "... at any time".
3. For A & D on the basis of following the precedent set by the decisions in *Macob* and *Outwing*.

Importantly the judge clarified his reasoning for following the *Macob* and *Outwing* decisions, saying:

"For this court to review the Adjudicator's decision, given that he has been properly appointed under the Scheme and was considering matters under the contract, properly within his remit, would be to go behind the intention of

Parliament that his decision should be binding. The correctness of the decision may be reviewed, revised or challenged where appropriate in subsequent arbitration proceedings or legal proceedings or by way of an agreement. In the instant case there are the pending legal proceedings commenced by the Defendant ... where the disputes between the parties, now provisionally adjudicated by the Adjudicator, will be finally determined by the court."

So A & D were awarded their money in the enforcement proceedings, but as stated above there were no winners—only losers all round. Pagehurst then called in the Receiver and the money never got to A & D, who themselves were not only carrying the debt, but also all their legal costs. If there was a case for the adjudicator using his commercial initiative and ordering the money—at a more certain and lower level than that actually determined by the adjudicator—to be paid into a stakeholder account pending immediate arbitration, but with an interim finance charge provision as suggested above, this might have been the appropriate situation. It might just have enabled both parties to live and fight another day.

Then came an unpopular decision, given by a district judge in the Liverpool Technology and Construction Court and involving plastering and screeding works in a chocolate factory in Speke—*John Cothliffe Ltd* v. *Allen Build (Northwest) Ltd* (1999). Again it had been a Scheme adjudication and in this case some £28,000 had been awarded on the merits, and the successful party, Cothliffe, asked for their costs in bringing the adjudication. Allen Build opposed the application on the basis that the Scheme made no such provision for the adjudicator having power to decide the parties' costs, but the adjudicator considered he had such power under the wide powers conferred by section 13 and awarded Cothliffe £13,500 out of £26,000 claimed as costs. Allen Build then paid the £28,000, but refused to pay the costs as awarded, so Cothliffe applied for enforcement on the outstanding costs element.

Most commentators consider this was a freak decision, and not to be relied upon, especially as it was not given in the London TCC, but this author begs to differ with the majority view that the adjudicator does not have the power. The alternative view begins with the primary argument that as both the HGCR Act 1996 and the supporting Scheme are silent on the point, the adjudicator *was* arguably entitled, both in the interests of natural justice and in order to resolve the totality of the dispute, to decide he had such power. As it was, he cut down the Referring Party's costs by almost half.

The secondary argument is that the judge in *Cothliffe* was referred to the consultation paper commissioned by the government before the HGCRA was published. The substantial majority of respondents advocated the provision for both sides in an adjudication to bear their own costs—

presumably as a disincentive to one side spending large and disproportionate sums on lawyers and experts, or preparing "ambushes".

It therefore follows *that in rejecting this high level advice* Parliament must have perceived good public interest reasons not to be prescriptive, and to leave the assessment of parties' costs in adjudication to the common sense and discretion of the man on the spot, i.e. the adjudicator. If the adjudicator is to be trusted to administer first-level justice and order the payment of potentially millions of pounds as between the parties, he can surely be trusted to see fair play on parties' costs—typically in the order of £2,000 to £5,000 in the average non-payment adjudication so far reported, and up to £20,000 for multi-issue referrals.

The public interest reasons are not difficult to perceive:

— Firstly there is the long-established principle that the successful litigant is entitled to his costs, unless there is good reason why not—as endorsed by the Lord Chancellor's Department's 1998 Consultation Paper, when discussing Conditional Fees, and as subsequently confirmed as public policy in the Access to Justice Act 1999.

— Secondly, over a third of the adjudications to date have involved statutory default under sections 110 and 111 of the HGCRA. The paying party has not only *not paid*, but has *failed to say why he is not paying*, however unjustified his reasons might be. The Notice provisions at sections 110 and 111 of the HGCR Act 1996 and Part II of the Scheme, sections 9 and 10, are there *for both parties' benefit*. The payee needs reasonable financial certainty so he can pay his suppliers and labour, or refer any queries back to them, whereas the paying party, who has reason to question the bill he has been presented with, is a fool to himself if he doesn't make use of this essential safeguard.

— As such, the non-paid party is perfectly entitled to chase his money via adjudication, citing statutory default under HCGRA sections 110 and 111 or the Scheme paras 9 and 10. It is iniquitous therefore if his eventual recovery is to be devalued by adjudicators not also awarding him his reasonable costs.

— Thirdly in a "merits of issues" adjudication, it is probably right in principle that both parties bear their own legal costs, except when one party misbehaves or misconducts himself to try to gain an advantage. There must be the power of sanction in this situation and leaving this to the adjudicator by way of the unstated, but discretionary, power to assess parties' legal costs sits four square with the thinking of the new Civil Procedure Rules.

— Fourthly, although adjudication is only a first-stage dispute resolution procedure, to be taken on to arbitration or litigation at the losing party's option, in theory therefore all costs will be reviewed in the final decision. However, in reality, most adjudication decisions will not be subsequently arbitrated or litigated. As such the adjudication "winner" never will get the opportunity to recover his legal costs in a final reckoning.

— Fifthly, the adjudicator is required to give a decision by Part I, para. 20 of the Scheme on "... the matters in dispute", and if winning parties' costs are not otherwise reimbursable, it could encourage inflation of claims.

The JCT, ICE, CIC and ORSA (as was, now the TeCSA) published Adjudication Procedure Rules all require both parties to bear their own costs—but *John Cothliffe Ltd* v. *Allen Build (Northwest) Ltd* and the question of parties' costs was then helpfully reviewed in February 2000 by the TCC in *Northern Developments (Cumbria) Ltd* v. *J. & J. Nichol Ltd* (2000). It was held that on the wording of the present legislation an adjudicator has no jurisdiction to order the loser to pay the winner's costs, but at the same time the judgment in *Cothliffe* was apparently upheld. This was because in *Northern Developments* each party had submitted costs claims in the event of being successful, and neither had suggested to the adjudicator that he had no such power. Neat decision! Whilst this might now be regarded as settled case law, there is no reason to regard the debate as closed pending the promised review of adjudication in action, and no reason why on the particular facts of a new case, e.g. flagrant abuse of the rules, one cannot distinguish that case.

Undoubtedly the most difficult area for adjudicators is deciding their own jurisdiction in the first instance. The RICS as an ANB, on legal advice, do not enquire into the details of the contractual arrangement and whether a referral falls within the HGCRA definitions, even if on the face of the Referring Party's application for the appointment of an adjudicator it is plain that the contract pre-dated the operative date of 1 May 1998—as indeed happened to this author as representative of the Defendant Party.

So often an adjudicator will find himself appointed and then the Defendant Party will refuse to accept his authority for various reasons. In this situation, the accepted practice is that the adjudicator only proceeds if there is a respectable argument that he is duly appointed and the adjudication proceeds on the basis that the Defendant Party's position is reserved, allowing him to seek a judicial declaration on the adjudicator's jurisdiction—immediately or when he has seen the Decision, and presumably the reasons for that Decision. As such, the adjudicator proceeds to decide the technical issues as put, but he does not have binding authority to finally determine his own jurisdiction.

This difficulty came before the court by way of an "appeal" from the decision of an adjudicator in *Project Consultancy Group* v. *Trustees of the Gray Trust* (1999), where PCG had provided professional services for the conversion of a house into a nursing home and there was a dispute as to fees—notably the first professional services adjudication to be reported. Both parties had agreed that the adjudicator should first decide on his jurisdiction, which depended on whether or not the contract pre-dated 1 May 1998, and then decide on the substantive issues, but with the Defendant Party having expressly reserved his position should the adjudicator decide it was a compliant contract under the HGCRA.

The adjudicator duly decided the contract post-dated 1 May 1998 and proceeded. The Defendant Party co-operated, but only on a reserved basis, and the adjudicator's decision duly went against him. When the monies awarded were not paid on the basis that the Defendant Party did not accept the adjudicator's jurisdiction and therefore his decision, the Referring Party took enforcement action by way of Summary Judgment.

However, the judge refused to give Summary Judgment under CPR rule 24—not on the basis that the adjudicator was actually wrong on the date of contract formulation, but on the principle that the adjudicator could not, as a matter of law, finally decide his own jurisdiction. Given that there was reasonable doubt and a respectable legal argument to suggest it was not a compliant construction contract the matter remained to be decided by the court. By implication the adjudicator's decision would then be enforced if the contract was found to post-date 1 May 1998.

Summarising the position thus far, some commentators have likened the adjudicator's standing to that of an independent Expert appointed to determine a defined issue. He may form his own judgment, even to the extent of making a mistake in fact or law, but he must stay within the scope of his terms of reference. In particular he is not entitled to answer a question or issue not put to him unless both parties agree to extend his remit—*Morgan Sindall Plc* v. *Sawston Farms (Cambs) Ltd* (1998) arbitration.

If it is sensible and agreed by the parties that the dispute is to be widened, it may be appropriate to reschedule the adjudication into effectively two adjudications such that the tight timetable can be adhered to and monies paid, particularly if there are third parties waiting to be paid, and holding back themselves in good faith from issuing their own Notice of Intention to Refer.

So far we have not heard of any multi-party adjudications, but it can only be a matter of time given that provision for such proceedings is obliquely included at para. 8(1) of Part I of the Scheme. This is done by expressly allowing one adjudicator to deal with more than one dispute on the same contract at the same time. At para. 8(3) all the parties involved "may" agree to extend time, but the chances of two, let alone four or even six parties agreeing anything must be as low as Foinavon's chances of winning the 1963 Grand National—but he did, as a 200–1 outsider when the remaining horses fell over one another at Beecher's the second time round!

Most adjudicators give their decisions and order monies to be paid on a peremptory basis under Part I, para. 23(1), but this is probably unnecessary as the adjudicator is empowered to decide when any payment should be made (Part I, para. 20(b)), and if the adjudicator fails to specify a payment date then at Part I, para. 21 it is provided that "... the parties shall be required to comply with any decision of the adjudicator immediately on delivery of the decision to the parties in accordance with this paragraph."

Another adjudicator got himself into difficulties in *Lathom Construction Ltd* v. *AB Air Conditioning* (1999)—a factory job in Skelmersdale. It was the usual story of alleged payment slippage, time overrun and the deduction by AB, as the employer, of Liquidated and Ascertained Damages. So Lathom called for an adjudicator, who was duly appointed.

However, the parties then started talking and believed they had reached a compromise settlement. Seemingly the adjudicator had failed to formally close matters down by a consent Decision, as would a good arbitrator bring matters to a conclusion with an Award by Consent.

The dispute erupted again over the detail of the supposed agreement and Lathom applied afresh to the RICS who questionably reappointed the same adjudicator, who equally questionably accepted a new appointment to disentangle the compromise agreement and essentially hear the same matter. Now some would say it was the original adjudication revived, and others might say it was a second adjudication of the same issues—which is out of order. AB were not happy and challenged the adjudicator's jurisdiction, contending that the compromise agreement was not a construction contract within the meaning of the HGCRA! On the other hand, AB contended it was a stand-alone collateral contract.

Par for the course; the adjudicator pressed on, effectively enquiring into his own jurisdiction and then dealing with the original issues. In the meantime the employer, AB, was having none of it, going on record from the start of the second adjudication to say that whatever the result, they did not recognise the adjudicator's jurisdiction. The adjudicator duly decided in favour of Lathom, but of course AB didn't pay, and Lathom went for enforcement by way of Summary Judgment. The Court decided however that there were triable issues of jurisdiction, so AB succeeded and kept the money, pending final determination.

Another challenge to the jurisdiction of the appointed adjudicator arose in *Palmers Ltd* v. *ABB Power Construction Ltd* (1999). The main contract was for a power generating plant, so was clearly outside the HGCRA definition of a "construction contract", but how about the scaffolding sub-contract with which the two parties were concerned?

There was the usual payment and set-off dispute and on the basis of alleged non-payment under the Scheme provisions the scaffolding sub-contractor, Palmers, both suspended work and called for an adjudicator. ABB contended breach by Palmers on the basis that scaffolding was not a "construction operation" within the meaning of the Act, so there was no right to suspend; whereupon ABB did the sensible thing and applied to the court for a declaration as to the status of their contract. The judge duly considered this all too possible situation and decided that he saw no reason why there should not be a construction contract for sub-contract works within a larger contract, which was excluded from the HGCRA by virtue of the end purpose definition within the Act.

Another technicality arose in the case of *A. Straume (UK) Ltd* v. *Bradlor Developments Ltd* (1999). This was an insolvency situation and the concern was that, given that the contract had specifically excluded any right for the employer to arbitrarily set off, if the employer was now allowed to call for an adjudicator and was successful, this would give rise to set-off by the back door and prejudice the recovery of the preferential creditors.

It was duly decided that a Referring Party wishing to go against a party, who has called in the Receiver etc, needs the permission of the court to be allowed to adjudicate, as in the judge's view adjudication was "a form of arbitration". Whether this decision would hold given a contract that didn't expressly deny the employer the right to set-off remains to be seen.

Now we come to what can only be called a "lulu" of a decision. Certain projects have a capital T for trouble written all over them and this one was a classic. Firstly it was one of those Private Finance Initiative funded BOOT schemes—**B**uild, **O**wn, **O**perate for a specified number of years, typically 20 years, and then **T**ransfer ownership back to the original owner, in this case a combined Medical School Trust.

European procurement rules resulted in a French main contractor, employing largely Portuguese labourers for the structure, who thought lift shafts and service risers were old-fashioned *garde de l'eau's* (living apparently on site, literally), Danish mechanical contractors and Irish electricians! Not surprisingly it was a disaster job, in more ways than one.

Firstly a major dispute broke out between the French and the Danes, with issues of under-certification of the mechanical services, extensions of time denied, direct payments by the contractor to the sub-contractor's workforce when they went on strike, defects, overpayments, disputed variations, Liquidated and Ascertained Damages, and even the tax status of operatives.

Upon the referral to adjudication by the Danish mechanical sub-contractor, a solicitor was appointed as the adjudicator, who promptly appointed an engineering quantity surveyor to assist him, with the consent of the parties. Presumably the extra 14 days was requested and agreed, and off they went.

In fairness, it must have been a tall order to steer a way through all the problems, even without the multi-national dimension, but just before the adjudicator could publish his decision the Danish sub-contractor went into voluntary liquidation. Nevertheless, in due course the adjudicator published his decision, with lengthy reasons, together with detailed calculations, and then it all went horribly, horribly wrong.

When the French contractor was ordered to pay £207,741, plus the full cost of the adjudicator's fees, he refused and a fundamental issue arose:

— What is the position if on the face of the decision, or in the attached reasons, it is apparent that the wrong result has been given, i.e. the other party should have won? In this case the adjudicator had clearly got the calculations wrong, confusing gross and net values.

So the case came to court as *Bouygues UK Ltd* v. *Dahl-Jensen UK Ltd (In Liquidation)* (1999), with the latter seeking Summary Judgment. Bouygues contended that the figures didn't work, whichever way you stacked them, and that if the adjudicator was remotely correct it could only be because he was effectively releasing the final moeity of retention, which he had not been asked to do by either party. Consequently he had exceeded his authority and the decision was void. Dahl-Jensen contended it was part of his remit, but he had simply made a mistake, so the decision was a valid, if not a very clever, decision.

Seemingly the adjudicator was invited by the Claimant to reconsider his decision, but he stood by his published result and reasoning—so what was the judge to do? He then held that the adjudicator "... was doing precisely what he had been asked to do, and was answering the right question, but he was doing so in the wrong way."

The judge restated his previous opinion in *Macob* that "The purpose of the Scheme is to provide a speedy mechanism for settling disputes in construction contracts on a provisional interim basis, and requiring the decisions of Adjudicators to be enforced pending final determination ... whether those decisions are wrong in point of law or fact."

With particular relevance to this case, the judge said:

"It is inherent in the Scheme that injustices will occur because from time to time Adjudicators will make mistakes. Sometimes those mistakes will be glaringly obvious and disastrous for the losing party. The victim of mistakes will usually be able to recoup their losses by subsequent arbitration or litigation, and even by a subsequent adjudication. Sometimes they will not be able to do so, where, for example, there is an intervening insolvency, either of the victim or of the fortunate beneficiary of the mistake."

The judge then went on to say that the court should "guard against characterising a mistaken answer to an issue that lies within the scope of reference as an excess of jurisdiction."

In short the judge was saying that even if the adjudicator addresses a question within his remit, but gets it manifestly wrong in fact, as evidenced by his own reasons, then that is tough luck and the decision must be acted upon until the wronged party institutes the appeal process by arbitrating or by litigation.

With respect, this strict legal interpretation of the HGCRA cannot be reconciled with the real world in which the construction industry and rapacious bank managers operate. From a lender's point of view, there is no better time to call in an overdraft, quite legally on demand, than when a contractor or sub-contractor has just received a large cheque. The cash flow is temporarily improved, so now is the time to cease trading and try to collect the remaining assets, and bank managers have no interest in being Defendants in litigation or arbitration. That is the harsh, real world.

There have therefore to be safeguards and who better to apply those safeguards than the judges in the TCC. Under the Woolf reforms we are told judges have the power to appoint technical assessors, so why couldn't the judge in *Bouygues* have appointed an experienced Quantity Surveyor assessor to go to the adjudicator and say "Look here old chap, your decision and your reasons don't make much sense, so could you please explain them to me, such that I am satisfied, and can report back to the judge."

However, the real mystery in *Bouygues* is why Bouygues and in particular their Counsel didn't point out to the judge the potential injustice of a wrong decision given in favour of an insolvent company. According to the instructing solicitor for Dahl-Jensen they couldn't believe their luck—firstly at the adjudicator's decision, but then secondly at Bouygues' failure to play the insolvency card at the enforcement proceedings. Even the case title fails to carry the fact that Dahl-Jensen had ceased to trade—all very intriguing!

Now as I said, some projects have a capital T for trouble and this same site was the scene for the adjudication referred to in Chapter 8 and the author's uncomplimentary comments on bank managers. The author represented a sub-sub-contractor, who had carried out first fix electrics in the basement and ground floor. My client was underpaid by some £100,000 for which no Section 110 or 111 Notices had been served, so we went for adjudication on the basis of statutory default under the Scheme.

As often happens the Notice of Referral prompted peace talks, so I visited the site, the building having been handed over to the combined

Medical School some two weeks earlier for the start of the University year. On arrival I found large temporary generators in the limited car park and heavy duty cables all over the place. Yet another disaster had struck: water from a burst main up the road had got into the hospital service tunnel complex and then found its way round the site and through the double doors into the basement plantroom. All the high voltage switchgear instantly tripped and put the five-storey building into darkness, trapping people in lifts etc. The "high water mark" was two thirds of the way up the plantroom wall and all the electrics had now to be replaced! At least it took care of any silly arguments about defective work by my client!

Then came the case of *Sherwood & Casson Ltd* v. *Mackenzie* (1999). Whereas Part I, para. 9(2) of the Scheme provides that "An Adjudicator must resign where the dispute is the same or substantially the same as one which has previously been referred to adjudication, and a decision has been taken in that adjudication", no similar provision appears in the Act itself.

In the above case there had been a dispute concerning alleged under-valuation on an interim certificate of structural steelwork being erected in a new grandstand for a rugby club in Barrow—and this had been adjudicated. A few months later the sub-contractor, Sherwood & Casson, put in another application, increasing the value of work done, and now including a Loss and Expense claim. When this was not paid another adjudicator was called for, and predictably the Defendant contractor, Mackenzie, challenged his jurisdiction, citing section 9(2) of the Scheme. The court subsequently had little difficulty, given the claim element, in deciding it was a different dispute, and therefore that the second adjudicator was validly appointed—but this is unlikely to be the last word on what is potentially adjudication's Achilles' heel, i.e. repeated visits to the Final Account.

The reason for this is simple. Each month the work and the value thereof moves on, so let us assume as in the above case an adjudication has sorted out a dispute, which a month later is history. If the paying party has had to pay more than he believes was right, all he has to do is issue a section 110 Notice against a subsequent interim valuation, and then help himself to the disputed money, giving reasons dressed up so as to make it arguable that it is not "substantially the same" dispute.

So in this event, not only does adjudicator No. 2 have a problem, but so do the lawyers. The whole principle of adjudication is that it is binding until overturned by subsequent arbitration or litigation—so in practice the sub-contractor will contend that:

— The Defendant Party has reversed or partly undone the previous adjudication decision—and that he is not allowed to do.

— It is the same dispute and accordingly the Defendant Party must refer the matter to arbitration or litigation.

Of course, the Defendant Party will argue the exact opposite, his strongest card being to say that *not* to allow one interim valuation to be corrected by a subsequent valuation runs contrary to the whole regime of interim certification and the express terms of the subject contract.

This dilemma will of course be particularly contentious where the first adjudication decision was, as often happens, given simply on the grounds of no section 110 or 111 Notices. In order, therefore to make the Notice provisions effective and to guard against the situation, where such a Notice is issued months after the money in question has been paid, and then snatched back, further amendment to the initial legislation is urgently required. If not, the payment abusers will be back in business, and adjudication will lose its current effectiveness and reputation.

At this point a line has to be drawn, and no doubt by the time this book is actually in print, various further problem areas will have been addressed by the courts—hopefully by a wider panel of judges, and also on some larger-value decisions by the Court of Appeal.

9.8 ADJUDICATION—UNANSWERED QUESTIONS

(1) *Reasons–*
when should they be given and how far should one go? What if they show that the adjudicator has answered the wrong question, or simply given an impossible answer? The start point must be the statutory provisions, i.e. Part I, para. 21 of the Scheme requires the adjudicator to give reasons if so asked by one of the parties. If not under the Scheme, but an adjudicator is appointed under one of the various ANB's procedure rules, then he is tied by whatever is prescribed. But supposing an adjudicator is not so tied, does he give reasons in the interests of natural justice? The thinking is that he gives minimal reasons or an indication of reasoning so at least the losing party can see why he lost.

(2) *Letters of Intent–*
will continue to be a difficult area for the lay adjudicator in deciding whether there is a respectable argument for the Defendant Party to contend "No Contract", and thereby to resist the adjudicator's jurisdiction. Here the thinking is that the adjudicator should suggest to both parties that they make application to the courts for a declaration as to the status of the contract, before incurring potentially wasted time and costs.

However, this is unlikely to satisfy a cash needy sub-contractor and probably the Referring Party will want to press on to a 28-day (or quicker) decision. Equally the reluctant Defendant, not wanting to be parted from the disputed money, will not be willing to go anywhere near a court! If so, the adjudicator can do little other than proceed, noting the Defendant Party's challenge and reserved position.

(3) *Bespoke contracts–*
these will need to comply with the basic requirements of HGCRA section 108 as discussed in detail earlier in this Chapter. Any one-off self-protection clauses, such as requiring any monies awarded by an adjudicator to be paid into a Trust Fund and not released pending the final resolution by arbitration or litigation, are certainly contrary to the spirit of the HGCRA. If objected to by a Defendant Party in the course of a referral what does the adjudicator then do? Accept the express term of the contract, supposedly freely entered into by both parties, and leave alone? Or take the bull by the horns and order "A will pay B forthwith"?

(4) *Pay when paid etc–*
Similarly, any attempts to introduce "Pay-when-certified", or to call a "dispute" by any other name, such as a "difference of opinion" as a holding tactic, or to prescribe a credit note system to delay actual payment, are considered to be automatic "Red Card" offences. Any party trying to play such games will have to accept the summary procedure of the Scheme provisions.

(5) *Securing the adjudicator's fees–*
unfortunately the old arbitration practice of only releasing the award/ decision once both parties have paid their half, or one party has paid the lot, lives on, e.g. the ICE Adjudication Rules. In the context of adjudication where the time is of essence this simply can't work satisfactorily and there is simply no provision in the HGCRA allowing Adjudicators to exercise liens pending payment in full. The reluctant payer, almost inevitably the Defendant Party, may well use such an opportunity, if offered by the adjudicator, to delay publication of the adjudication decision and so delay the evil day of being parted from his money. He might even try crying "foul" when the Decision is not published within the required 28 days—although he is the cause of the delay! So the message for all adjudicators, and the ICE in particular is: Don't give hostages to fortune. So long as the adjudicator has got a properly drafted and signed Form of Appointment, on a joint and several liability basis, that should be sufficient to secure payment, even if it should mean a visit to the County Court.

However, this author's practice avoids all these potential difficulties and is simple:

> — In your Terms and Conditions of Appointment provide that the Referring Party will be invoiced the full cost of the adjudicator's fees.

— Then provide that such fees will be allocated or apportioned as appropriate and any value payable by the Defendant Party will form part of the decision.
— Usually the Refering Party wins, so will be happy to pay!

(6) *Assessment of parties' costs–*
as discussed the jury is out on this most contentious of subjects following the *Cothliffe* and *Northern Developments* decisions and no doubt this is an issue which will be considered and clarified on the promised statutory review.

(7) *Ambushes–*
where one party expensively prepares a voluminously detailed case and there is obvious prejudice to the other party in not being able to mount an equally detailed defence in a matter of a week or so. The Scheme Part I, para. 13(g) empowers the adjudicator to limit the length of written documents or oral submissions. This has yet to be tested and it is suggested an adjudicator could well refuse to admit a six-volume submission and insist it is summarised in a six-page executive summary. The adjudicator would then have started with a reasonably level playing field, and can control the detail and volume of any supplementary information he considers necessary.

(8) *Reverse ambushes–*
where the paying party effectively issues a section 110 or 111 Notice and takes back monies he has been paying in previous months. Except in instances of clear mistake or an adverse test result on quality of workmanship or materials, etc, such practice should be severely dealt with, as discussed above. Such practice is an abuse of Latham principles and makes a mockery of the Fair Payment provisions, running contrary to the fundamental concept of transparency and certainty of cash flow.

(9) *Payment to stakeholder accounts–*
discussed in detail earlier in this Chapter. This subject is coming back onto the agenda following some recent decisions. Having been one of the recommendations of the Latham Report, which did not find its way into the HGCRA, no doubt this area will also be revisited by the promised statutory review.

(10) *The Human Rights Act 1998–*
this is likely to become effective from 1 October 2000, but current thinking is that adjudication is an *interim process*, subject to final decision by arbitration or litigation, or by agreement between the parties. It therefore does not offend the principle of having a fair and public hearing. Whether arbitration will be deemed compliant might be more arguable.

(11) *Case law–*
As noted, further developments in this fast-growing area of dispute resolution are inevitable. In particular we still await a case on the specific issue of whether, in the absence of a section 110 Notice, the "amount due" is *de facto* proven and therefore whether an adjudicator is acting beyond his jurisdiction, if on the request of the Defendant Party he subsequently enquires into the proper value of work done—before the issue of contras etc under section 111.

(12) *Current usage of ANB's–*
The number of applications for the appointment of adjudicators since *Macob* etc. hit the construction press has increased exponentially. In the first year of the HGCRA, to the end of April 1999, the RICS had only been called upon 80 times, i.e. on average, 6.5 appointments a month, whereas in the second year the RICS appointment rate is now running at over 50 referrals per month, and rising.

It is to be expected that there will eventually be a levelling off in the applications for appointments of adjudicators as the current abusers of the Fair Payment provisions learn their lessons the hard way, but the pattern of who is doing the business is clear. Currently the RICS is receiving more applications per month than all the other ANBs added together—yet there continue to be new entrants as self-appointed ANBs, such as TecBar, writing their own Adjudication Procedure Rules and drawing up Panels etc!

9.9 NON-STATUTORY ADJUDICATION

So far all discussion in this book has concerned statutory adjudication as arising from the HGCRA and the supporting Scheme for Construction Contracts, other than the passing mention of more limited applications of adjudication prescribed in some standard forms of contract or sub-contract and pre-dating 1 May 1998.

Increasingly, however, adjudication is being suggested as a binding or non-binding method of potentially unlocking disputes, and is being inserted in new construction contracts where the jurisdiction of the HGCRA does not apply, e.g. international contracts or where the activities fall outside the definition of "Construction operations".

Hopefully we will see an increasing use of adjudication in such international construction contracts and also at home—literally. At present the lower end of the HGCRA spectrum excludes all owner-occupier construction contracts, yet this is a vast area of business for many genuine and competent building contractors, who daily face unfair and unregulated competition from the "cowboy builder".

So long as the government of the day fails to realise that avoiding paying VAT at the rate of 17.5% on the cost of domestic building work is a very powerful, if selfish, reason for commissioning work *"sur le noir"* as the French say, and so long as it fails to abolish VAT on domestic work or reduce the rate to 5% as the French have done, the evil will remain. However, one initiative recently launched by the JCT and the RICS is a new and simple (some say too simple) standard form of contract for domestic work–the JCT Building Contract for a Home Owner/Occupier. Underpinning the whole concept is the right for either party to call for the appointment of an adjudicator, who will then operate on a modest maximum fee basis of £750 and give a decision in 21 days.

This has to be the way forward, as even the JCT Standard Form of Contract for Minor Works is inapplicable for a large proportion of domestic works, and is only usually used where there is an Architect or Building Surveyor administering the project. This, however, is the exception rather than the rule, so the great majority of domestic works contracts are arranged, often informally, on exchange of letters, verbal agreements, etc. Very rarely is there a proper definition of the original scope of the work, and even more rarely an adequate mechanism for adjusting the price when the inevitable changes are instructed.

Hopefully the new JCT/Home Owner contract will focus minds at the outset and thereby help avoid some of the potential for disputes, but inevitably there will continue to be disputes of every shape and size. So enter Mr Adjudicator, empowered by the contract as opposed to statute, and as politely and even-handedly as possible let him give a decision—enforceable until otherwise decided by arbitration or litigation.

The challenge now is to "sell" the JCT Building contract for a Home Owner/Occupier to the typical domestic extension type client and the small builder who doesn't belong to any trade federation or read *Building* magazine. One idea is that a pamphlet about the Home Owner contract should be sent out with every application for Planning or Building Control Approval, and another is that it be featured on TV on a "Cowboy" building drama, just as various medical conditions are featured each week in *Peak Practice*.

However, the point is that it is just as much in the genuine builder's interests as the houseowner's interests to adopt such a contract. When it comes to the crunch, as it will on various projects, it will be for the adjudicators appointed under this particular form of contract to make it work in practice by giving prompt and sensible decisions, which hopefully both parties respect. If any party then thinks justice is expensive at £750, maybe it should be pointed out to him that this is equivalent to two hours of a London solicitor just looking at the file.

CHAPTER 10

THE ARBITRATION ACT 1996

10.1 WHY ARBITRATION?

Before anyone coined the term Alternative Dispute Resolution (ADR) there were only two recognised methods of settling a construction dispute when normal negotiations failed: in front of a judge, or in front of an independent professional, expert in the subject matter of the dispute and vested with judge-like power by virtue of successive Arbitration Acts. For an arbitrator to be preferred to a judge it was necessary that either the contract as signed before the dispute arose provided for arbitration as a final method for resolving the dispute, or that the parties so agreed after the dispute had occurred.

Now it must be remembered that the successive Arbitration Acts were not brought in for the exclusive benefit of the construction industry—far from it. Arbitration has for centuries underpinned the commercial world, particularly in fast-moving industries such as perishable cargoes and financial transactions, and accordingly London has for a long time enjoyed a pre-eminent reputation as the arbitration capital of the world. This represents considerable foreign earnings so it has been necessary to protect this position by amending the Arbitration Act from time to time. For a long time the 1950 Arbitration Act was the Bible, but the arbitrator was almost a prisoner in his own court—sitting at the top of the table in almost magisterial silence, and as construction dispute practice developed, often open to challenge on procedural irregularities or points of law. Then came the Arbitration Acts of 1975 and 1979, and greater autonomy for the arbitrator to take charge of the procedure and to take a more inquisitorial role when matters were not clear to him.

About this time construction claims proliferated and we saw the development of specialist construction solicitor practices and specialist construction chambers. Not surprisingly, construction arbitrations also proliferated, as did appeals from arbitrators' awards—heard in the Official Referee's Court, as was, now the Technology and Construction Court.

For many years the appointment of construction arbitrators was badly co-ordinated between the professional bodies, with the RICS refusing to adopt a policy of only appointing RICS members who were also members of the Chartered Institute of Arbitrators and on their panel of approved arbitrators.

Further, it was only 20 years or so ago that the CIArb tightened their rules and insisted on all new panel members undergoing training, examination and pupilage. In the meantime many names on the historic lists continued to be appointed and, not having been trained as arbitrators, some were soon found out by Counsel on one side or the other, such that if their client lost the decision they knew they had pretty certain grounds of appeal. So the reputation and reliability of arbitration suffered, particularly as arbitrators tended, like tortoises, to go back into their shell and proceed very slowly for fear of giving grounds for appeal.

In one case the author was involved in, we were in the hearing for two and a half months, Mondays to Thursdays. Of that time we spent 40% arguing procedural issues, such as whether to let in fresh evidence, and 60% actually dealing with the technical evidence—a quite disproportionate imbalance mimicking litigation.

Changes were long overdue, and the RICS now work very closely with the CIArb and have got the appointments system for both arbitrators and adjudicators down to a fine art. Also the old school of "amateur" arbitrators, appointed by successive Presidents on the "good old boy" network, is now dying out naturally, or being culled, and the quality of the decision-making process now enjoys a high level of respect, even from losing parties.

Previously arbitration was generally perceived to be the most cost effective method of dispute resolution, as compared with litigation. This was mainly because the parties could actually run their own timetable, more or less, and having got to trial state they could reasonably expect the chosen or appointed arbitrator to be available. Whether they then got a properly controlled hearing and a quality decision was the big risk.

On the other hand going to court seemed to carry more weight, and certainly deterred some parties, who assumed litigation was necessarily much more expensive than arbitration. However, the real downside of litigation, as discussed elsewhere, was the sheer unpredictability of being allocated a trial date at some time in the distant future and then when the date eventually drew nigh, the odds were that one leading individual, usually Counsel, would not be available. This was both psychologically and financially crippling to the party supposedly stood out of his rightful monies.

Now, as we shall see in Chapter 11, Lord Woolf has listened to this criticism and stolen the arbitrator's clothes metaphorically speaking. Case management and early trial dates, after some form of ADR, are now the order of the day, with even the largest cases being disposed of after a full trial within a year of being commenced. At least that is the promise, but we have yet to hear of this actually happening in practice.

If, following the Civil Procedure Rules introduced in 1999, the new court procedures work in practice as promised, then arbitration will have lost its decisive advantage, almost overnight, and we may expect to see the dispute resolution clauses in contracts increasingly altered in favour of litigation.

So with many construction solicitors already amending contracts in favour of litigation due to the provision in section 9 of the Arbitration Act 1996 (power of court to retain action where an arbitration clause exists), and many more disputes now being effectively settled by adjudication, it is entirely possible that the professional construction arbitrator will shortly become an endangered species!

So far no figures for the number of arbitrator appointments since 1 May 1998 have been published to assess the impact of adjudication and the new Civil Procedure Rules. Only time will tell, but the betting must be that the graph of arbitrator appointments will be the mirror image of the adjudicator appointments graph.

10.2 INCORPORATED OR NOT INCORPORATED?

One might have expected the Arbitration Act 1996 to clear up the old chestnut of when an arbitration clause is effectively incorporated in a contract by reference to another document. Section 6(2) attempts to do just this, but sadly leaves us none the wiser. As an exercise in non-plain English, section 6(2) must be a candidate for a special award. It reads: "The reference in an agreement to a written form of arbitration clause or to a document containing an arbitration clause constitutes an arbitration agreement if the reference is such as to make that clause part of the agreement."

However, this very point came before a judge in *Trygg Hansa Insurance Ltd* v. *Equitas Ltd* (1999). There were two contracts, one of which had a full-blown arbitration clause, and the other merely referred to the arbitration clause in the former. As a result it is clear that, if arbitration is to be the preferred final resolution option, then it is necessary to say so expressly, and of course to put it in writing, albeit by reference to another signed document—not omitting to properly conclude the second contract.

10.3 THE POWERS OF THE ARBITRATOR

When the Arbitration Act 1996 was published there was universal rejoicing in the construction arbitrator fraternity—at last the powers of the arbitrator were confirmed and he could adopt a much more pro-active role without fear of being appealed.

The other major change is the provision at section 9 that if a Claimant should choose to ignore an arbitration clause and issue court proceedings under the contract, then the court no longer has the power to decide to retain the action—even if there are joinder complications and possible prejudice to third parties. Whilst this provision can be commended on the basis of giving certainty as to how to proceed it does reopen the old *Crouch* debate, as referred to in Chapter 1.

For 14 years construction industry law had been constrained by the case of *Northern Regional Health Authority* v. *Derek Crouch Construction Ltd* (1984) where the Court of Appeal had decided that where there was a valid arbitration clause in the contract, then only an arbitrator, not a judge, was empowered to resolve any dispute, including opening up and reviewing Architect's certificates as to time and money.

Then the House of Lords in *Beaufort Developments (NI) Ltd* v. *Gilbert Ash (NI) Ltd and Others* (1998) overturned their earlier ruling in *Crouch* and decided that after all a judge could deal with construction cases, even where there was an arbitration clause, if there were reasons to do so.

It must be remembered that the intervening 14 years had seen the rapid growth of non-standard forms of contract and alternative forms of procurement, such as Design and Build, where there is no third party referee. Main contractors were effectively certifying their own payment each month and disputes had proliferated accordingly.

However, in the meantime there had been a very late amendment to section 9 of the Arbitration Act 1996 restoring the *status quo*, i.e. as in *Crouch* the courts could not get involved if the parties had signed up to an arbitration clause—to which the JCT responded in their 1998 review of standard contracts by making it a straight choice between arbitration and litigation.

So assuming there is a valid arbitration clause, unless the Claimant can reasonably contend that there is some defect in the contract, which would then knock out the arbitration clause, the court *must* now grant the Defendant a stay of proceedings, if requested, in favour of arbitration given a dispute arising *under*, as opposed to *in connection with* the contract.

This seemingly fine distinction came about by virtue of two cases. Firstly in *Halki Shipping Corporation* v. *Sopex Oils Ltd* (1997) the Claimants commenced court proceedings for recovery of damages consequent to a failed charterparty agreement which had been factually pleaded. The Defendants then sought a stay under section 9 of the Arbitration Act 1996 on the basis of the existence of an arbitration clause. The Claimants responded that it was a factual breach and no basis of dispute was pleaded by way of defence—so the arbitration clause was not triggered. Unfortunately the court played safe and decided a "dispute" could include one party just simply not wishing to pay the other. As such the arbitration clause applied.

The other case, *Al-Naimi* v. *Islamic Press Agency Ltd* (1999), concerned a contract where substantial additional works were ordered and a dispute broke out concerning those additional works. The question for the court was therefore: did the arbitration clause govern just the original contract works or the mutually extended contract? If the latter was correct then the arbitration clause was applicable and the Defendant would be entitled to an arbitration. Somewhat controversially the court decided, presumably on the facts of how the further works were ordered, that there were two separate, but linked contracts—so the dispute could be heard by the court. Hence the "... in connection with ..." finesse.

Importantly sections 30 to 32 and 72 to 73 of the new Act confirm that an arbitrator may decide on his own authority to act, e.g. where there is a challenge from the Defendant as to the existence of the necessary arbitration clause, or indeed the existence of a binding contract. However, this does not shut out a party from making application to the courts to determine an arbitrator's jurisdiction, or from taking an active part in the arbitration proceedings, provided he has first reserved his right to subsequently take the matter before a judge (assuming he might come second in the arbitration).

However, at section 34 the arbitrator has his power restricted—under the old premise that he is the servant of the parties. Through what is now termed "Party autonomy" the parties are free to jointly instruct the arbitrator how they would like him to proceed. If this causes him a real problem he will no doubt discuss it with them before he proceeds, but if all else fails he can resign.

Then at section 34 there is a statement by Parliament of a major policy change. Expressly the arbitrator is released from necessarily following an adversarial form of proceedings, as typified by court practice over many years. This option is consistent with the principle of the arbitrator being the master of the proceedings, but does have its dangers if the arbitrator can see that one party is "being economical with the truth". In seeking "further clarification" an over-zealous arbitrator could well end up effectively promoting the other side's case, and so be open to a charge of bias. However, in larger cases both sides will be legally represented, so any variation to the conventional adversarial procedure can be discussed and agreed in advance.

As already discussed, multi-party disputes are the problem area, and whilst at section 35 the arbitrator is empowered to hear consolidated disputes, he has no power to order consolidation if the parties are unwilling.

As regards the power to order a Claimant, or to order a Counterclaimant, to provide security for the other side's costs, this now appears at section 38. But whether or not it is equitable to order such costs against the Claimant in a financial dispute where arguably he has been put in financial distress by the very subject matter of the dispute is a fine call, just as it was under the old Act.

Finally, the arbitrator's power to enforce timely procedure by both parties is effectively unchanged. If the Claimant is deemed to be responsible for "inordinate and inexcusable delay" the arbitrator may strike out his claim. But if the Defendant refuses to comply with the required timetable the worst the arbitrator can do is proceed to an award, after satisfying himself that the Claimant has made out his case, which the Defendant has then failed to answer, after due time and warning.

All the above are of course new in so much as they are new statutory provisions, coming out of the Arbitration Act 1996, but it should be appreciated that arbitration practice has over the years been codified by various bodies, notably the JCT and the ICE, who published their own Arbitration Rules. As such, all the above powers of the arbitrator existed, depending on which rules were being adopted, before the 1996 Act, and the Act effectively collated perceived best practice.

Even so, a further codification was required to provide just one set of further practice rules to supplement the 1996 Act. This is the CIMAR Rules (Construction Industry Model Arbitration Rules), a joint production by the ACE, the BPF, the CIArb, the CIOB, the RIBA, and the RICS. Now if this combination of the great and the good can't get it right between them, then who can?

10.4 TECHNICAL ARBITRATOR OR LAWYER?

The two most commonly heard criticisms of arbitration continue to be:

— Arbitration is no more than litigation in private.
— You are more likely to get a maverick arbitrator than a maverick judge.

Hopefully, the Arbitration Act 1996 will encourage arbitrators to be more robust and to meet the three stated overriding objectives of the Act:

— To achieve a fair and impartial resolution without unnecessary delay or expense.
— To allow the parties to decide how their dispute should be resolved, subject only to possible public interest issues.
— To limit the power of the court to intervene.

If this can be achieved then the first criticism should be answered, but the second criticism is more difficult to achieve.

It has always been a principle of arbitration that the professional person appointed should be appointed primarily because he is a respected practitioner in the subject matter of the dispute. Very much as a secondary consideration, he is also expected to be a safe pair of hands as to knowledge of the law and the required procedure. However, in recent years we have seen the growth of the professional arbitrator, who would be hard pressed to complete his annual Continuing Professional Development record if he was limited to the profession of his original calling—and this is the dilemma.

The response from the CIArb has been officially stated as a policy of trying to ensure that arbitrators of the future should have the equivalent skills of a first class honours graduate in law, and to create three tiers of members, i.e. practising arbitrators, aspiring arbitrators and "Friends" of the CIArb. If an analysis were done, the latter category would probably account for 75% or more of the subscription income.

Now this is laudable on paper, but wholly unrealistic in practice. Who in this day and age, unless enjoying a source of private income, can afford to take the necessary time out from his main practice and drop fee earning work to undertake the extensive study necessary? Then having done this he has to go on weekend courses and submit to interrogation by his peers, who themselves have not necessarily achieved the new standard required. If his face doesn't fit, so be it—all the personal investment has been for nothing.

Cynical you might say, but realistic would be the reply. Further is the CIArb not losing sight of what the commercial customer actually wants? If he wants a double-first lawyer to decide his dispute he can go to the TCC in St Dunstan's Lane and pay good fees for legal advice along the way. On the other hand if he wants a fair decision within the parameters of the contract, given by an expert in the area of the dispute and sensible enough to apply the CIMAR rules, he can instruct solicitors to carry out the basic necessities of case preparation—and then get the case heard within a month or so by a technical arbitrator.

Alternatively, if liability turns on a point of law, why not have a two-part hearing—the first decided by a lawyer arbitrator—and if the fight goes to the second round, then call up a technical arbitrator in place of the lawyer?

With adjudication fast taking the lower ground of construction disputes, and the new Civil Procedure Rules taking the higher ground, arbitration will only survive if it goes back to its roots of being a commercial tribunal—and a lawyers' tennis match only when absolutely necessary.

10.5 ARBITRATION CLAUSES—TO DELETE OR LEAVE IN?

It must be remembered that in real life it is the purchaser who has the option of setting the contract conditions and deciding whether to put out the tender enquiry with or without an arbitration clause. It is also a fact of construction life that it is usually the supplier of services who has to commence proceedings when for whatever reason the purchaser suspends payment.

Thus whether one is acting for the employer, or for a main contractor sub-letting a part of the works, the tactics are to choose the dispute resolution procedure that is perceived to make life most difficult for the supplier—and safest for oneself.

Thus before the reform of the court system, contractors would often place sub-contracts on their own sub-contract terms and conditions without arbitration clauses—purely on the basis that a small sub-contractor might just chance his arm in a dispute by calling for arbitration, but would be unlikely to commence litigation, rightly perceiving it to be a more drawn out and costly process.

As explained, the court system has now been radically overhauled so this perception should soon disappear. So what does the party drafting the contract now choose to do? Prefer to be sued in arbitration or in litigation?

The unique benefits of arbitration, i.e. privacy and having the option of trying to choose the arbitrator, may have their attractions, but if court procedures are now seen to be efficient and not noticeably more expensive than arbitration why not settle for the greater certainty of the decision-making process? At least the courtroom is free, whereas the arbitration rooms usually have to be expensively hired.

On the other hand, an employer may well be swayed by the fact that section 9 of the Arbitration Act 1996 denies the court any discretion as regards whether or not to grant a stay to arbitration. If there is an arbitration clause, any dispute between the employer and the contractor can only be resolved by an arbitrator.

As the employer nominates the Architect or Contract Administrator, and presumably has every confidence in his ability, at least at the outset, does he want to give a judge (lawyer) or an arbitrator (building industry professional) the right to overrule any Certificate, and thus the final decision as to what the employer might owe the contractor on Final Account?

Certainly solicitors acting for employers are likely to have more bad experiences of arbitrators than judges, but equally how many times have we seen cases turn on fine legal decisions, only to be overturned on appeal, and then on occasion turned back again? On the other hand, in arbitration there is a perception that legal issues will be given due consideration, but not to the extent of producing a result—as sometimes happens in litigation—which appears to be inequitable.

However, the deciding factor from an employer's point of view is probably the risk of defects and the economic damage that flows from a development that cannot generate a secure income stream. Should serious defects arise, the employer will wish to pursue the guilty party, but is that the contractor, the Architect, the Engineer, etc?

The prospect of having to arbitrate against the contractor, but at effectively the same time having to litigate against the professionals, alleging negligence, is of course unattractive and fraught with the risk of conflicting decisions; one consolidated action is required. So given section 9 of the Arbitration Act 1996 shutting out the litigation option, there is compelling reason, from an employer's point of view, to avoid this obvious hazard by deleting the arbitration clause.

From the contractor's point of view, if the head contract does not have an arbitration clause, what do you do in respect of the sub-contracts you need to place? What if you opt for inserting arbitration clauses, and then find yourself caught in the middle of a dispute which is essentially a specialist sub-contractor v. consultant argument, but you are the Defendant? What if the arbitrator orders you to pay the sub-contractor substantial additional monies?

The employer may well honour that decision, especially if you have kept him fully informed, but all too often disputes are not single-issue disputes and the employer may well disassociate himself from the arbitration decision. In this case you have no option but to pay the sub-contractor and commence litigation against the employer in your own name.

In short, you cannot afford to be otherwise than in a back-to-back position, so you should also delete all arbitration clauses down the supply chain. On the other hand, with most sub-contractor disputes now being taken care of by adjudication, if you do prefer to use arbitration clauses in your sub-contracts, the likelihood of actually having a parallel litigation and arbitration on the same matter should be reduced accordingly.

10.6 HOW TO SELECT YOUR ARBITRATOR

Unlike adjudication, arbitration is a final and binding dispute resolution process, so it is essential that at the end of a hearing both parties feel that they have been allowed to present their respective cases to the best advantage, that they have been allowed to challenge the other party's case and that the arbitrator has been even handed. Whether the losing party is as happy when he picks up the award is of course unlikely, human nature being human nature. It is therefore important that the quality of the arbitrator is as high as possible, so the question is how can one be more certain of getting a good arbitrator?

Sometimes employers will nominate an arbitrator in the head contract, assuming they haven't deleted the arbitration clause, and often contractors will put the same name in all their sub-contracts. This practice may have been acceptable when Presidential appointments were something of a lottery, but now that the quality of such appointments has improved immeasurably in recent years there is no need for it.

The last thing anyone wants is any suggestion or perception of possible bias, and however experienced and well respected a named arbitrator might be there is inevitably a question mark as to how he came to get his name into the documents. Equally there has to be a suspicion that should he give a decision against the interests of the party who nominated him, then he might lose his sinecure.

The preferred method of appointment is therefore to leave the personal appointment slot blank and to name one of the professional bodies. Some are well organised and have a proven list of experienced arbitrators covering the whole of the UK and overseas, categorised by skill base. Some also operate a quality control system, writing to both parties after an arbitration and asking them to rate the arbitrator's performance on various aspects of the process.

Unfortunately most professional bodies who appear as ANBs under the statutory adjudication scheme of the HGCR Act 1996 are run on shoestring budgets, with a handful of dedicated staff—and consequently they cannot readily offer the same range of trusted arbitrators as are available through the larger appointing bodies such as the RICS and the ICE.

A Chartered Institute of Arbitrators 1999 survey of arbitration practice in the construction industry came up with the following findings:

— Of arbitrators, however appointed, 36% were Quantity Surveyors, 17% Civil Engineers, 16% Architects, 10% Barristers—and 77% were construction industry professionals when other surveyors and engineers were added in.
— The typical arbitrator will have had between 30 and 50 years experience in his primary profession.
— Thus the most common category of arbitrator is a Quantity Surveyor aged 60 to 65.

Interestingly the survey also revealed that only 46% of arbitrators were institutional appointments—thus 54% were mutually agreed. However, this would also catch those arbitrators named in the contract by the party putting out the tender, and who are therefore tacitly agreed by the other party. As discussed, this practice of pre-naming should decrease as confidence in the quality of institutional appointments rises, as will the practice of parties agreeing a name as and when a dispute arises. This last alternative should of course be the safest selection process of all.

In the past the mutual agreement of an arbitrator when a dispute arose tended to be just another tactical game to be played between solicitors, with neither party minded to agree anything and usually trying to run the other to the wire on costs. Typically one side would submit three names, after enquiring as to their availability, but this would be regarded by most of those so approached as the "kiss of death" as inevitably the other side would reject all three, and submit their own list of three different names. This would then be rejected, almost as a matter of form, and after two further exchanges if a name was agreed it was usually a third choice appointment—who happened to be available. One interesting variant of this game was that each party submitted six names simultaneously, and the Claimant had first pick of any common names. Another variant was to get a list from one of the institutions, put them in random order then each side in turn had the right to veto the name at the top of the list. However, now that a new culture of good conduct is required amongst the parties and their legal representatives involved in a dispute, agreeing a well known arbitrator should not be the problem that it used to be!

In this context, and by way of a closing comment in this section, certain Institutions are now operating a compulsory retirement policy. Some say this is ageism and therefore contrary to public policy. Others say it is necessary to make way for younger men to gain the necessary experience. However, what it does mean is that there is an available pool of semi-retired 65 + arbitrators, who have proved themselves over many years and have seen all the wrinkles. So long as they have kept up with their CPD requirements and still have all their marbles about them, then why not dip into that pool by mutual agreement? It is still far safer than a Presidential appointment.

CHAPTER 11

THE WOOLF REPORT AND THE CIVIL PROCEDURE RULES

11.1 BASIC PRINCIPLES

In April 1999 the most radical overhaul of the English civil procedure system for hundreds of years became operative, all as a result of a mould-breaking report by Lord Woolf, *Access to Justice*, published in 1996. This then led to the publication of draft Civil Procedure Rules, and extensive discussions, both inside and outside the legal profession, as to how the new CPR would work in practice.

Indeed it was noticeable how, in the last few years before the Woolf Report, leading figures in the judiciary made themselves available at social functions and went out of their way to show themselves as ordinary people. Well do I remember a very personal finger-wagging lecture, delivered from all of two feet away, by Helena Kennedy QC, now a Baroness, on the terrace of the House of Commons when I wound her up with a question on sexual discrimination! Equally I remember somehow, after some excellent Bordeaux at a solicitors' evening bash, discussing the sinking of the bulk carrier the *Derbyshire* in the South China Seas—a subject of which I know nothing—with a lovely old gentleman. Only in the morning was I told I had been giving free advice to the senior Admiralty judge! Sadly I also remember, after a seminar and over a cup of tea, discussing with the late and well respected judge, John Newey QC, why he personally disregarded any small print on the back of contractors' quotations!

So whereas "*Liberté, Égalité, Fraternité*" sounded the French Revolution in 1789, so in 1999 "Equality, Economy, Proportionality" heralded the Woolf Reforms, made flesh in the new Civil Procedure Rules (CPR). These three key elements of "The overriding objective" of the new CPR are set out at Part 1.1:

> "(1) These Rules are a new procedural code with the overriding objective of enabling the court to deal with cases justly.
>
> (2) Dealing with a case justly includes, so far as practicable:
> a. ensuring the parties are on an equal footing;
> b. saving expense;
> c. dealing with the case in ways which are proportionate—

  i. to the amount of money involved;
  ii. to the importance of the case;
  iii. to the complexity of the issues; and
  iv. to the financial position of each party;
 d. ensuring that it is dealt with expeditiously and fairly; and
 e. allotting to it an appropriate share of the court's resources, while
  taking into account the need to allot resources to other cases."

The new CPR now govern the whole civil court system right down to your local District Court, and are indirectly a fundamental criticism of the old system.

The new CPR are specifically designed to:

— Make justice more affordable—the "level playing field" objective, overhauling the flawed and discredited Legal Aid system.
— Make justice more efficient—cutting out the "games" played by solicitors at both parties' expense and so saving excessive and unnecessary costs.
— Make justice relevant to the commercial world—limiting the level of recoverable costs to the actual value in dispute, and allowing Claimants, not just Defendants, to make settlement offers.

Then at CPR Part 1.3 the "Duties of the Parties" are unequivocally set out, sounding the cultural theme running throughout the Woolf reforms: "The parties are required to help the court to further the overriding objective."

The above is a brief synopsis of the new thinking, but there are many other fresh initiatives. However, first it is necessary to get to know "The New Legal Dictionary":

Old term	*New term*
Plaintiff (Litigation)	Claimant
Claimant (Arbitration)	Claimant
Defendant (Litigation)	Defendant
Respondent (Arbitration)	Respondent
Writ or Summons	Claim Form
Defence	Defence
Interlocutory Summons	Application Notice
Pleadings	Statement of Case
Discovery	Disclosure
Further and Better Particulars & Interrogatories	Further Information
Leave	Permission
Taxation of Costs	Assessment

There are also some wholly new terms, which are briefly explained in the course of this chapter:

Pre-Action Protocols
Particulars of Claim
Listing Questionnaire
Allocation Questionnaire
Case Management Conference
Track Allocation
Statements of Truth
Interim Applications
Summary Assessment
"Part 36" Offers and Payments

Now applicable to the whole of the English legal system, the new procedures owe a large measure of thanks to the old Official Referees, OR's Court, now the Technology and Construction Court, TCC. Over the years the judges in the old OR's Court had become increasingly frustrated at the public criticism of the wasted costs associated with uncertain trial dates, tactical posturing by legal representatives, and in particular the lack of objectivity displayed by many Expert Witnesses, so they resolved to tackle these issues by introducing pro-active case management on a trial basis.

Lord Woolf was then appointed to develop the best of the radical ideas and see if they could be adapted for a wider application in commercial litigation. So the new CPRs came into being via the Lord Chancellor's Office—and everyone connected with the civil law from judges downwards had to be hurriedly retrained! Nice work if you were one of the very few training companies qualified to undertake such a task.

Inevitably there will be a learning curve until the system is bedded down, and to help that process various Court Pre-Action Protocols, applicable to specific specialist areas of litigation, e.g. Medical Negligence, are in the course of being developed, tested and issued.

The construction industry is no exception and the TCC have now issued the following documentation, picking up where the Civil Procedure Rules (CPRs) leave off, and dealing with specific problem areas:

— A TCC Practice Direction—supplementing CPR Part 49—see Appendix G.
— A TCC Case Management Conference Directions Form—see Appendix G.
— The ORSA Expert Witness Protocol—see Appendix H.

The essential requirement of Pre-Action Protocols is that the solicitor acting for the Claimant fully sets out his client's grievances to his opposing number so that there can be every opportunity for the two parties to reconcile their differences before commencing litigation, including exploring the options offered by various forms of Alternative Dispute Resolution (ADR). If, when the case comes to court, it is apparent to the judge that one party has not made a genuine effort to comply with both the letter and the spirit of the Pre-Action Protocol then the judge is empowered to make an adverse costs award on the application of the other party.

Thus Pre-Action Protocols give the new message: it is no longer the parties and their respective solicitors but the courts who will now dictate the procedure and the required pace of litigation, once action is commenced. Assuming one has gone through this first hoop, and served a Claim Form, setting out one's Statement of Case, then the first decision required by the court is the appropriate Track Allocation. As such three alternative "Tracks" have been defined:

1. Small Claims Track—Part 27: Value of dispute up to £5,000.
2. Fast Track—Part 28: Value of dispute £5,000 to £15,000.
3. Multi-Track—Part 29: Value of dispute over £15,000, or non-monetary claims, or matters likely to require more than one day in court.

These indicative value limits may yet be revised, but it is safe to say it will only be the Multi-Track that will apply to construction litigation, except some domestic disputes.

Hopefully, over the remainder of this Chapter the principle changes involved in the new CPR will be covered, but as the Americans say "It's a whole new ball game", and so far very few of us have had the experience of actually having to play by the new rules.

11.2 STATEMENTS OF CASE

Pleadings—now known as Statements of Case—had under the old system become little more than tactical opening shots. Often they were generally framed by the Plaintiff, pending the detailed repleading of his case after Discovery. Opening Pleadings therefore almost inevitably met with little better than a blanket denial from the Defendant. Sometimes Pleadings prompted more serious settlement discussions, but the determined "non-payer" in the construction industry usually called them for the bluff that they often were—particularly where the Defendant was a larger and more financially stable company than the Plaintiff.

All that has now changed, and under CPR Part 7 the Claimant is required to:

— Have complied with the required Pre-Action Protocol.
— After which he may apply to the court for a Claim Form, but must serve this within four months of issue by the court.

Presumably the two actions above can run in parallel, and then, as before, proceedings are formally commenced by service of the Claim Form, formerly the Writ. However "Service" is inadequately defined—first class post is good enough according to the procedures, but this can lead to deliberate abuse by determined non-payers.

This happened to the author in a County Court action, where we were suing a removal company for having conveniently "lost" over £8,000 worth of antique china. No Defence was entered and we were granted Summary Judgment. This was then sent by first class post to the removal company's registered office address—their auditors in London, where the originating notice of Claim had also been sent. Somehow they received the second letter, but not the first, so they applied to have the Summary Judgment set aside. Now the "Green Book" (Lower Courts) suggests judges should give Defendants the benefit of doubt if Service is disputed—so Summary Judgment was overturned and we were ordered to re-serve, losing four months in the process!

Why in this day and age service is not required to be by Recorded Delivery or proven fax transmission only the Lord Chancellor can answer. In our small domestic case, at time of writing, we are now 10 months gone since original service and still have no "Track" allocation. If the matter does go to full trial we will have been battling probably over 15 months to recover monies from a Defendant who may well cease trading at any time. So much for Lord Woolf's supposed reforms at County Court level!

So assuming the Defendant doesn't play games about receiving service, he is entitled to receive, either with the Claim Form, or within 14 days of receipt thereof, the Claimant's Particulars of Claim. Under the CPR provisions the Defendant then has three options, within 14 days of service of the Particulars of Claim:

— To file an Acknowledgement of Service (Part 10).
— To admit liability, and request time to pay (Part 14).
— To file a Defence, i.e. Defendant's Statement of Case, which may be delayed a further 14 days if an Acknowledgement of Service, as above, has first been returned to the court (Part 15).

Another welcome new feature is that both the Claimant's and the Defendant's Statements of Case are required to be accompanied by a Statement of Truth. This is not to be treated lightly, and is a contempt of court, punishable by imprisonment *in extremis*, if it is other than the personal belief as to the truth, signed by the principal representative of each party in an individual capacity—not by instructed solicitors.

The significance of Statement of Truths signed at an early stage by both parties is that it is very difficult, and tactically damaging, if one subsequently has to seek leave of the court to amend either an overstated claim or an embarrassing first defence. Thus there should be a regime of "getting it right first time", which certain contractors and sub-contractors would have had trouble complying with under the old scheme!

A key feature of the new provisions is that cases are dealt with justly, and accordingly the courts now have power to set their own procedures without waiting for one side to make an application. Accordingly if the court perceives that the Statement of Case discloses no reasonable grounds for bringing an action or defending a claim it may on its own initiative strike out an action. Likewise an action may be struck out if it is perceived to be an abuse of process, an obstruction of the proceedings, or in defiance of a court order.

Thus the big difference between the old system and the new CPR is that:

— Litigation should be a genuine last resort, after all other dispute resolution options have been exhausted.
— If a party does commence an action, that party must have a fairly advanced and detailed case to put before the court, and to the other side.
— Once the clock is started, the timetable will be brisk, with the court prepared to deal robustly with non-performing parties.

11.3 CASE MANAGEMENT AND COSTS

As the title of this book implies, the emphasis of the new CPR is case management—by the judges, as opposed to case management by two rival legal teams, who have no incentive to necessarily agree anything. After each party has completed an Allocation Questionnaire the court will then give directions for the management of the case, allocating the case to a Track (e.g. Multi-Track), with an allocated case judge, and setting a timetable culminating in a trial date.

However to assess the complexity and demands of the case the court may well order:

— a Case Management Conference, followed sometime later by
— a Pre-Trial Review.

Typically the Case Management Conference will involve each side in:

— Preparing a synopsis of its case—maybe in no more than 500 words.
— Listing the facts agreed, the matters in dispute and the areas of evidence on which the case will turn.
— Stating the areas of expertise considered relevant and the names of the experts they propose calling.
— Stating what disclosure they consider will be necessary.

The judge may then also require each side to:

— Give an estimate (non-binding) of their likely legal costs, given alternating procedures, including those incurred to date.
— Consider how they may jointly make use of computer technology.

All the above are eminently sensible provisions, aimed at saving wasted costs and focusing the minds of the parties on the key areas of the dispute itself—a far cry from the old "White Book" tactical posturing. Further, a recurring theme of the new CPR is the power of the court to deal with any bad behaviour by adverse costs awards against the offending party, payable as the case proceeds if so ordered.

In complex construction cases involving claims and counterclaims it will sometimes be necessary to hold a second Case Management Conference once the real issues in dispute have been flushed out and narrowed. At this stage all options are still open as to how to resolve the dispute. For instance the judge may be thinking of a Trial of Preliminary Issues, or even a Mini-Trial. Alternatively the judge may not be satisfied that the parties have exhausted other options and may order an adjournment to allow one of the forms of ADR to be pursued.

On the other hand, the Claimant chasing his long outstanding money may take the view that the dispute has run long enough and that according to the dispute resolution provisions in the contract he is entitled to his day/week in court, and a final determination. Why should he be forced to submit to yet another costly, delaying and eventually non-binding process? Quite possibly the Defendant will cease to trade in the meantime—so what about Lord Woolf's "Overriding objective", in particular element (d) "... expeditiously and fairly ..."?

As regards costs at the end of the case, the old principle—the winning party is entitled to his costs—still applies, but in modified form. Firstly, under the second and third elements of the overriding objective, i.e. "Economy", and "Proportionality", the judges are empowered to take a firm line on what may be perceived to be unnecessary case preparation or posturing to effectively delay the trial. Thus one side may "win" the case, but if their conduct has been devious or dilatory they can expect to have a significant proportion of their costs disallowed.

The same applies if the winning party has engaged a top-heavy legal team in relation to the value in dispute, although of course they are perfectly entitled to spend whatever the client will sanction. This imbalance of representation is perhaps one of the more difficult areas, particularly where a Claimant is impoverished because of his alleged non-payment by the Defendant.

Such a situation arose in the Commercial Court in *Mars UK Ltd* v. *Teknowledge Ltd* (1999). Contract negotiations had been protracted and inconclusive, following which Mars lost patience and brought an action for infringement of copyright and breach of confidence against the much smaller company. Mars succeeded with their first claim but the judge took a dim view of the breach of confidence issue, and Mars' bully-boy tactics generally. Accordingly he made an interim costs award pending detailed assessment, reducing Mars' winning costs from £200,000 to £80,000.

Also relevant to any costs award will be to what extent both parties genuinely tried to settle matters before trial, or whether one party was willing, but the other party was not.

As referred to above, there is a new provision, operative since 1 March 1999 for "costs in any event", to be ordered to be paid, not at the end of the trial as previously, but within 14 days of the award, or by a stated date. This new power for the judges is intended to impose good behaviour, before and during proceedings, and to put an end to the old tactics of interlocutory applications. Now if Counsel for one side is running a poor point, as a tactical each way bet, he runs the risk of having to ask his client to put him in funds when he comes second. Known as "Summary Assessment" this could then result in a claim or a defence being struck out, if the costs as ordered are not paid into court in due time.

The major concern, however, is how the courts will interpret "Proportionality" and whether it will be applied consistently. Given that any case of whatever value can be complex in terms of both legal principle and proof, a certain level of costs is inevitable if justice is not only to be done, but to be seen to be done. Proportionality will apply to the majority of cases, particularly those in the TCC, as only in respect of Small Claims and Fast Track cases can the court apply fixed costs for various stages of the proceedings.

One of the suggested effects of the requirement for Proportionality is a possible relaxation of the level of proof required in respect of causation and proof of attributable loss in disruption claims. Often the Defendant will in effect ask the Claimant to prove the impossible, and at disproportionate cost. Now it is suggested the test will be balance of probability, subject to proper records.

Another far-reaching new provision is the power given to the court to call for forward estimate of costs from both parties at any stage in the proceedings, or to call for a statement of costs incurred to date. The parties can also be asked how much they would seek to recover should they be successful.

Hopefully some guidelines will be published in due course, but if both sides comply with the spirit of case management it should be possible for evidence parameters to be agreed at the Case Management Conference, with the judge giving a strong indication as to how he will apply the requirement for Proportionality.

Finally in this Section, readers are referred to Appendix I for a flow chart setting out how a typical TCC Multi-Track action might run.

11.4 ALTERNATIVE FORMS OF DISPUTE RESOLUTION

Alternative Dispute Resolution (ADR) comes in several different guises, the current variants being:

— Formal ADR
— Mediation
— Conciliation
— Expert Determination
— Adjudication
— Early Neutral Evaluation.

What they all have in common is that they are:

— non-contractual—they are consensual and only binding if the parties so agree;
— cheaper than arbitration or litigation;
— approved by the courts as part of the new CPR process;
— but only work if both parties are minded to let them work.

Dealing first with formal ADR, the Centre for Dispute Resolution (CEDR) is the well established body, sponsored by the Confederation of British Industry, who run training courses for mediators and who retain a list of approved mediators. The RICS, RIBA and CIArb also offer ADR services as do the British Academy of Experts.

Where formal ADR differs from arbitration and litigation is that:

— ADR can be agreed between the parties before solicitors get heavily and expensively involved.
— Commercial reality can take precedence over law.
— The parties directly control the timetable and procedure.
— Parties can agree a "Key issues only" agenda to save costs.
— All meetings and discussions are totally confidential.

— The personal interaction of the ADR process should not prejudice on-going trading relationships.

Much however will depend upon the personality of the appointed mediator, in particular whether he can build a basis of trust with both sides and then find the middle ground, acceptable to each. Part of his armoury is of course getting both sides to consider the commercial reality of *not* settling, but this aspect should not be overplayed at the expense of actually finding a solution which can be seen as a qualified "win-win" by both parties.

The basic procedure in a formal ADR is as follows:

— Each party produces to the mediator and to the other side an "Executive Summary" of its case.
— On the day of the mediation each party presents its case in the presence of the other.
— The mediation then goes into "caucus" sessions where in turn each party talks openly and confidentially to the mediator.
— The mediator then conducts "shuttle negotiations" between the parties—revealing only authorised confidences until hopefully a resolution is achieved.

In practice a formal ADR may result in a considerable narrowing but not an actual closure of the dispute. In this event a "moratorium period" is sometimes recommended by the mediator for both parties to reflect before commencing arbitration or litigation, and usually the parties get on the telephone to one another in that period and do a deal.

ADR can be used tactically in parallel with arbitration or litigation, at least in theory, but the critics of ADR will rightly point out that this could spoil one's chances by showing one's full hand too soon, if at the end of the ADR the Defendant won't settle and simply walks away. If this happens costs, and perhaps more importantly time, may have been wasted, which the Claimant will have difficulty explaining to his bank manager, pressing him on cash flow.

It is dangerous to generalise, but ADR is probably more applicable where the two parties have expectations of repeat contracts, but simply can't agree on the existing dispute. Both know they need to settle without losing face, so the intervention of a sensible third party often unlocks the impasse.

However, in a one-off contract dispute where "Goliath" is standing "David" out of his money Goliath's only actual need to settle is commercial nuisance value, i.e. the time and the individuals being diverted from new and profitable work. In this situation David would be far better advised to go for statutory adjudication under the HGCR Act 1996. If he should lose, or not get all he thinks he should have done, he can always have a second bite of the cherry, if he can afford to do so, through arbitration or litigation.

The trend will inevitably be a decline in ADR and a greater use of adjudication, particularly in disputed Final Account situations. When the 28-day adjudication rule was promulgated everyone was thinking in terms of interim payment disputes. It will therefore be interesting to see if on the promised review an exception will be made in respect of Final Account disputes, which properly might require more than 28 or 42 days for an adjudicator to sort out.

Mediation and Conciliation are really synonymous with ADR, but are usually even more informal and private affairs with the mediator or conciliator agreed between the parties, rather than appointed by CEDR. If a distinction is to be drawn between Mediation and Conciliation it is that in the former the mediator can be more pro-active, almost to the point of gently cross-examining the parties, whereas a conciliator has a relatively passive role more akin to a facilitator.

Expert Determination on the other hand is a more formal process, often with the parties agreeing to be bound by the decision and where the expert is usually appointed by one of the construction industry institutions. To put the role of the Expert Determiner in context, it is probably between an arbitrator and an adjudicator.

As for adjudication there is more than sufficient coverage elsewhere in this book so there is no need for repetition here.

That leaves Early Neutral Evaluation—ENE, or maybe Ears, Nose and Eyes might be more appropriate. The latter in fact sums up this approach in that it is in fact a "shadow" trial. Rather like tasting the wine, one is putting skeletal arguments to a judge on a "What if?" basis. If he likes the arguments, fine—but if he finds them hard to swallow he can spit them out, in polite form of course.

This alternative form of ADR was pioneered in the Commercial Court and then tried in the old OR's. The beauty of the above process is that:

— It is in court, which tends to focus minds rather more than other more mundane settings.
— Being a fairly short process the Managing Directors and other senior management of both parties should be able to spare the time to attend, and get the full flavour of what might happen at full trial first hand.
— All statements and disclosures are on a strict "Without prejudice" basis.
— Each party is to pay their own costs of the ENE.

Typically an ENE in the TCC might go as follows:

— Both parties submit Statements of Case—limited to 12 sides of A4-sized paper a week before "trial".
— On the day of the "trial" the senior executives of each party are in attendance.
— Each side is then allowed 30 minutes to open their case and 10 minutes to reply.
— There is then a slot of one hour for the judge to explore the issues as he sees fit, with the parties allowed to put questions to one another, but only through the judge.
— The court then adjourns whilst the judge considers a notional judgment.
— Notional judgment is then read out, with the judge explaining his line of reasoning.

ENE is still a fairly new initiative, but so far it has had the desired effects, most actions settling (if not immediately), based on the indicative views of the judge, but it does seem to get both parties minded to settle a few weeks later if they can and before real fees start to be incurred.

Obviously in a real case much will depend on the quality of evidence, how witnesses perform, and above all the value in issue, but nevertheless a short sharp dress rehearsal complete with the principal boy and girl might just stop the real pantomine.

Where ADR is a required step in the dispute resolution procedure written into the contract, a dispute can arise on whether the prescribed procedure has been complied with—the Claimant chasing money being anxious to press on to a final and enforceable determination. Just such a situation arose on the Channel Tunnel project, the Claimants contending that the prescribed ADR process had broken down and/or was taking too long, so they sought to commence arbitration.

In *The Channel Tunnel Group Ltd* v. *Balfour Beatty Construction Ltd* (1993) the House of Lords held that the courts have an inherent jurisdiction to refuse to hear proceedings brought in breach of an agreed dispute resolution procedure, or as the leading judgment put it: "... those who make agreements for the resolution of disputes must show good reasons for departing from them ...". It was "quite beside the point" that the party seeking payment found their "... chosen method too slow to suit their purpose."

As previously stated however, the vast majority of disputes are sub-contractor squabbles where the unlocking of monies arguably due is vital to the continuation of the business. In these circumstances, adjudication is the short form of ADR most applicable, leaving other forms of ADR to the bigger project disputes.

11.5 OFFERS AND SETTLEMENT

Under the old system it was only the Defendant who could make an offer, in a sealed envelope marked "Without Prejudice, Save as to Costs", to settle the action, which would give costs protection from that point in the action if the Claimant declined the offer. In litigation involving monetary claims Defendants' offers took the form of payments in, as indeed they still do under the CPR. Similarly, in arbitrations, and non-monetary civil action claims, the Defendant could make a "Caldebank" offer to the Claimant and if it was not accepted this would be submitted to the tribunal in a sealed envelope, for opening when it came to awarding costs of the dispute.

Now some of us who regularly meet at one of the Arbitration Club lunches had previously wondered why this tactic was not available to Plaintiffs and Claimants. So when the new CPR were published it was particularly gratifying to see that just such an option had been introduced at Part 36, provided the case is on a Fast or Multi-Track procedure.

The significance of the Claimant, as opposed to just the Defendant or Respondent, now being allowed to make a settlement offer, at a lower value than claimed, is to put commercial pressure on the Defendant, and at the same time encourage a more realistic attitude from the Claimant, who may well be under cash flow pressure from his bank manager.

In the event of the Defendant not agreeing to pay the proposed settlement figure, and the trial continuing to a result *more than* the Claimant's offer, the court can award both indemnity costs and interest at 10% above Base Rate against the Defendant, without prejudice to finance charges as a head of claim in their own right.

The question now is: will Claimants be expected to make Part 36 Settlement offers in order to assist the process and therefore, if they decline to do so, will that count against them when costs are finally assessed? Not impossible, given the discretion given to judges to pro-actively manage cases, but probably unlikely is the considered view.

From the Defendant's point of view, the position on cost exposure remains much the same as before, except that the new rules provide the following further conditions:

— Any offer made by either party 21 days or more before the trial date must be stated as remaining open for acceptance for 21 days from date of offer.

— If, however, some time after the 21-day time limit one party wishes to accept the offer, then they may only do so if liability for costs to date have been agreed, or the court gives permission.

— If a Defendant wishes to make a Part 36 settlement offer he must also serve a Part 36 Payment Notice and *at the same time pay the offered amount into court*—the thinking being that Defendants will be expected to make such offers, or risk the displeasure of the judge!

Another feature is that offers may even be made before proceedings have been formally commenced in court. No doubt this provision has been introduced in recognition that under the new CPR it is necessary to do much more serious and costly case preparation before serving a Statement of Case—as opposed to a writ followed by notional pleadings under the old system.

Thus a prospective Defendant may make a pre-action offer to settle, which if not accepted will put the Claimant at considerable risk. If the offer is not beaten then the court will inevitably take the view that the court's time could have been saved, and will be severe on the Claimant, even if he goes on to win the litigation.

For such a pre-action offer to be effective the Defendant must, once the action has been formally started, make the payment into court within 14 days of the service of the Claim Form, and the written offer will have needed to set out:

— The offered settlement value, or proposed remedy.
— Whether the offer relates to the whole of the claim, or only to part of the claim.
— Whether it takes into account any counterclaim.
— The current payment situation as understood by the prospective Defendant—it is surprising just how often when disputes break out the two parties have two different versions of how much has actually been paid, VAT and retention usually confusing the factual position, and if so how it has been calculated.

The above conditions for a valid Pre-Action Defendant's settlement offer under CPR Part 36 also can be applied to offers generally, except that the offeror may for his own commercial reasons choose to impose a time limit for acceptance by the other side. Otherwise, where a Part 36 offer, made by either the Claimant or Defendant, is accepted by the other side, then the general rule remains that the other side are entitled to their reasonable costs up to the date of notice of acceptance.

11.6 DISCLOSURE OF DOCUMENTS

It seems to be a rule of construction disputes—at least in the author's experience—that the Claimant starts out with far less documentation than the Defendant. Typically the Claimant will be a sub-contractor going against the main contractor, or an employer bringing a counterclaim against the main contractor, and it stands to reason that if one is "piggy-in-the-middle" one will have much more paperwork. It also stands to reason that "piggy" will have been trying to face both ways most of the time. Inevitably, therefore, the party with the least documentation will usually have most to gain by full disclosure of all paperwork, and vice versa.

The author has often started a case as expert witness for a Claimant with little more than a sense of injustice and a "bad smell". Only on full discovery/disclosure, has the key information been found establishing causation. Without such paper digging, hard won from the other side's files, winning cases would have been lost, and justice would have been denied.

On the other hand the mere fact of allowing full discovery undoubtedly was the single biggest cause of excessive costs, and often what started out as a simply pleaded single or two-issue case, ended up after full discovery, as a multi-issue major litigation, and/or a significant counterclaim—a good example being a case previously referred to where the author was called in to advise whether a client had a defence to a fee claim for circa £50,000 and we ended up running a major counterclaim for professional negligence, winning a £2m settlement from the Quantity Surveyor and his insurer!

So it is with some apprehension, but understanding of the reasoning, that one views the more restrictive rules on Disclosure at Part 31 of the new CPR. There are now three types of Disclosure:

— Standard Disclosure, Part 31.6, as described below.
— Specific Disclosure, Part 31.12, i.e. as requested by document or class of document by each side, of the other side.
— Third Party Disclosure, Part 31.16, a potentially case breaking provision.

Quite rightly the onus is now on each party to be more focused on what they believe the other side holds, and why it is relevant to the issues in dispute. No longer can either party simply go on an undisclosed "fishing trip", simply in the hope of turning up some information which then gives that party a stick with which to beat the other side.

However, the new rules on Disclosure do give cause for concern as to how they will be complied with by a "guilty" party in practice. Assuming Standard Disclosure has been ordered, each party will be required to list:

- The documents on which they wish to rely.
- The documents which adversely affect their case or support the other party's case.
- The documents which they are required to disclose by a relevant practice direction.

It is in respect of the last two that there will be a natural temptation to be less than enthusiastic—and which could possibly be challenged when European law is enforced in the UK. Recently, a motorist caught by a speed camera refused to disclose who might have been driving his car. When prosecuted for obstructing justice he invoked some human rights provision, which allows one to remain silent when to do otherwise might incriminate oneself, and got the case thrown out.

No doubt we shall be hearing more of this, both in terms of motoring law, but also as regards where the line is to be drawn when it comes to Disclosure. How the European Human Rights law—due to take precedence over all national laws as from October 2000—will sit with the English legal system will probably be the next "big issue" in the construction legal columns, once adjudication enforcement decisions have exhausted themselves.

However, as regards the practicalities of Standard Disclosure, a party is required to make a reasonable search in respect of these two discretionary categories of documents, and what is deemed to be a reasonable search is to be determined by:

- The number of documents involved.
- The nature and complexity of the proceedings.
- The ease and expense of retrieval of any particular document.
- The significance of any document which is likely to be found during the search.

There is then another catch: the duty to disclose is not limited to documents within each party's control, but is extended to those documents which have been in their control, but no longer are. This provision could well create all sorts of mischief, and what the courts will do when potentially key information is proven to have been conveniently lost remains to be seen.

To complete the Disclosure process each party must produce a statement:

- Listing those documents on which he claims privilege.
- Setting out the extent of the search that has been made to find the documents that must be disclosed.
- Identifying any category of document for which he has not searched and the grounds on which it is claimed it would be unreasonable to carry out an extensive search.

— Identifying any document which was once in his power but is no longer, explaining what has happened to it.

— Certifying that the disclosing party understands the duty to disclose documents.

— Certifying that, to the best of his knowledge, the disclosing party has carried out that duty.

Further, the responsibility for honest Disclosure is now placed on the party—the signatory to the Disclosure statement declaring his status—not as before by the party's solicitor. No doubt this is to link the power of the court as regards wasted costs to the conduct of any transgressor, albeit the solicitor will continue to play a key role.

Another new initiative in the CPR (Part 31.16) is the provision that either party may apply to the court to be granted specific pre-action disclosure if it can be reasonably shown that to do so will save substantial time and costs, or of course that it may lead to an early settlement.

Already this latter provision has been put to the test in *Burrell's Wharf Freeholds Ltd* v. *Galliard Homes Ltd* (1999). This was a massive building defects case, principally lack of fire compartmentation and fire alarms in a large top-quality development in London Docklands, and some 400 flats were to varying degrees unlettable or unsaleable until the full extent of non-compliance issues had been established and rectified.

Key to the whole issue was to what extent the flats had been inspected and signed off by the Local Authority Building Control. The Claimants therefore applied to the court for pre-action disclosure. The Defendant naturally took the line that if and when there was any litigation such information would be disclosed in the normal way. The judge was unimpressed by the arguments put up by the prospective Defendant, and could see the force of the Claimant's application—presumably to decide whether or not to also issue proceedings against the Local Authority in the same action.

So will the new CPR achieve their objective of limiting costs, yet at the same time not denying justice by allowing a "guilty" party to be "economical with the truth" in the Discovery process? In the author's experience the CPR will not in themselves save costs. What is needed is more effective document handling and more intelligent inspection.

In the past too often one would get to the conference stage with Counsel and the trial bundles would be assembled in neatly labelled files on Counsel's carousel. The only problem was that the files were no more than photocopies of all sources of files; consequently much of the correspondence and other documentation repeated itself up to six times over. Not only was this very wasteful of paper, it was particularly wasteful of expensive time, and very frustrating to all concerned. Surely it has to make sense for a master bundle to be prepared from the earliest stage of the case, and if Information Technology can be used, e.g. scanning and pagination, there is no reason why both parties should not agree to co-operate and share the bundling costs. Indeed it will be surprising if this is not a feature of "best practice" in the TCC in future years, given the increasing power of laptop computers.

The other area where greater efficiency could be achieved is in respect of inspection of one's own as well as the other side's documentation. The current practice of solicitors relying on paralegals—often trainee solicitors between Law School and their first regular job—is usually focused on whether documents might be privileged, with limited instructions as to key words and issues. By all means have a team of such paralegals, but do have your lead Expert or one of his assistants sitting in on the process to answer any technical queries. It is surprising how one stray comment will make the necessary connection, and disclose a key line of enquiry.

When it comes to inspection of the other side's disclosure it is all very well rushing off and inspecting, but the real question is whether there are other files which should also have been disclosed. In practice it is vital that the retained expert knows where the other side is likely to be vulnerable, and where to find that embarrassing information, if not disclosed.

Some solicitors certainly have a very myopic view of "relevancy". On the other hand to allege non-disclosure by the other side can be a double-edged sword. In one case we had given the other side a really hard time over the dripfeed disclosure they had given—then very late on the author visited one of our client's offices on another matter. On the way out a passing comment as to what might be in a particular cupboard revealed some 30 files on the project in question, which no one knew were there!

On another case where the author was brought in to a 10-year-old action concerning a leaking podium slab in a shopping centre it became clear that there was other information not so far disclosed to us. However, my instructing solicitor was reluctant to make an issue of it, confiding in me that we had an embarrassment of our own. Seemingly our client had decided to clear out an old warehouse in his yard, and have a staff bonfire night party. Some 50 + tea chests of documentation from old projects had been forklifted onto the bonfire and doused in petrol; it had not been realised that 20 + tea chests related to the project being litigated. Apparently they burnt beautifully!

So the new provision requiring a party to disclose even those documents he has lost, burnt or otherwise destroyed could well be critical. A good Quantity Surveying expert will know exactly what files he would have needed to run the project, and if they are not on any of the lists, then they must be accounted for.

Even more critical will be the extent to which the new provision at CPR Part 31.16 for Third Party Disclosure is used, such usage requiring permission from the court. Typical application might be when one is acting for a sub-contractor on a loss and expense claim and it is essential to know when the main contractor completed his activities in a preceding trade, e.g. plumbing, lining and levelling of structural steelwork.

In three recent claims the release of the successive steelwork surveys as between main contractor and Structural Engineer, and thus the delayed steelwork release dates, would have embarrassed our opponent and probably have led to early settlement of our claim—whereas under the old rules one had to get well into the litigation process before being able to force this key information out on Discovery.

Thus under the new rules one might make early application to the court for permission, and then to write to one of the consultants, the Employer, or other sub-contractors, seeking specific information which one has reason to believe exists. Alternatively the mere threat of such a third party approach may well persuade one's opponent to give early Disclosure.

A final word of warning: the new rules on Disclosure are far reaching. Typically progress on troublesome projects is minuted in Board Meetings. Whilst any legal advice given by a solicitor would be protected by legal privilege, any discussion of tactics in a Board Meeting will almost certainly be disclosable. Thus a request for disclosure of Board Meeting Minutes is fair game—whether it will be successful is another matter. On the other hand one might advise one's client to avoid this possible attack by means of appointing a sub-committee, attended by the solicitors advising the company, to review all litigations and keep separate Minutes! The Board Meeting Minutes could then be little more than a one-liner.

11.7 THE ROLE OF EXPERTS

Under the old system the position was less than clear as to how expert witnesses could and should be used. Whereas it was clear that once matters got to court the expert had but one duty, i.e. to the court, giving his factual and unbiased opinion on the issues to the judge, this was inherently unrealistic. That it led to criticism of expert witnesses generally was not so much the fault of individuals called to take the oath as of the system itself.

The legal mindset allows a solicitor or barrister to argue a point of law one way one day, but to argue the same point for a different client exactly the other way round on the following day—so why shouldn't an expert be Jekyll when not in court, and then nice Mr Hyde when in front of the judge? The underlying reason is of course that in the UK we run on the adversarial system of law, and inevitably the expert comes to a case as a "hired gun" in the first instance.

The solicitor needs to get into the technical detail and flush out factual strengths and weaknesses, which either support or conflict with the legal lines he is adopting to promote or defend the case. Who better than an experienced professional in the subject matter of the dispute to dig for dirt and hopefully strengthen the case in time for the next report to the client? Alternatively, if it is not a strong case the sooner this can be identified the better, albeit there is a natural reluctance to advise the client that he shouldn't really be risking his money in major fees, but should settle.

Inevitably the solicitor's opening position when instructing an expert is "Of course this matter should never go to trial—it should be capable of settlement" and in the next breath one is usually instructed to prepare an initial report designed to do just that—hit the other side so hard he will have to seek a settlement. So off one goes firing from the hip metaphorically, looking for some easy targets in the project documentation. However, this author, although very happy to accept such an instruction, will adopt a more cautious if no less robust approach: imagine one has been similarly instructed by the other side—i.e. where is the incoming fire likely to be coming from?—then seek to silence it early, or at least meet it head on.

So inevitably there is a culture of "us" and "them", "kill" or "be killed", and when the case doesn't settle it requires an unnatural act of self-conversion, rather like St Paul on the road to Damascus, to suddenly see the light and become the totally objective, unbiased professional man assisting the court, and thereby turning one's back on one's client.

In one case the author had been instructed on behalf of an employer wishing to sue his Structural Engineer for delays resulting from inadequate foundation designs on a residential development in the old Hull docks. The designed piling scheme failed when the rigs encountered the old oak baulks of the original docks, but in the meantime the residential sales market had also collapsed.

As quantum expert my report dealt with the costs of the alternative foundation schemes and the other losses claimed by the employer. At the first case conference Counsel spent over an hour dealing with the employer and the engineering expert before turning to the author and, after thanking me for my report, he posed the question: "Now Mr Hackett, reading between the lines of your report, am I to assume that you would be more comfortable if you were the quantum expert for the other side?" In other words I had supported my client's case as far as I could, but had made it very clear that there were other factors which probably accounted for most of the losses claimed. The case then settled, but I got no thanks from that particular client or instructing solicitor.

All that has now changed. Lord Woolf recognised the artificiality of the expert witness's position under the old system and resolved to change it.

On simple cases, or single-issue cases such as occur in Insurance or Medical Negligence litigation there is no reason why the Single Joint Expert option of CPR Part 35.7 should not be applicable, provided each party is allowed reasonable costs of taking expert advice as part of its case preparation.

However, life is not so simple in a messy construction industry litigation. Almost inevitably there are allegations and counter-allegations, and several different issues ranging from legal points, practice and procedure, money, time, quality, and/or building defects. As such, each side may wish to employ a team of experts—and in reality the principal use of such experts is to assist the solicitor and Counsel. Both during case preparation and at trial, the legal team need to understand the technical issues, and then direct where such issues are leading, focusing on the strengths and weaknesses of their case.

Single Joint Experts are therefore unlikely to be imposed on the parties in construction cases of significant value, but there are new rules at CPR Part 35 to control costs:

— The permission of the court is required before a party may appoint an expert. In practice this will often be a formal second-stage instruction given by the solicitor to the professional already instructed to assist with case preparation.

— The expert's report must be addressed specifically to the court, and not to those instructing him.

— The court may, as part of the consent procedure, decide on the number of experts to be allowed on each side and set a limit on recoverable costs for those experts.

— If a party fails to exchange an expert's report then it is most unlikely to be allowed to do so later, and will not be allowed to rely on that report.

There are then further provisions clarifying how an expert's report may be used or challenged, as well as some unanswered questions:

— If a party (after presumably naming an expert in the Listing Questionnaire and obtaining the court's permission to call him) fails to disclose his report it may not call him—but can the other side call him or force disclosure of what may well be an unfavourable report?

— A party may put written questions to the expert appointed by the other side on matters arising from his report, provided such questions are:

(a) put once only;

(b) are put within 28 days of disclosure of the report;

(c) are for clarification purposes only.

— The expert's answers (presumably in writing) are then deemed to be incorporated in the report.

— Should the expert decline to answer a question, the court may order that:

(a) the expert's evidence is not to be relied upon;

(b) the costs claimed in respect of that expert are not to be recovered from any other party, whatever the result of the action.

The above are draconian powers and of course there is a world of difference between refusing to answer and deflecting the question. Whether or not the court will allow supplementary questions or whether the judges will themselves press for further clarification remains to be seen. Will they also disallow some questions? Only time will tell.

11.8 CONTENTS AND FORM OF EXPERTS' REPORTS

Firstly an expert's report must comply with any relevant practice direction, e.g. the TCC Protocol, covering all matters required to be set out. To comply with CPR Part 35 an expert's report *must* then meet four basic requirements:

— State the substance of all instructions, written or oral, given by the client or by the instructing solicitor.

— State that the expert understands his duty to the court.

— State that the expert believes he has complied with that duty.

— Be accompanied by a signed Statement of Truth: "I believe that the facts I have stated in this report are true and that the opinions I have expressed are correct"; or a fuller version as recommended by the Expert Witness Institute, and as set out at Appendix J.

This last requirement draws attention to the necessity of the expert making it clear for the benefit of the judge as to when he is setting out a fact—which if not challenged by the other side can then be relied upon by the judge—as opposed to other statements which are opinions or conclusions. Certainly it is for the other side to take issue with such opinions and conclusions as they see fit, but it is for the judge to assess their validity in the context of the case and give them credibility accordingly.

It is often the case that an expert's instructions are at best unclear and at worst devious. The new requirement to disclose all instructions should therefore lead to better practice and certainty all round—and is to be welcomed. However, to guard against "hidden agendas" the courts are now empowered to allow cross-examination of the expert on the stated details of his instructions where there is reason to believe they might be incomplete or inaccurate.

In addition to stating his relevant professional qualifications, an expert's report and subsequent conduct should follow the established principles set out in *The Ikarian Reefer* (1993). The seven basic principles are that:

— Expert evidence must be independent and uninfluenced by the exigencies of litigation.
— The report must be unbiased and objective and the witness should not assume the role of advocate.
— The witness should state the facts or assumptions upon which his opinion is based and should not omit material facts which might detract from his opinion.
— The witness should make clear whether a particular matter falls outside his expertise.
— If his opinion is not properly researched due to insufficient data, he must state that his opinion is provisional.
— If he changes his opinion after exchange of reports, this must be communicated to the other side without delay.
— Where the plans or other documents are referred to in expert evidence they must be supplied to the other party with the report.

In addition to the above, the CPR have introduced another recommendation for the completeness of an expert's report: where the expert gives an opinion, he should assist the judge by stating a range of opinion, as applicable. This last requirement puts the onus on experts to demonstrate that they still practise in their main calling, and if they can support the discussion of the possible "At best" and "At worst" scenarios by reference to any current published material this will lend credibility to the report. It is then for the judge to decide where, in the scale of things, justice lies.

Already we have seen expert witnesses in trouble under the new CPR provisions—the first case to hit the headlines being dealt with by Lord Woolf himself in the Commercial Court. In *Beachley Properties Ltd* v. *Edgar* (1999) the Plaintiff sought to serve witness statements very late, which if allowed would have prejudiced the trial date. In disallowing late service, using the then existing procedures, Lord Woolf gave notice for the future, saying that time limits were not targets, but requirements of the court, to be broken at the litigant's own risk.

Then in another case, *The Mortgage Corporation* v. *Sandoes* (1999), Lord Woolf again disallowed late service of a witness statement, expressly stating that under the new procedures the courts should be very strict on time limits, albeit each case had to be examined on its merits, as there might be extenuating circumstances and justice might be denied.

Then in July 1999 came a landmark case flagging up the death of the "hired gun" type of expert witness. Seemingly an all too typical Final Account dispute had broken out as between builder and employer. The latter then employed a Building Surveyor expert who produced a counterclaim for alleged defects valued at £127,000 and the Architect was joined in the action.

The court, acting under the old rules, ordered experts to meet etc, but when the Building Surveyor failed to comply the judge in the County Court switched to the new CPR and ordered the Defendant to comply. When the Defendant's Building Surveyor expert put in a very adversarial report, failing to comply with the new requirements for experts' reports, he was not allowed to give evidence and his client's case collapsed.

So *Edwin Stevens* v. *R.J. Gullis & David Pile* (1999) came to the High Court and earned the stinging rebuke of Lord Woolf, who said the errant Building Surveyor had "demonstrated by his conduct that he had no conception of the requirements placed upon an expert". In the meantime the Defendant engaged another expert, who reviewed all alleged defects and found valid complaints worth £10,000 at best—a real life demonstration why the new rules require experts to give ranges of opinion and value.

In *Matthews* v. *Tarmac Bricks and Tiles Ltd* (1999) both of the Defendant's two experts were unable to attend on the date set for trial and the Defendant applied for a deferment, Counsel not being able to offer a valid explanation. The trial date seemingly remained as set and the Court of Appeal supported that decision, taking the opportunity to remind experts that they could no longer rely on trial dates being set to suit their diaries. Strangely, Lord Woolf also added the opinion that he did not believe the trial judge would allow the Defendant's case to be prejudiced if neither of his two experts presented themselves! This must indicate that in future courts will rely in some cases on written reports only.

Then in *Rollinson* v. *Kimberley Clark Ltd* (1999) the Defendant's solicitors only instructed their expert six months before the set trial date, having been informed he was unlikely to be available for a year. Needless to say their adjournment application got short shrift.

In *Barron* v. *Lovell* (1999) the Defendants deliberately delayed serving their expert's report till after the time limit and until the Defendant was in a position to make a settlement offer. Again they came second, the case being ordered to proceed on the basis of Claimant's expert report only. Whilst this may seem unjust, there were apparently only narrow differences of opinion in the opposing experts' reports.

The courts are, in accordance with the new CPR, looking critically at the need for expert witness evidence, and its particular relevance to issues on which the case will turn. In *Pozzolanic Lytag Ltd* v. *Bryan Hobson Associates* (1998) both the Claimants and the Defendants produced various experts' reports on different aspects of the case, going well beyond what the court had authorised on a pulverised fuel ash plant at the memorable address of "Fiddlers Ferry".

Seemingly, various experts strayed outside their areas of specialist knowledge, so the court was very severe in what was allowed by way of expert evidence and which experts' costs were recoverable by the winning party. Final judgment included the following extract:

> "This case provides a good illustration of a problem which is endemic. Modern civil litigation without expert witnesses is becoming something of a rarity. Of course I accept that expert witnesses fulfil a vital role in many cases. I strongly suspect, however, that in many cases, insufficient thought is given by parties (and in particular their legal representatives) first to the question whether an expert is really necessary at all, and secondly to what issues the evidence of the expert should be directed. ..."

Finally in this section a word of warning to solicitors and experts alike. In the case of *Prince Jefri Bolkiah* v. *KPMG* (1997) the High Court reaffirmed the position on client's privilege with the statement that: "It is of overriding importance for proper administration of justice that the client should be able to have complete confidence that what he tells his lawyer will remain secret."

Given the new rules on disclosure of instructions it is therefore important that the expert is not embarrassed by knowledge of confidential information, particularly if it compromises his official instructions or prejudices his objectivity. On the other hand the expert must not be kept in the dark of material facts by his instructing solicitor. Should the expert find himself so embarrassed he may now apply direct to the court under CPR Part 35.14 for directions to assist him in carrying out his function— but he is unlikely to impress his client or instructing solicitor in so doing! Thus the golden rule for experts' instructions is that they should be open and transparent—so setting a working agenda of the issues for trial.

11.9 EXPERTS' MEETINGS

Any genuine attempt to keep a major construction dispute out of court will already have seen meetings of experts—usually discussing quantum and time issues, held on a "Without Prejudice" basis. Assuming these have failed to achieve a settlement, formal Experts' Meetings almost certainly will then be ordered as part of the Case Management procedure.

However, this may be good in theory, but on past experience under the old system it rarely works in practice in respect of complex construction disputes. Sometimes solicitors tried to influence what experts could reveal or commit themselves to, which of course tended to defeat the object of the exercise before it started, and in such instances it was very difficult for experts to go against instructing solicitors.

Usually such formal meetings leading up to the trial were set up on a "Without Prejudice" basis and this could be helpful—particularly so to the expert with a bad case to protect. He could make admissions and attempt to trade information and issues by way of damage limitation, but then if his solicitor or client didn't like it, it had all never happened!

At one such experts' meeting, where the author represented the employer in a subsidence dispute, the builder had obtained an expert from his trade body. His report made various unsupported statements and when these came to be discussed he was not able to support his case, and being an ex-local authority employee virtually admitted he was out of his depth. He made various concessions and an agreed note was made of the meeting, signed by both of us for passing to our respective solicitors. I therefore confidently expected a settlement proposal, but no. The other side's instructing solicitor invoked privilege and claimed his expert had no authority to make such admissions! What a waste of effort on our part.

Hopefully this sort of charade will now be impossible as CPR Part 35.12 now provides for:

— The court having power to instruct opposing experts to meet either before carrying out their analysis of the detailed facts, or, as previously, only after exchange of reports.
— The court directing experts to discuss specific areas of disagreement and proposing a structured agenda for addressing such issues.

The new procedures suggested involve a combination of the following:

— A limited timescale for meetings of experts.
— Experts and solicitors agreeing an agenda in advance.
— Agreement of attendees at the meetings—usually experts only.
— Use of teleconferencing.
— Independent Minute taking.
— Minutes jointly agreed and signed.

The court can, as appropriate, direct that after such discussions between experts a formal joint statement be prepared confirming:

— Those issues on which the experts can agree.
— Those issues on which the experts cannot agree and the basic reasons why they differ.

Assuming the above has happened, at least any progress is on the record, and consequently it will be almost impossible for one party, or their solicitor, to try to retrieve any concessions.

Nevertheless, under CPR Part 35.12 any jointly signed Minute of an experts' meeting is "open, but not binding", unless the parties agree to be bound, so it will be very interesting to see how this will work in practice. Hopefully this is an area where after an initial trial period it will be possible to incorporate proven best practice in a TCC Protocol.

11.10 SINGLE JOINT EXPERTS

When the Woolf Report was first published, and then when the CPR followed, this proposal, namely that the court might see fit to impose just one joint expert on the parties, probably caused the most consternation in the construction litigation fraternity.

How would each side be able to prepare the technical aspects of a claim or defence if they were not to be allowed to employ experts in the necessary skills involved, or, more precisely, would the costs of employing such "shadow experts" be recoverable as costs for the winning party? Would they be chargeable as paralegals? How would the court select a single expert and would the parties have any choice in the matter?

The above were some of the typical questions that this radical proposal provoked, but then reality dawned. The way was led by the Commercial Court who very quickly endorsed the spirit of the CPR, but made it clear that parties would generally be allowed to appoint their own experts and expect to recover the reasonable costs thereof, if successful.

The use of Single Joint Experts in construction cases is therefore likely to be:

— very much the exception rather than the rule;
— seen in lower value cases allotted to the Fast Track procedure;
— by consensus between the parties, probably on specific issues.

This last possibility could well be the way forward, but only after the "shadow experts" have done their forensic investigations.

Personally speaking as an expert witness I would be happy to agree with my opposite number the name of a fellow professional to examine a specific list of issues where we have failed to agree, and for him to make his recommendations to the judge. I would however require just one caveat. I would not be happy if having reached his initial view he did not give each party the opportunity in private to discuss that view jointly with both "shadow experts", before making his submission to the judge.

This suggested procedure is in fact nothing new—it is how Party Wall disputes have generally speaking been kept out of the courts, i.e. by the use of a "Third Surveyor". Originally applicable in London, The Party Wall etc. Act 1996 extended this highly successful concept to the whole of the UK. Certainly it has no doubt worked partly because most Party Wall surveyors in London know one another, apart from being members of the aptly named Pyramus and Thisbe club, but why should it not also work under the auspices of the TCC in a wider context?

Alternatively, provision is now made for the court to appoint an Assessor, but this is presumably intended for technical guidance on particular aspects, e.g. evaluation of disability, rather than as a substitute for the judge's own function of weighing the evidence adduced in a typical construction case.

However, should the judge decide that a Single Joint Expert should deal with a particular issue or the totality of the case, it raises various procedural issues. If the parties cannot agree on a single name then the court may invite the parties to propose names, and then select the Single Joint Expert from that list. Alternatively the court may decide on some other criteria for selection.

Once appointed the Single Joint Expert will need to take instructions from both sides—and of course this may cause problems. The rules provide that each set of instructions is communicated to the other side as well as to the court, and that if this does not set a clear agenda for trial, then the Single Joint Expert may apply to the court for further directions.

Further, CPR Part 35.8 also allows the court to limit the amount to be spent on engaging a Single Joint Expert before his appointment, and unless the court directs otherwise the costs of such an expert are to be split on a jointly and severally liable basis between the parties.

Perhaps the final word on SJEs (as they are referred to) should go to Lord Woolf himself:

> "I do not recommend a uniform solution, such as a court-appointed expert, for all cases. As a general principle, I believe that single experts should be used wherever the cost (or the issue) is concerned with a substantially established area of knowledge or where it is not necessary for the court directly to sample a range of opinions."

As such, it will be surprising if SJEs are seen in Multi-Track construction disputes—but then there is always a danger that some judge will have a bee in his bonnet, and not have actually read what Lord Woolf had to say as quoted above.

CHAPTER 12

THE ACCESS TO JUSTICE ACT 1999

12.1 THE SCOPE OF THE ACT

Up to now this book has focused on only the part of Lord Woolf's Report *Access to Justice* that addressed how procedures in the civil courts might be made more user friendly.

When I was writing this chapter the papers were full of a typical construction industry legal disaster. A lady flat owner, who 12 years ago had property and other assets worth over £500,000, was bankrupted and forced to move with her two young sons no less than 18 times in those 12 years—all because she had a falling out with her builders over a refurbishment project in Gloucester Road, London, originally costed at £130,000.

The supervising Surveyors and their insurers are now seeking leave to appeal to the House of Lords from the Appeal Court decision awarding the lady over £1m in damages and interest. However, the real point of the story is that it was the legal system itself that had failed, if it took 12 years and another £3m in both sides' costs to obtain justice, including legal aid once her original £500,000 had been swallowed up.

The all too typical problems identified in the reports of the above case had in the meantime been well recognised. Following Lord Woolf's Report *Access to Justice*, published in 1996, the government then issued *Access to Justice with Conditional Fees—A Lord Chancellor's Department Consultation Paper* in 1998. The opening paragraphs, titled "The Way Ahead", are particularly relevant and bear repeating:

> "1.1 Justice should be there for all of us, when we need it. It should not be just for the wealthy. But justice always has a cost, in time and money, and we always want to encourage fair settlement of disputes before they go to court, whenever possible. We do not want to create a litigious society, but one in which people respect one another's rights.
>
> 1.2 The present civil justice system falls woefully short of this ideal. It is too complex, takes too long to deal with cases and it is too costly. The number of people entitled to legal aid has gone down. A huge swathe of ordinary people on modest incomes are deterred from starting legal

action by the potential costs of litigation—their own costs, and the risk of ending up paying the costs of the other side ...

1.3 The current system does not encourage lawyers—who are paid the same, win, lose, or draw—to weed out weak cases. This means that too many people undergo the strain of lengthy legal disputes for nothing.

1.4 At the same time the cost of legal aid goes up and up ...."

Among the key proposals were:

— "Promote access to justice for the majority of the population in England and Wales through the wider availability of conditional fee arrangements."

— "Refocus legal aid by removing cases which can be financed in some other way and promote access to justice for the needy by directing the legal aid budget to priority areas."

— "Developing a way of supporting cases which have a significant wider public interest but which might otherwise not be brought."

Underpinning the Lord Chancellor's thinking on conditional fees was the concept of risk assessment and risk sharing as between client and solicitor, but with a vital third dimension, i.e. Litigation Expenses Insurance (LEI): "To provide peace of mind against the possibility of having to pay his opponent's costs, a client can take out insurance ...".

The proposal was that conditional fee arrangements, first allowed by the Courts and Legal Services Act 1990, section 58(3), for claimants in personal injury, insolvency and European law cases, should now be allowed for all non-family civil actions. But if CFAs backed by insurance were now to be the key that unlocked the door to justice for commercial disputes generally there were two problems.

Firstly, given that CFAs had previously not been allowed for commercial disputes, where might individuals or companies find a LEI policy? Secondly, where were they to find solicitors and Counsel prepared to take on such work, which previously had been regarded as poor quality work, best left to small practices in the country?

There then came a consultation period. While the legal world took stock of how these radical proposals might be accommodated they knew that the new Lord Chancellor would have his way sooner or later, with his ex-pupil now installed as Prime Minister, backed by a huge majority in the House of Commons. In due course the Act was drafted and passed into statute law without much comment in the Construction press, where the total focus was still on the HGCR Act 1996 and how adjudication might or might not work.

The Access to Justice Act 1999 therefore sets out to update procedures for obtaining financial assistance to bring or defend an action in either the civil or criminal courts. It then goes on to review the procedures for challenging decisions in the lower courts and allowing cases which have particular points of law touching public policy to go all the way, if applicable, to the House of Lords.

However, it is Part II of the Access to Justice Act 1999—"Other Funding of Legal Services"—with which we are concerned, and in particular with the following sections:

27. Conditional Fee arrangements.
28. Litigation funding arrangements.
29. Recovery of insurance premiums.
30. Recovery of where a body undertakes to meet cost liabilities.
31. Rules as to costs.

In this respect it is important to note that Contingency Fees are still not permitted and that it is only the wider use of CFAs which Lord Woolf advocated, and which, after the Lord Chancellor's discussion paper, became law under the Access to Justice Act 1999.

12.2 CONDITIONAL FEE ARRANGEMENTS

First of all some definitions might be helpful:

— LEI—Legal Expenses Insurance—introduced into the English legal system in 1967, but allowable in French law since 1885 and in German law since 1925, comes in two basic forms:
  (a) a "Pre-Event" litigation costs policy, bought speculatively to guard against the possibility of becoming embroiled in a dispute, either as a Claimant or Defendant;
  (b) an "After-the-Event" litigation costs policy, purchased as and when needed.
— A Contingency Fee is where the legal team agree to undertake the work speculatively, and if successful to be rewarded by a percentage of the damages awarded—common in the USA, but not allowable in the UK.
— A Conditional Fee can come in two basic forms:
  (a) "No Win–No Fee"; or
  (b) a structured fee arrangement—typically where a basic fee is to be charged irrespective of "result", but should the result be achieved, then a pre-agreed "Win Fee" or bonus will be payable. Usually this will take the form of an uplift on the basic fee.

Prior to 1990 the general rule had been that nobody could act on other than a full fee basis if appearing in court—therefore many Claimants (or Plaintiffs as they were known until 1999) simply could not afford the basic cost of engaging lawyers, even if they had strong cases.

The reasoning behind this was that the ancient law of champerty, i.e. the maintenance of a litigation by a third party for personal gain, simply did not allow a professional person with a duty to the court to have any interest in benefiting directly from the outcome of the case, and this was reinforced by the fact that Solicitors' Practice Rules, unlike other Professions' Practice Rules, are governed by statute.

This was the basic position until *Thai Trading* v. *Taylor* (1998) when Mrs Taylor instructed her husband in a dispute with Thai, the arrangement being that no fees would be paid unless the action was successful and costs were recovered from Thai. Thai responded that such a cosy fee arrangement was champertous and therefore objectionable in the public interest.

The case went to the Court of Appeal where the judges found nothing objectionable in Mr and Mrs Taylor's solicitor and client arrangement, so creating a significant departure from the strict interpretation of the law of champerty. The key extract from the judgment was:

> "There is nothing unlawful in a solicitor acting for a party to litigation to agree to forego all or part of his fee if he loses, provided he does not seek to recover more than his ordinary profit costs and disbursements if he wins."

Until July 1998 Solicitors' Practice Rules had forbidden any Contingency or Conditional Fee Arrangements, but following the *Thai Trading* case the rules were amended and Conditional Fee Arrangements are now permitted between solicitors and their clients for all types of litigation. Only expert witnesses are rightly restricted, and must charge normal fees irrespective of outcome.

Conditional Fee Arrangements, or CFAs as they are referred to, are now allowable for all types of civil litigation, except for certain family law matters, and are also now admissible in arbitration proceedings, following the case of *Bevan Ashford* v. *Geoff Yeandle (Contractors) Ltd* (1998). However there are strict rules with which solicitors have to comply in order to seek to recover such Conditional Fees, if successful.

As part of the Lord Chancellor's consultation paper five specific questions had been posed:

— What changes to the law might assist the development of conditional fees?
— Should the success fee and any insurance premium be recoverable against the losing party?
— If the success fee is to be recoverable, when should a party disclose the success fee he has agreed with his lawyer?
— What rights should the party liable to meet the success fee have to question the basis on which it had been agreed?

— How should any disagreement be resolved?

The responses to the five main questions posed by the consultation paper produced some interesting ideas, among them that:

— Insurance should be made compulsory in conditional fee arrangements.
— Conditional fee arrangements should be imposed by law for all cases involving litigation.
— The government should not regulate solicitors' conditional fee agreements, but should allow them to charge as much uplift as they can negotiate.
— Over 75% of respondents were in favour of the success fee being recoverable by the winning party.
— Likewise over two thirds believed that the insurance premium should also be recoverable.
— One respondent even suggested that an insured Claimant was a benefit to the Defendant—on the basis that should the Defendant win, the recovery of his costs was underwritten.
— The success fee, although not calculated as a percentage of damages, should nevertheless be capped at 25% of the damages. This has since been made irrelevant by the provision in the Access to Justice Act that success fees are recoverable as costs in their own right, subject to the discretion of the court.

Naturally there were concerns as to the operational details, particularly over disclosure by the Claimant of cover and the level of the success fee, but the response was very positive that Conditional Fee Arrangements backed by LEI were the way forward.

So the Access to Justice Act 1999 was drafted and enacted, with Part II incorporating the following provisions:

— Section 27(1) amended section 58 of the Courts and Legal Services Act 1990 to allow Conditional Fee Arrangements, subject to certain basic rules:
(a) CFAs must be in writing.
(b) CFAs must not be used for classes of action which are specifically excluded from the general provision that CFAs are applicable to all classes of litigation.
(c) The success fee must be defined.
(d) The success fee must not exceed the maximum uplift prescribed from time to time by the Lord Chancellor.
(e) CFAs and success fees are permitted, not only in litigation, but in all types of dispute resolution procedure.

(f) The success fee is recoverable as costs by the winning party who has proceeded under a CFA.

— Section 28—similarly section 58 of the 1990 Act was amended to define and allow litigation funding arrangements, the main provisions being:

(a) The arrangement between funder and the litigant must be in writing.

(b) Such arrangements must not be used for classes of action excluded by the Lord Chancellor.

— Section 29—where a successful party has previously taken out an insurance policy as against the eventuality of losing and therefore running the risk of an adverse costs award, then premium payments are a recoverable cost.

— Section 30 allows "... a body of a prescribed description ..." to underwrite the potential liabilities of members of that "body", or the liabilities of other persons who are parties to a particular litigation—presumably on the basis of public or commercial interest to the concerned "body".

So the main thrust of the *Access to Justice* Report, i.e. a shift from state-sponsored Legal Aid, with all the attendant problems of qualification and fair distribution of scarce funds, to the private insurance sector, has now been enacted. The big questions are: Can it work? and How will it work, when applied to the construction industry?

12.3 "PRE-EVENT" LITIGATION COSTS INSURANCE

Most people can think of the more obvious insurable risks a contractor or sub-contractor faces in the normal course of his business activities. Should an insured peril occur, then a procedure swings into action and as far as possible the damage or loss is made good with the minimum interruption to the contract, or to the business.

However, probably the two biggest threats to any business are the Inland Revenue and one's own bank. Whereas the former are regulated and one can help oneself by having good accounting systems and records, the latter are effectively unregulated and can all too easily bite off the hand that feeds them, with very little warning.

With the introduction of the right to adjudication by the HGCR Act 1996, finally enacted in May 1998, sub-contractors only have themselves to blame if they do not get paid promptly, always assuming of course that they have reasonably performed their obligations. However, this applies only to non-contentious measured work and all too often a sizeable variation account and/or contractual claim arises for Loss and/or Expense.

All the party receiving such applications each month has to do is to issue a reasonably detailed section 110 Notice disputing "the amount due"—and keep the money. The Claimant then has a stark choice: try to obtain the money quickly by adjudication, at the risk of the adjudicator only awarding the "easy" money, or go for full arbitration or litigation straight away. It follows that if the "easy" money has been recovered, the risk of not winning the subsequent arbitration or litigation is that much higher. Either way it makes a dent in the cash flow.

So all too often an otherwise solvent company, with a strong balance sheet record and impressive margins in preceding years, can suddenly find itself in temporary financial difficulties. A visit to the local bank manager usually results in extended loan facilities, and quite genuinely both parties believe that it is a temporary blip caused by a third party not paying his bills.

It is at this stage that the critical mistake is often made—a softly, softly approach is made at executive level to see if the other party will see reason and pay his bill, but inevitably the answer is "Yes, but only if you can persuade me that the bill is correct." Attempting to prove the "if" can be like a donkey and a carrot—the other party keeps moving the carrot.

So valuable time, often weeks, if not months, is lost. Eventually an adjudication is reluctantly commenced and even if it goes through in the basic 28 days it can be too late—a new directive may have gone out from the bank's Head Office in London (or Edinburgh) as the case might be, requiring local bank managers to call in outstanding loans, especially those which have gone past their temporary facility limit or end date. So in a matter of months a long-standing and otherwise profitable company can be put under, just because of interruption to cash flow.

A prudent contractor or sub-contractor must therefore have a structured approach to potential bad debts, with little room for sentiment—and very much part of that approach is a willingness to litigate or arbitrate when necessary after allowing an initial period of time for commercial settlement. The second rule of successful negotiation is don't blink—if you issue a threat with a deadline, go for it, as the timescale in debt collection is all important.

Thus the prudent contractor or sub-contractor will have considered the bolt-on option to their main insurances of a Pre-Event Litigation Costs policy, either as potential Claimant or Defendant. But all too often the decision is taken that this is one cost which can be saved, as the company never needs to get into the hands of solicitors. Unfortunately, as the contractor caught in the act of practical completion in the wrong jacuzzi (Chapter 5) found out to his cost, one never quite knows when one will need a solicitor, and just how expensive their services can be.

Pre-Event Litigation Costs policies are not therefore as popular as they ought to be. They represent good value, premiums being related to turnover and being set against tax as a business cost. Should a claim arise, either as Claimant or Defendant, the insurer will need to vet the details, via a professional assessor, and if he is satisfied as against the "Reasonable Prospects" clause of the policy, then the insurer will take on the claim, subject to regular review as the case progresses.

12.4 "AFTER-THE-EVENT" LITIGATION COSTS INSURANCE

This is a further option for contractors and sub-contractors who find themselves in a serious contract dispute and who therefore need to engage expensive professional advice to try to recover the monies which they perceive to be rightfully theirs by virtue of their understanding of the terms of the contract. It stands to reason that the other party may well have a diametrically different reading of the contract, or have good reason to withhold the disputed monies by way of set-off or counterclaim.

Either way, "After-the-Event" insurance policies are available for Claimants, but not for Defendants. The only possible exception might be where the Defendant in the main action is also the Claimant in a counterclaim and therefore, in theory at least, able to obtain insurance cover on the basis that the counterclaim issues are distinctly different from the main issues. Even so there can be no certainty that costs can or will be separately accounted for, so in reality it is unlikely that such cover can be obtained.

The usual form of After-the-Event litigation costs insurance cover is that the policy will only respond in the event of the Claimant losing the case. This is because a winning case or an agreed settlement will decide damages, following which costs are awarded, agreed or taxed, and whilst the successful party may not recover all his claimed costs, he will in principle be recompensed for having to bring his case.

Whether the insurance industry will respond to the new Civil Procedure Rules, where judges are allowed greater discretion to split costs, and so let in policy conditions covering adverse costs awards against winning parties, remains to be seen. However, the likelihood must be "No", even where the stated reason for splitting costs was a multi-issue trial and, in boxing terms, the net winner won by five rounds to four with one round tied.

However, the reality of After-the-Event litigation costs insurance is that Claimants, whether individuals or companies, now have a means of affording justice, i.e. seeking to enforce their perceived legal rights under a contract, whereas previously the sheer uncertainty of the financial risks involved, particularly of losing and therefore incurring effectively double costs, was simply too great for personal or company trading reasons.

In the past this "unlevel playing field" scenario favoured the larger company defending a claim from a smaller company, and many were the instances of such larger companies enforcing wholly unfair commercial settlements on such smaller companies or individuals in the certain knowledge that they would never dare sue, or if they did actually issue a writ the sheer threat of an application for Security for Costs would probably force them to withdraw the action.

This has all now changed thanks to Sir Michael Latham and Lord Woolf. What adjudication doesn't catch, the Access to Justice Act 1999 should provide for. Quite specifically Lord Woolf pointed the way to impecunious Claimants purchasing such After-the-Event insurance policies, taken out in conjunction with Conditional Fee Arrangements, as between Claimant and his legal team—premium costs and success fees, subject to certain rules, being allowed as recoverable costs for the winning party.

The insurance industry however is a volume business and having played with After-the-Event insurance schemes prior to the Access to Justice Act 1999, the industry does not perceive it to be a strong business stream, particularly with all the previous hang-ups over the law of champerty and the limitation on the categories of action previously allowed.

Some specialist construction insurers are now being persuaded otherwise and the next year will undoubtedly see new products coming onto the market. However until CFA cases start going through the Commercial Court or the TCC it is unlikely that a range of such After-the-Event insurance products will be readily available on the open market.

The dynamics of CFAs and After-the-Event insurance is that the financial risk is laid off by the Claimant, in return for the premium paid, and then picked up by both insurer and the legal team. On the face of it the Claimant has laid off all risks, but this is not so. He must continue to fully assist the legal team to advance and win the case, whatever it takes in staff resources, or cover will be withdrawn, and if the case should go down, the reimbursement of the other side's costs and his own costs up to the level of cost protection purchased will be scant consolation for not having collected all or part of the damages claimed.

From the legal team's point of view they are in the same boat as the insurer. Whilst they may collect a basic hourly rate based fee each month—typically one third of their normal charge out rate—this in fact represents a considerable loss to them as against normal fee earning work.

On the other hand, if solicitors and Counsel back their initial case prospects judgement, and are proved right, they are duly rewarded by the payment of the balance of normal fees, plus the pre-agreed success fee, making CFA work even more profitable than normal fee earning work.

Thus all three partners in a CFA case, backed by After-the-Event litigation insurance, are incentivised to share the risks and pull together to achieve a successful result for the Claimant—a result that, but for the new procedures now allowed under the Access to Justice Act 1999, simply would not have been within the reach of the typical construction or property industry Claimant. This triangular sharing of risks and reward ensures that the case is kept on the move with no "sleeping" partners, or paperwork relegated to the "too difficult" tray.

Obviously, close attention to policy terms and conditions is essential, particularly the definition of what constitutes a "result" in the event of a settlement, and whether in those circumstances the policy will respond. However, a properly structured and defined After-the-Event litigation costs insurance policy should contain no unpleasant surprises, and should in principle put the insured Claimant in essentially a "Win-Win" situation— either he gets costs paid by the other side, or his costs bill is met by the policy, subject to the level of cover purchased.

Some After-the-Event polices require a substantial single premium for an agreed cover level, but frankly this is unhelpful to the cash-strapped Claimant. The action may settle quickly once the other side realise their exposure, defending against an insured Claimant. Alternatively the action may run its full course, especially if Professional Indemnity insurers are involved for the other side.

So what is required is a structured policy written by underwriters with a maximum level of indemnity, say £1m of litigation costs, but with staged premiums—a reasonably low first-level entry premium and then three or four more premium stages, with increasing premium to cover ratios at each stage. Each further cover level is purchased at the insured's option, as and when the solicitor with care and conduct of the case advises that both sides' cost levels are approaching the next cut-off level. If the insured decides to dispense with further cover that is his commercial decision, but he is good for the level of cover already purchased. Equally, if the Claimant in a big case requires more than the standard policy cover level, special terms should be negotiable.

So how does the insurer and his underwriters decide which cases to take on? In the past, certain winners have been easy meat for insurers whereas any doubtful cases have generally been refused or have attracted onerous premium levels—thus slamming the door in the face of the cash-strapped Claimant.

Now, with adjudication and the new CPR flushing out the strong cases, which would previously have been defended using every tactic allowed by the "White Book", just for the sake of trying to retain the other (smaller) man's money, it will probably only be the larger, more complicated disputes which will reach arbitration and litigation as a tribunal of last resort.

Thus the insurance industry must respond and come to terms with the fact that there is a volume business to be done in insuring Claimants' litigation costs as now positively encouraged by the Access to Justice Act 1999—but the business has to be profitable for the ultimate insurers, i.e. the underwriters at Lloyd's.

Risk assessment and management is therefore the key, and this comes in two main stages:

— At initial proposal.
— Once cover is in place.

As any solicitor will tell you until you have seen the evidence, i.e. the other side's hand after close of pleadings and disclosure, it is very difficult to advise a client that his case is likely to succeed, let alone agree to take the case on at financial risk to oneself. Yet this is precisely what the Lord Chancellor is encouraging solicitors to do by entering into CFAs, backed by Pre-Event or After-the-Event litigation costs insurance!

So how is an After-the-Event policy put in place in relation to construction cases? Firstly, the insurance proposal—usually from a solicitor already involved with a case—is independently reviewed by external assessors appointed by the insurer after payment by the proposer of an appraisal fee. On one particular policy this appraisal fee is then credited back to the proposer against the first premium if cover is subsequently offered.

The legal aspects of the proposer's case are then reviewed by a solicitor, including Counsel's opinion, and the technical aspects are reviewed by a construction professional—usually a Quantity Surveyor specialising in claims, as at the end of the day it is all about financial recovery.

Occasionally cover is refused, the most likely reason being wholly unsatisfactory records and poor quality evidence generally—even if it is an obvious hard luck story. The burden of proof in court will be with the Claimant, so this is likely to be the most critical area in initial case assessment.

The second stage of case appraisal, assuming case prospects are positive, is the question of the level of "result", to be agreed between proposer and insurer. If case prospects are good then the result level may be as high as 75% of claim value. Conversely it might be as low as 25%.

Assuming there is then a formal offer of cover, the proposer then has to make his own commercial decision as to whether to accept the offer of cover, including the result level, and pay the first premium. Costs protection then commences from this point—so the sooner a Claimant proposes, the lower his commercial exposure will be.

However, it is never too late to think of taking cover with an After-the-Event policy. Provided the legal team are prepared to switch to a CFA fee basis, cover can be purchased at any stage in a case, subject to positive appraisal.

So how can case prospects be assessed and all parties' positions safeguarded should that initial assessment prove misleading? Firstly, the initial assessment is based on the initial information only, and it is very much a combination of looking for essentials and then applying one's experience of just how the case might develop—a meeting with the proposer and some fairly robust questioning, as well as file investigation, usually being required. Secondly, the monthly review process, led by the solicitor appointed by the Claimant, is crucial—if the prospects are diminishing the previously agreed result level must be reviewed.

Happily for the legal and technical assessors there is case law to suggest that the giving of *bona fide* early advice on case prospects cannot be negligent, the case in question being the Court of Appeal decision in *Hodgson* v. *Imperial Tobacco Ltd* (1998).

The case then proceeds with the insured and his legal team, other than his expert witnesses, acting on a CFA basis—the solicitor now having a dual responsibility. Firstly, he is responsible for having the normal care and conduct of his client's case, and secondly he must keep the insurer informed on a monthly basis of case progress and any change in case prospects.

Some might see this as a conflict of interest, but in reality his duty to his client, and to his quasi-employer, the insurers, is very similar—to manage the case and achieve the best result given the constraints of the need for early income, cost of litigation and the risk of losing. In this last respect it is important to remember that the solicitor is essentially backing his own judgement by undertaking the work at a considerable loss, as against normal fee earning work, so is incentivised not to throw away his own money in continuing to run a doubtful case rather than seeking insurer's and client's consent to broker a settlement—the triangular risk partnership referred to earlier.

Certain insurers have in the past insisted that cover only be granted on the basis of the insured switching from his usual solicitor and preferred experts (usually already involved in preparing the claim) and employing one of a small panel of solicitors (and their own experts). In practice this leaves the insured badly exposed and at the whim of the insurer, who naturally will stop the action at the first real sign of possible problems, i.e. when the Defendant fully pleads his case or when disclosure reveals areas of weakness. Inevitably the insured then feels he has no control over the case and resents deploying staff time in assisting the case, let alone paying further fees or premiums. That is why it is so important in an After-the-Event litigation costs insurance backed case that all three partners—insured, solicitor and insurer—share the risks via a CFA and jointly manage the case to a conclusion. The preferred approach is therefore for the insurer to approve the proposer's existing team of solicitor and expert—which is not a problem providing they have a trade record in construction litigation.

However, the real benefit of being able to purchase an After-the-Event litigation costs insurance policy is the certainty factor. No longer is the contemplation of going to law to chase a major claim a matter which sends shivers down the Finance Director's spine: the premium costs can be written into the Company's Business Plan, as can the monthly CFA based fees from the legal team, plus experts' fees (not on CFA basis) as and when they are likely to occur. Then, on the "Win-Win" basis discussed above, such costs can be credited back, maybe 18 months later, into the Business Plan.

Better still, the fees are not only reasonably quantifiable by calendar date (thanks to the new CPR), but there will be no need to make a substantial provision for the risk of losing and being ordered to pay the other side's costs as well—albeit some modest provision should be made for the inevitable costs not allowed on assessment, even if the case is won. Alternatively the policy will respond up to the level of cover purchased should the case not succeed.

However, even the servicing of a CFA, paying premium costs as and when payable, plus the legal team's base fees each month can put a financial strain on a company struggling to maintain liquidity, so some After-the-Event providers are now offering loan facilities for the premium payments. Also, in the event of the Defendant making a serious application for Security for Costs, some providers offer to arrange a form of Advance Payment Bond.

As such the only uninsurable risk for a Claimant with LEI is the risk of enforcement, i.e. actually collecting damages and costs as against the Defendant calling in the Receiver. This is obviously a very real risk, especially as the successful legal team will be invoicing for their well earned success fee. In real terms the only safeguard is to do one's homework before starting in order to decide on the financial status of one's opponent. If they are a subsidiary of a larger company this should be sufficient, and probably the best one can hope for in the absence of a Parent Company Guarantee provided as part of the contractual arrangement.

Nevertheless we are seeing an increasing trend in losing Defendants then turning to their bank managers and calling in receivers. This has to be an abuse of the legal system, if they knowingly enter the process on a "heads I win, tails you lose" basis and something that must be urgently examined by Parliament.

The Lord Chancellor's Department discussion paper rightly identified other tactical considerations, e.g. the disclosure by the Claimant of the fact that he is acting with the benefit of litigation costs insurance and/or on a CFA basis. However the Access to Justice Act 1999 made no specific provision for:

— whether and when an insured Claimant should inform the other side of the existence of cover; or
— the amount of premiums involved, or the level of the success fee agreed with his legal team.

In the absence of statutory guidance this will be an area of trial and error before accepted best practice emerges. However, it should be noted that the Act has various clauses which clearly allow for future fine tuning by the Lord Chancellor directly, or through the Rules of Court, to regulate the operation of CFAs and litigation insurance generally.

12.5 THOUGHTS FOR THE FUTURE

Undoubtedly once the wrinkles of adjudication enforcement have been exhausted by the series of "appeal" cases now being referred to the TCC the next big topic in the construction legal press will be the effect of European human rights legislation, and how the Human Rights Act 1999 will work alongside UK law and established legal procedures such as arbitration, when the Act comes into force in October 2000.

On the face of certain details already being circulated this will create big problems of co-ordination with current UK law—and in certain areas direct conflict. Whether this will have the effect of actually undoing existing well established law and case precedents relied on in the construction and property industries remains to be seen.

The Contracts (Rights of Third Parties) Act 1999 and the Late Payment of Commercial Debts (Interest) Act 1998, when fully enforced, will no doubt be fruitful territory for solicitors, and sooner or later there will surely be legislation to clarify liabilities concerning latent defects.

This author would also like to see a tightening of requirements in the area of Professional Indemnity insurance—the present position being an anomaly in that whilst most professional institutions covering the construction industry require their members to carry a minimum level of cover, when it comes to pursuing an Architect, Engineer or other design team professional for alleged negligence and losses there is no certainty that he was actually insured at the time the claim was first made.

As such, one can get into a court action only to find that, for whatever reason at the material time, there was no effective P.I. cover. Worse still, as the case evidence emerges there is apparently nothing to stop a Defendant P.I. insurer stepping out of the action on the basis of material non-disclosure—leaving the Claimant going against a "man of straw", with his assets conveniently redistributed in other people's names. Surely there has to be a system that once service has been acknowledged a Defendant P.I. insurer remains the Defendant, and if he loses he must pursue the errant professional in the event of policy non-disclosure.

Otherwise probably the biggest developments will necessarily be in how the insurance market will respond to the new opportunity presented by the endorsement of CFAs backed by some form of LEI. Both Pre-Event and After-the-Event policies should become a generally accepted form of business protection, and hopefully as underwriters gain experience of a radically enlarged market then we shall see premiums coming down to more affordable levels.

The old Legal Aid system has already been consigned to history, with the Legal Services Commission supposedly applying "funding assessments" on the basis of "Whether a reasonable person able to fund out of his or her own resources [but presumably unable to] would be prepared to pursue it", plus case prospects in the order of 75%. Quite how many applicants obtain litigation funding on the new Legal Aid system remains to be seen.

Lord Woolf in his Report *Access to Justice* reckoned that 80% of the population were "cut off from justice" and that only some 13% of personal accident victims pursued a claim. The first figure is shocking in its own right, but the second figure is simply incomprehensible—particularly when personal injury insurance and litigation costs insurance are now very inexpensive bolt-on options to household insurance policies.

Certainly solicitors who sign up with insurers to handle bulk claims have be clear as to where their duties lie—to their employer, the insurance company, or to their employer's clients, the various insureds making claims. When normal fee earning work is available, the temptation must be to ignore the insurance claims, and the insurer, unless chased by their client, will rarely press for urgent resolution. Even when the files are attended to the chances are that the claim is against another insurer—who has absolutely no incentive to do other than stall the matter. Maybe this, coupled with poor quality legal advice, is why only 13% of personal injury claims actually get to court.

So how can we expect the insurance route to construction claims recovery to perform any more satisfactorily than the personal injury sector has performed to date? There are hopefully good reasons to believe the CFA system backed by LEI will work once the principle is more widely accepted and a better range of such policies come on the market. The main reasons for optimism are, in the author's view:

— Having paid up front premium costs and monthly base fees the Claimant will be looking for an early "result" to repair the damage done to his cash flow, so he will not allow the matter to set a pace of its own.
— Assuming the Claimant has been allowed to appoint his own solicitor to run the case he only has to pick up the telephone to chase progress.
— Even if a panel solicitor has been nominated, the Claimant's contract should be with that solicitor, so again the Claimant should be in control.
— The nature of the business—each claim in the construction industry will be unique, requiring individual attention unlike typical road traffic accident claims.
— The fact that on CFA work the solicitor, until he successfully resolves the case, is acting on a loss-leading basis and solicitors, just like contractors and sub-contractors, have to account for their cash flow to their bank managers—not to mention his other Partners in different sectors of the practice!

However, perhaps the biggest culture change required is in how solicitors and barristers actually manage their businesses. Gone are the days of what the Lord Chancellor refers to as "taxi meter" charging, and both insurers and private clients will soon be looking to place their litigation instructions on various forms of CFA.

Lord Woolf identified the need for flexibility and negotiation of fee arrangements to make litigation a more viable commercial option, strongly encouraging the legal profession to move towards CFAs. The common basis of any CFA must be incentivisation to deliver a winning result and the options might be:

— "No Win–No Fee" agreements.
— Fixed Fees with a "Win bonus"—probably applicable to the smaller value cases.
— A "Hold-back" Contingent Fee—where normal fees are charged up to an agreed stage and then no final fee is paid until the case is decided, with no further fee payable, or a reduced hourly rate payable, if the case is lost.
— Minimum Base Fees with "Win bonus"—typically one-third of usual hourly charge out rates paid monthly, plus 100% normal billing when the case is won.
— "Collared" Fees—a combination of a fixed fee and then a variable fee based on recorded time, but where any excess over the agreed cap is absorbed by the solicitor and any savings below the bottom of the "collar" are shared.

— Sliding scale fixed fee, time related—a variant of a fixed fee where the sooner damages are recovered the larger the fee.

What is certain is that construction industry dispute resolution procedures have been fundamentally reformed, with the emphasis on Claimants and Defendants having the opportunity of sensibly managing and settling their differences without recourse to the courts. If the parties do not take such opportunities they must then expect the judges to seize control of their dispute, and not to suffer fools or non-performing parties gladly, and to be robust with costs awards, payable within 14 days. Likewise all concerned with the court process will have to sharpen up their act, particularly expert witnesses who will risk being barred if they are not focused on the task required.

However, as I seek to close this book on what is essentially still a moving target, two major concerns are being expressed privately, if not yet publicly in the construction legal press:

— The sudden trend for employers under main contracts and main contractors under sub-contracts issuing negative valuations— inevitably in the last two months of a project. This author's view, following comments on "reverse ambushes" in Chapter 9, is that a "Nil" valuation might be permissible, but to seek to take away monies previously paid drives a proverbial coach and horses through the HGCR Act 1996 and the Withholding Notice requirements of section 111, unless there is a very genuine reason for doing so, e.g. discovery of a significant defect.

— The apparent reluctance of judges in the TCC to actually move cases on to the next stage in the Multi-Track procedure. Seemingly the trend is for weekly case management conferences being ordered, almost as if the judges have nothing much else to do. Of course, with the emergence of adjudication in the last six months as a dispute show stopper, backed by the robust approach of the TCC judges themselves, maybe clients are now reluctant to let their cases go to court and are opting for adjudication as perhaps the answer to their prayers—at a fraction of likely litigation costs.

The "honeymoon" period for the effective changeover to the new Civil Procedure Rules is almost over. What is needed is some positive reports as to how the new CPR are working in practice; otherwise the solicitors and others drafting contracts will be deleting the litigation option recently introduced expressly into the standard JCT family of contracts, and the construction arbitrators, far from being an endangered species, will be back in business with a vengeance.

Thus it is strange how the Lord Chancellor's star is beginning to fall, just as the political star of his two former pupils, now living in No. 10 Downing Street as man and wife, is seemingly taking a sharp dive!

APPENDIX A

THE JCT FAMILY OF STANDARD FORMS OF CONTRACT AND ASSOCIATED SUB-CONTRACTS

Main Contract Full Title	Revision Year	Abbreviated Title	Suggested Value Range £ [2]	Sub-contract Forms (see Chapter 2, section 2.1, for full titles)							
				NSC/A 98	NSC/C 98	NAM/T 98	NAM/SC 98	NSC/T (PCC) 98	IN/SC 85	DOM/1 Articles	[1] DOM/1 Conditions
The JCT Standard Form of Building Contract	1998	SFBC 98		#	#					#	#
The JCT Intermediate Form of Contract	1998	IFC 98	Up to 300k			#	#		#		
The JCT Agreement for Minor Building Works	1998	AMBW 98	Up to 90k								
The JCT Standard Form of Management Contract	1998	SFMC 98									
The JCT Standard Form of Contract With Contractors Design	1998	WCD 98									
The JCT Standard Form of Prime Cost Contract	1998	SFPCC 98						#			

Notes

[1] Standard Forms of Sub-Contract published by the Construction Federation for use with JCT Standard Forms of Main Contract
[2] At 1998 Tender Price values

EXTRACT FROM THE ICE FORM OF DEFAULT BOND

(Reproduced with the kind permission of Thomas Telford Publications Ltd)

Date

Parties

SURETY (1)

CONTRACTOR (2)

EMPLOYER (3)

Background

(A) By a contract defined in the Schedule hereto the Contractor has agreed with the Employer to construct and complete the Works.

(B) The Surety has agreed to provide this Bond in favour of the Employer in order to guarantee the performance by the Contractor of his obligations under the Contract.

Surety's obligation

1(1) If the Contractor fails to pay the Excess Sum within 28 days of receipt by the Contractor of a copy of a certificate issued by the Engineer under clause 65(5) of the Contract the Surety hereby guarantees to the Employer that the Surety shall subject to the terms and conditions of this Bond pay the Excess Sum in accordance with Clause 1(3) up to the Bond amount.

(2) It shall be a condition precedent to the payment by the Surety that the Employer serve on the Surety a copy of the certificate issued by the Engineer under clause 65(5) of the Contract as served on the Contractor and certified by the Engineer as being a true copy of such certificate.

(3) Subject to Clause 1(4) payment by the Surety shall be made not later than 14 days after the later of

    (a) the expiry of the 28 day period referred to in Clause 1(1) (save in respect of any payment made by the Contractor within that time) and

    (b) service on the Surety of the copy certificate referred to in Clause 1(2).

(4) If the Surety objects to the contents of or entitlement to issue a certificate under clause 65(5) of the Contract in respect of which the Employer seeks payment from him the Surety shall have the right to refer the matter to adjudication in accordance with the adjudication provisions contained in sub-clauses 66(6) and 66(8) of the Contract as if the Surety were a party to the Contract in place of the Contractor.

(5) Any adjudication under Clause 1(4) shall be commenced by the Surety within 14 days of receipt by the Surety of the documents referred to in Clause 1(2) and the Surety shall have no right to refer the matter to adjudication after that time.

(6) If the content of or entitlement to issue the Certificate under clause 65(5) of the Contract in respect of which payment is sought by the Employer is or has been the subject of an adjudication between the Employer and Contractor under the Contract (in respect of which both parties have made submissions to the adjudicator) the Surety agrees to be bound by the result of such adjudication and shall have no right to refer the matter to adjudication under Clause 1(4).

(7) In the case of an adjudication under Clause 1(4) payment by the Surety shall be made within 7 days of the decision in such adjudication.

Surety's rights

2(1) The Surety shall be entitled to receive copies of any notice given by the Employer under clause 65(1) of the Contract (with any Engineer's certificate referred to) within 7 days of such notice or certificate being served on the Contractor.

(2) The Surety shall be entitled at any time within 7 days of receipt by the Surety of the copy certificate to in Clause 1(2)

    (a) To request the Employer to provide the Surety with such further information and documentation as the Surety may reasonably require to verify the Excess Sum (including information or documentation held by the Engineer) and/or

    (b) to request to inspect the Site and the Works upon reasonable notice (the Employer may require that a representative of the Employer accompanies the Surety during such inspections).

Accounting

3(1) If the Excess Sum is subsequently determined by reason of a subsequent certificate issued by the Engineer under clause 65(5) of the Contract or by adjudication arbitration litigation or agreement between the Surety and the Employer to be less than the amount paid by the Surety the difference (if the Excess Sum has already been paid by the Surety) shall be repaid by the Employer to the Surety with Interest within 14 days (or such other period as the adjudicator arbitrator or Court may direct) after the date of such determination or agreement.

(2) If the Excess Sum is subsequently determined or agreed to be greater than the amount already paid by the Surety any difference (up to the Bond Amount) shall be paid by the Surety to the Employer within 14 days (or such other period as the adjudicator arbitrator or Court may direct) after the date of such determination or agreement.

Interest

4 Subject to the amount payable by the Surety being varied in accordance with Clause 3 above in the event that any amount payable by either the Surety or the Employer under this Bond is not made by the date determined by Clause 1(3) or in accordance with Clause 3 (the Due Date) then the payer shall pay Interest on the sum from the Due Date until the date of payment.

Expiry

5 Save in respect of any failure to pay the Excess Sum in respect of which a claim in writing has been received beforehand from the Employer by the Surety this Bond shall expire on the earlier of the date stated in a certificate of substantial completion issued by the Engineer and the Final Expiry Date.

Forebearance

6 The Surety shall not be discharged or released by any alteration variation or waiver of any of the terms and conditions and provisions of the Contract or in any extent or nature of the Works and no allowance of time by the Employer under or in connection with the Contract or the Works shall in any way release reduce or affect the liability of the Surety under this Bond.

Governing Law

7 This Bond shall be governed and construed in accordance with the laws of the country named in the Schedule ("the Country") and the courts of the Country shall have exclusive jurisdiction.

Assignment

8 This Bond may only be assigned by the Employer with the prior consent of the Surety and the Contractor which consent shall not be unreasonably withheld. In the event of any such assignment the Employer and assignee shall remain jointly and severally liable for any repayment due to the Surety under Clause 3(1). Notice of assignment shall be given to the Surety as soon as practicable.

Author's further comments

1. Please note that this Form of Default Bond is limited to default as defined by Clause 65(1) of the Standard ICE Form of Contract, *and the Contractor has in consequence been expelled from site by the Employer.* The Engineer is then required to certify the residual value of the works, yet to be completed, including damages etc, and it is only this certificate, issued under Clause 65(5) by the Engineer, which can trigger the calling of the Bond by the Employer.

2. The Contractor's rights are of course preserved by the statutory provisions of the Housing Grants Construction and Regeneration Act 1996, as incorporated in the contract. If the same issue has not already been adjudicated the Surety, under the terms of this Bond, has the right to call for an adjudicator, albeit this would be a non-statutory referral.

3. Please also note that the Bond expires on the certification by the Engineer of substantial completion, or a "Final Expiry Date", whichever is the earlier, i.e. this back-stop date has to be written into the further standard provisions covering definitions, which follow the above extract, in the Standard ICE Form of Contract.

FLOW CHART OF THE HGCRA STATUTORY PAYMENT PROVISIONS

HGCRA Compliant Contracts and Section References

HGCRA Non-Compliant Contracts therefore "Scheme" Applies, and Section References

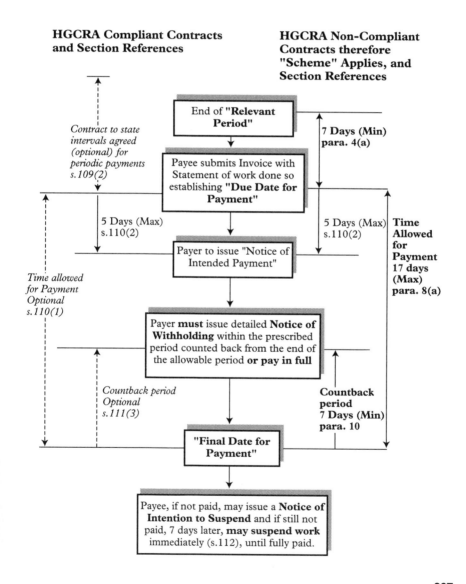

Contract to state intervals agreed (optional) for periodic payments s.109(2)

End of **"Relevant Period"**

7 Days (Min) para. 4(a)

Payee submits Invoice with Statement of work done so establishing **"Due Date for Payment"**

5 Days (Max) s.110(2)

5 Days (Max) s.110(2)

Time Allowed for Payment 17 days (Max) para. 8(a)

Payer to issue "Notice of Intended Payment"

Time allowed for Payment Optional s.110(1)

Payer **must** issue detailed **Notice of Withholding** within the prescribed period counted back from the end of the allowable period **or pay in full**

Countback period Optional s.111(3)

Countback period 7 Days (Min) para. 10

"Final Date for Payment"

Payee, if not paid, may issue a **Notice of Intention to Suspend** and if still not paid, 7 days later, **may suspend work** immediately (s.112), until fully paid.

FLOW CHART OF THE HGCRA STATUTORY ADJUDICATION RULES

RP = Referring Party   **DP = Defendant Party**

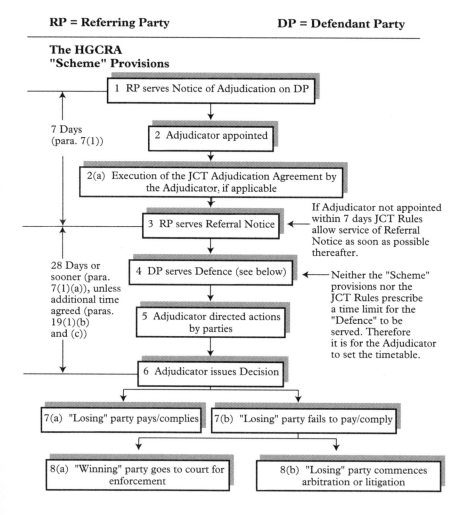

The HGCRA "Scheme" Provisions

1 RP serves Notice of Adjudication on DP

7 Days
(para. 7(1))

2 Adjudicator appointed

2(a) Execution of the JCT Adjudication Agreement by the Adjudicator, if applicable

3 RP serves Referral Notice

If Adjudicator not appointed within 7 days JCT Rules allow service of Referral Notice as soon as possible thereafter.

28 Days or sooner (para. 7(1)(a)), unless additional time agreed (paras. 19(1)(b) and (c))

4 DP serves Defence (see below)

Neither the "Scheme" provisions nor the JCT Rules prescribe a time limit for the "Defence" to be served. Therefore it is for the Adjudicator to set the timetable.

5 Adjudicator directed actions by parties

6 Adjudicator issues Decision

7(a) "Losing" party pays/complies   7(b) "Losing" party fails to pay/comply

8(a) "Winning" party goes to court for enforcement   8(b) "Losing" party commences arbitration or litigation

CHECKLIST FOR MONITORING THE CONTRACTOR'S CONSTRUCTION PROGRAMME

A. Actions required pre-tender

1. State the contractual status of the Contractor's Construction Programme in the tender enquiry document—the usual practice is that the Contractor's Construction Programme is the Contractor's preferred proposal for meeting the Employer's objectives, i.e. it is not a contract document per se but it is a contract requirement that immediately after contract award the contractor submits a detailed Construction Programme identifying his preferred construction sequence, and the key dates by which other parties will be required to have performed, e.g. design freeze dates.

2. It is also helpful to make a policy statement to the effect that the Contractor's Construction Programme is to be adopted as a statement of joint intent, with the twin objectives of:

— enabling both the employer and contractor to review site progress on a monthly basis;

— addressing any problems likely to affect the intended Completion Date as and when they arise.

3. It is therefore necessary to be prescriptive as to the format of the Contractor's programme, the usual provision being along the lines that:

(a) The Contractor shall produce a Master Programme—to record overall progress v. planned progress on a trade or elemental basis related to the Bills of Quantities, such programme to be updated each month, and to be revised as necessary for instructed Variations.

(b) The Contractor shall also produce a Detailed Three-Month Ahead Working Programme identifying the key interface of specialist trades, recording progress v. planned progress, updated on a weekly basis.

(c) Whether or not one specifies a particular software package is a matter of choice, but it is advisable to require the Contractor to support his construction programming with a written schedule of activities, numbered as per the Working Programme and showing Start Dates, Durations, Finish Dates and dependent links. The Working Programme should at all times show the "Critical Path", together with any essential information release dates.

4. It is then advisable to require the Contractor to pass down the above Construction Programming regime to all principal sub-contractors, such that if all goes according to plan there is an interlocking suite of programmes and sub-programmes.

5. For key trades it is also advisable to require, through the contractor, that submitted Programmes show proposed labour resources week by week and that these are supported by detailed Method Statements, identifying preferred gang strengths and planned productivity factors, with maximum and minimum variants thereof.

B.   Post-contract controls and Programme monitoring

1. The key to controlling the post-contract scenario is of course setting down the required procedures at tender stage. So often this is not done and projects commence on an ad-hoc basis, with the contractor effectively running the meetings and controlling the format, content and accuracy of Minutes of Meetings.

2. The recommended procedure, if not laid down in the contract documentation, is to hold a "Pre-Start-on-site" meeting, chaired by the Architect/Engineer/Contract Administrator, to:

  (a) Introduce Design Team individuals to contractor's staff.
  (b) Establish a hierarchy of meetings with prescribed dates.
  (c) Agree procedures for chairing, recording and signing off meetings.
  (d) Agree procedures for the issue of drawings and instructions generally.
  (e) Agree procedures for approving specialist sub-contractor drawings with design input, and issue thereof.
  (f) Agree procedures for the keeping of progress records, including regular photographs and formal reporting of progress each month.
  (g) Agree the monthly payment certification procedure with prescribed dates for application by sub-contractors, submission by the contractor, and issue of interim payment certificates by the Architect etc, via the Quantity Surveyor, if applicable.

3. Most standard forms of contract now provide an option for the pre-agreement of instructed variations—in respect of both value and time—with the further option of adjudication, if pre-agreement proves impossible. In order to keep such matters confidential and avoid delays, consider appointing an Adjudication Panel at the outset by agreement with the contractor, the panel to consist of an Architect, an Engineer and a Quantity Surveyor, each to act individually depending on the nature of any future dispute.

4. As regards the monitoring of the Contractor's Master and Working Programmes it is recommended that:

(a) Key individuals are nominated by the Architect and by the Contractor to be responsible for maintaining records etc, updating programmes, meeting regularly with one another and reporting to the monthly meetings.

(b) An agreed software package is used, with computer disks freely exchanged and hardcopy printouts agreed each month recording:

(i) Any revisions to Planned Progress in the last month arising from instructed variations, e.g. Extensions of Time awarded, Undefined Provisional Sums now instructed.

(ii) Actual Progress v. Planned Progress.

(iii) Variations awaiting formal instruction and their likely cost and time implications.

(iv) Any other contentious issues.

(v) Labour resources expended in the principal activities over the last month.

(vi) Any particular events occurring in the previous month that may be relevant to any claim for delay or disruption, e.g. exceptionally adverse weather.

5. Whatever progress monitoring systems are put in place, either via the contract documentation or voluntarily once the contractor is selected and appointed, review the Charge Order procedure. Make sure that it is understood by all concerned and supported by the appropriate forms.

SUMMARY OF KEY ADJUDICATION PROCEDURAL RULES: HGCRA "SCHEME" AND VARIOUS ANBs

—Once the Adjudicator is appointed as provided by the Contract conditions, or by default under the "Scheme" provisions, where

RP = Referring Party   and   DP = Defendant Party

Key Provision	HGCRA "Scheme" Pt.1	JCT	CIC	TeCSA	CEDR	ICE	TecBar
A *Timetable*							
1 RP to serve Referral Notice	Within 7 days of serving Notice of Adjudication: para. 7(1)	Within 7 days of serving Notice of Adjudication or the execution by the Adjudicator of the JCT agreement, if later	Within 7 days of serving Notice of Adjudication or as soon thereafter as the Adjudicator is appointed	Within 7 days of the Adjudicator notifying both parties of his appointment	Within 4 days of date Adjudicator appointed or when agreed Adjudicator confirms his availability	Within 2 days of confirmation of the Adjudicator being appointed	Within 3 days of appointment of Adjudicator
2 If RP fails to serve Referral Notice within 7 days of Notice of Adjudication	Silent, other than the three options under para. 15, none of which apply in this eventuality	No bar—Referral to be made as soon as possible	Silent	Silent	Silent	Silent	Silent
3 Latest data for Adjudicator's Decision	28 days from date of Referral Notice, unless: (a) DP asks for 42 days and RP so consents. (b) Other period as may be agreed: para. 19(1)	As for "Scheme"	As for "Scheme"	As for "Scheme"	As for "Scheme", but Adjudicator to give decision in 14 days if possible	As for "Scheme", but period starts from the date the Adjudicator receives the Referral Notice	As for "Scheme"

	Key Provision	HGCRA "Scheme" Pt.1	JCT	CIC	TeCSA	CEDR	ICE	TecBar
4	If Adjudicator fails to give Decision within time	Either party may stop and request a new appointment: para. 19(2)	Parties may agree to sack the Adjudicator, paying no fees	Parties bound if Decision given before appointment of new Adjudicator	Silent	Silent	Parties bound if Decision given before appointment of new Adjudicator, but subject to 7 days notice	Parties bound if Decision given before appointment of new Adjudicator
B	*Power of Adjudicator*							
1	To limit volume of documentation relied on by Referral Notice	Yes: paras. 13(a) and (g)	Yes: Adjudicator may set his own procedure	Yes: Adjudicator has wide discretion and need not follow court rules	Yes: Adjudicator has wide discretion	Yes: Adjudicator has wide discretion	Yes: Adjudicator has wide discretion	Yes: Adjudicator has wide discretion
2	To limit parties' wishes to be represented	Each party may be represented at a hearing by just one adviser of his choice, unless otherwise allowed by the Adjudicator: para. 16(2)	Yes: Adjudicator may set his own procedure	Yes: Adjudicator may set his own procedure	Must allow any representation either party requires	Yes: Adjudicator may set his own procedure	Yes: Adjudicator may set his own procedure	No, but may limit time allowed at any hearing

Key Provision	HGCRA "Scheme" Pt.1	JCT	CIC	TeCSA	CEDR	ICE	TecBar
B *Power of Adjudicator*							
3 To be inquisitorial	Adjudicator encouraged to be inquisitorial: para. 12	Yes: Adjudicator has wide power	Yes: Adjudicator has wide power	Yes: Adjudicator has wide power	Yes: Adjudicator has wide power	Yes: Adjudicator has wide power	Yes: Adjudicator has wide power
4 To obtain outside opinion	Adjudicator empowered to appoint experts, assessor or legal advisers, subject to reporting that advice to the parties: paras. 13(f) and 17	Yes: Adjudicator to advise parties including estimate of cost	Yes: Adjudicator to notify parties of his intention and issue copy of such advice	Yes: If one party requests or consents	Yes: If both parties agree	Yes, subject to notifying the parties of his intention to do so	May appoint an Expert or Assessor— no need to obtain consent
5 To deal with Adjudicator's own costs	Adjudicator empowered to determine reasonable value, and then apportion between the parties: para. 25	As for "Scheme"	As for "Scheme"	As for "Scheme" but capped at £1,000 per day or part day, plus expenses and VAT	As for "Scheme"	As for "Scheme"	As for "Scheme"
6 To award interest on damages as assessed	Only if a term of the contract so provides: para. 20(c), or if applied for by a party under other Statute law	Yes, but simple interest only	Adjudicator given total discretion	Adjudicator given total discretion	Silent	Adjudicator given total discretion	Adjudicator given total discretion

	Key Provision	HGCRA "Scheme" Pt.1	JCT	CIC	TeCSA	CEDR	ICE	TecBar
7	To deal with parties' case preparation and representation costs	Silent	Parties to pay own costs except if Adjudicator orders one party to pay costs of tests etc	Parties to pay own costs	Parties to pay own costs	Silent	Parties to pay own costs	Parties to pay own costs
8	To give, or not to give, Reasons with Decision	If requested by either party	No obligation, even if asked	Required to do so unless parties agree otherwise	Expressly forbidden	No obligation but may do so	No obligation but may do so	Parties may ask, but Adjudicator not bound
9	To withhold Decision until Adjudicator is paid	No such power: para. 19(3)	As for "Scheme"	Yes	No such power	Yes	Yes	No such power

Key Provision	HGCRA "Scheme" Pt.1	JCT	CIC	TeCSA	CEDR	ICE	TecBar
C	*Other matters*						
1 Standard Form of Agreement available for the appointment of the Adjudicator	No requirement	Yes	Yes	No	Yes	Yes	Yes
2 Joinder provision	Arguably—subject to the translation of para. 8(2) into plain English	Silent	Yes—if all parties agree	Silent	Silent	Yes—if all parties agree	Yes—if all parties agree
3 Final and binding	Until referred to Arbitration or litigation— HGCRA section 108(3)	As for HGCRA	As for HGCRA	As for HGCRA	Decision final and binding if not "appealed" within 60 days	As for HGCRA	As for HGCRA

PRACTICE DIRECTION— TECHNOLOGY AND CONSTRUCTION COURT

(Reproduced with the kind permission of the Lord Chancellor's Office)
This Practice Direction supplements CPR Part 49 and replaces, with modifications, Order 36 of the Rules of the Supreme Court

General

1.1 This Practice Direction applies to cases allocated to the Technology and Construction Court ("the TCC").

1.2 A TCC claim is a claim which involves issues or questions which are technically complex or for which a trial by a judge of the TCC is for any other reason desirable.

1.3 TCC claims may be dealt with either in the High Court or, subject to paragraph 2.3 below, in a County Court but cases allocated to the TCC will, unless and until a judge of the TCC otherwise directs, be dealt with by a judge of the TCC.

1.4 A judge will be appointed to be the judge in charge of the TCC (currently Mr Justice Dyson).

Commencement of proceedings

2.1 Before the issue of a claim form relating to a TCC claim, the claim form, whether to be issued in the High Court or in a County Court, should, if it is intended that the case be allocated to the TCC, be marked in the top right hand corner "Technology and Construction Court". The case will then be allocated to the TCC. The words "Technology and Construction Court" should follow the reference to "The _____ County Court" or "The High Court, Queen's Bench Division", as the case may be.

2.2 The TCC is a specialist list for the purposes of CPR Part 30 (Transfer) but no order for the transfer of proceedings from or to the TCC shall be made unless the parties have either:

(1) had an opportunity of being heard on the issue, or

(2) consented to the order.

2.3 A claim form marked as mentioned in paragraph 2.1 may not be issued in a County Court office other than:

(1) a County Court office where there is also a High Court District Registry; or

(2) the office of the Central London County Court.

2.4 Where a claim form marked as mentioned in paragraph 2.1 is issued in the Royal Courts of Justice, the case will be assigned to a named TCC judge (the "assigned judge") who will have the primary responsibility for the case management of that case. All documents relating to that case should be marked, under the words "Technology and Construction Court" in the title, with the name of the assigned judge.

Applications

3.1 Where a case form is to be marked in paragraph 2.1, any application before issue of the claim form should be made to a judge of the TCC.

3.2 If an application is made before the issue of the claim form, the written evidence in support of the application must state, in addition to any other necessary matters, that the Claimant intends to mark the claim form in accordance with paragraph 2.1.

3.3 Any application in a case which has been allocated to the TCC must be made to a judge of the TCC.

3.4 Where there is an assigned judge of a TCC case, any application in that case should be made to the assigned judge but, if the judge in charge of the TCC so authorises or if the assigned judge is not available, may be made to another judge of the TCC.

3.5 If an application is urgent and no TCC judge is available to deal with it, the application may be made to any judge who, if the case were not allocated to the TCC, would be authorised to deal with the application.

Case management

4.1 Every claim allocated to the TCC will be allocated to the multi-track and the CPR relating to track allocation will not apply.

4.2 Where a claim has been allocated to the TCC either on issue (i.e. in every case in which the claim form has been marked "Technology and Construction Court") or by transfer to the TCC, an application for directions (including an application for a fixed date hearing) must be made by the Claimant within 14 days of the filing by the Defendant of an acknowledgement of service or of a defence (whichever is the earlier) or, as the case may be, within 14 days of the date of the order of transfer.

4.3 If the Claimant does not make an application in accordance with paragraph 4.2—

    (1) any other party may do so or may apply for the claim of the Claimant in default to be struck out or dismissed; or

    (2) a TCC judge may on his own initiative fix a directions hearing.

4.4 The provisions of CPR Part 29 and the practice direction supplementing that Part apply to the case management of TCC cases except where inconsistent with this or any other TCC practice direction. But reference in those provisions to a listing questionnaire shall be read as references to a pre-trial review questionnaire and paragraphs 8 and 9 of the practice direction do not apply. Attention is drawn, in particular, to the following provisions of CPR Part 29 and the supplementing practice direction:

CPR Part 29

rule 29.3(2) (attendance of legal representatives)
rule 29.4 (agreed proposals)
rule 29.5 (variation of case management timetable)
rule 29.6 (pre-trial review(listing) questionnaire)

Practice Direction supplementing CPR Part 29

paragraphs 3.4 to 3.9 (general provisions)
paragraphs 5.1 to 5.8 (case management conferences)
paragraphs 6.1 to 6.5 (variation of directions)
paragraphs 7.1 to 7.4 (failure to comply with case management directions)
paragraphs 10.1 to 10.6 (the trial)

Case management conference

5.1 The first case management conference will take place at the directions hearing referred to in paragraphs 4.2 and 4.3 above.

5.2 When the court notifies the parties of the time and date of the first case management conference it will also send them a case management questionnaire and a case management directions form. These documents will be in the forms annexed to this practice direction, and marked respectively Appendix 1 and 2.

5.3 The parties shall complete, exchange and return both forms by no later than 4 pm two days before the date on which the case management conference is to take place. The parties are encouraged to try to agree directions by reference to the case management directions form.

5.4 If a party fails to exchange or return the forms by the date specified, the court may make an order which leads to the claim or defence being struck out, or impose such other sanction as it sees fit, or may hold a case management conference without the forms.

5.5 At the first case management conference, the court will usually fix the date for trial of the case and of any preliminary issue that it orders to be tried. It will also give case management directions. The directions will usually include the fixing of a date for a pre-trial review.

5.6 Whenever possible, the trial of a case will be heard by the assigned judge of that case.

Pre-trial review

6.1 When the court fixes the date of a pre-trial review it will also provide the parties with a pre-trial review questionnaire and a pre-trial review directions form. These documents will be in the forms annexed to this practice direction marked respectively as Appendix 3 and 4.

6.2 The parties shall complete, exchange and return both forms no later than 4 pm two days before the date on which the pre-trial review is to take place. The parties are encouraged to try to agree directions by reference to the pre-trial review directions form.

6.3 If a party fails to exchange or return the pre-trial review questionnaire or pre-trial review directions form by the date specified, the court may make an order which leads to the claim or defence and any counterclaim being struck out, or it may impose such other sanction as it sees fit, or it may hold a pre-trial review without the forms.

6.4 At the pre-trial review, the court will give such directions for the conduct of the trial as it sees fit.

The Civil Procedure Rules

7.1 The Civil Procedure Rules and the practice directions supplementing them apply to TCC cases subject to the provisions of this practice direction and any other TCC practice direction.

APPENDIX 1

First Case Management	In the County Court/High Court
Conference Questionnaire	Queen's Bench Division
	Technology and Construction Court
	Claim No.
To	Last date for filing with court office.

E.G. Buggins & Co. (Contractors) Ltd

Please read the notes on page 5 before completing the questionnaire.

Please note the date by which it must be returned and the name of the court it should be returned to since this may be different from the court where proceedings were issued.

If you have settled this case (or if you settle it on a future date) and do not need to have it heard or tried, you must let the court know immediately.

A.   Settlement

Do you wish there to be a stay to attempt to settle the case   Yes   No
by negotiations or by any other form of dispute resolution?
If yes, at what stage and for how long?
If no, please give reasons

B.   Transfer

If you think your case is suitable for transfer to another court or track, say which

Court: Chancery Division/Queen's Bench Division/another TCC
       Court/Commercial County Court
Track: Small claims/fast track

Please give brief reasons for your choice
. . . .
. . . .
. . . .

C. Pre-Action protocols

Have you complied with any pre-action protocol   N/A   Yes   No
applicable to your claim?

If Yes, state which protocol

. . . .

If No, please explain to what extent and for what reason it has not been
complied with

. . . .
. . . .
. . . .

D. Applications

If you have not already sent the court an application for   Yes   No
summary judgment, do you intend to do so?

If you have not already issued a claim in the case against   Yes   No
someone not yet a party, do you intend to apply for the
court's permission to do so?

Have you any other applications to make?   Yes   No
In such case, if Yes, please give details:

. . . .
. . . .

E. Witnesses of fact

So far as you know at this stage, what witnesses of fact do you intend to
call at the hearing?

Witness Name   Witness to which fact

. . . .
. . . .
. . . .

F.   Experts' evidence

Do you wish to use expert evidence at the   Yes   No
hearing?

Have you already copied any experts' report(s)   None   Yes   No
to the other party(ies)?   obtained
                                                 yet
Please list the experts whose evidence you think
you will use:

Expert's Name   Field of Expertise
                                           (e.g. architect, mechanical
                                           engineer)

. . . .

. . . .

Will you and the other party use the same   Yes   No
expert(s)?

If No, please explain why not:

. . . .

. . . .

Should any, and if so what, inspections, samples,   Yes   No
experiments or calculations by experts be
directed?

. . . .

. . . .

Do you want your expert(s) to give evidence   Yes   No
orally at the hearing or trial?

If Yes, give the reasons why you think oral
evidence is neccessary:

. . . .

. . . .

G. Location of trial

Is there any reason why your case needs to be   Yes   No
heard at a particular court?

If Yes, give reasons (e.g. particular facilities
required, convenience of witnesses; etc.)

. . . .

. . . .

and specify the court

. . . .

H. Representation and estimate of hearing/trial time

Do you expect to be represented by a   No   Solicitor   Counsel
solicitor or counsel at the hearing or
trial?

How long do you estimate it will take to   days   hours   minutes
put your case to the court at the
hearing/trial?

How long do you estimate for the whole   days   hours   minutes
of the trial, excluding judgment?

If there are days when you, your representative, expert or an essential
witness will not be able to attend court, give details:

Name   Dates not available

. . . .

. . . .

. . . .

I. Costs (only relates to costs incurred by legal representatives)

What is your estimate of your costs incurred to
date, excluding disbursements, VAT and court fees?   £ . . . .

What do you estimate your overall costs are likely to
be, excluding disbursements, VAT and court fees?   £ . . . .

J. Other information

Have you attached documents you wish the   Yes   No
judge to take into account when considering
what directions to make?

Have they been served on the other parties?   Yes   No

If Yes, say when   . . . .

APPENDIX 2

Case Management Conference Directions Form

( ) Signed statements of witnesses of fact to be served [and filed] by . . . .
am/pm on . . . . . 200. . . [Directions, if appropriate, for control of evidence
of fact under rule 32.1]

( ) [No expert evidence without further order] [Permission for expert
evidence on the following terms: (see below)].

( ) [Inspections to be made/samples to be obtained/experiments to be
conducted/calculations to be carried out as follows:

( ) Experts in like fields to hold discussions in accordance with rule 35.12
by . . . . am/pm on . . . . . 200. .on [all the issues arising in their common
fields] [the following issues:

. . . .
. . . .
. . . .
. . . .
. . . .
. . . .

Statements under rule 35.12(3) to be prepared and filed by . . . . am/pm
on . . . . . 200. . .

( ) The parties are to consult with each other and the court with a view to
arranging service and (where required) filing of statements of case, witness
statements, experts' reports, disclosure lists and other documents in
computer readable form as well as in hard copy. Format for court disks:

. . . .
. . . .

( ) [Time under paragraphs . . . . . above not to be extended without permission.]

( )

( ) Pre-trial Review: . . . . . Time allowed . . . . . Parties to complete, file and serve pre-trial questionnaire, after consultation, by . . . . am/pm on . . . . . 200. . .

( ) Liberty to restore, Costs in cause.

Permission to amend

The [Part 20] Claimant/Defendant to have permission to [re-]amend the [Part 20] particulars of claim/defence [and counterclaim/reply to defence] [and defence to counterclaim] in accordance with the draft initialled by the Judge. Re-service [to be effected by . . . . am/pm on . . . . . 200. .] [deemed to have been effected to-day]. The [Part 20] Defendant/Claimant to have permission to [re-]amend the defence/reply to defence [and defence to counterclaim] by . . . . am/pm on . . . . . 200. . limited to amendments consequential upon the amendment for which permission is first given above. The [Part 20] Claimant/Defendant to pay in any event the costs of and consequential upon that amendment, or thrown away thereby [and of this application].

Scott Schedule

Column headings:	1.	Serial number.
	2.	
	3.	
	4.	
	5.	
	6.	
	7.	
	8.	
	9.	
	10.	
	11.	
	12.	

Expert evidence

Party (or state "Joint")	Field	Name	Date for exchange	Whether leave for oral evidence
. . . .	. . . .	. . . .	. . . .	. . . .
. . . .	. . . .	. . . .	. . . .	. . . .
. . . .	. . . .	. . . .	. . . .	. . . .
. . . .	. . . .	. . . .	. . . .	. . . .
. . . .	. . . .	. . . .	. . . .	. . . .
. . . .	. . . .	. . . .	. . . .	. . . .
. . . .	. . . .	. . . .	. . . .	. . . .
. . . .	. . . .	. . . .	. . . .	. . . .
. . . .	. . . .	. . . .	. . . .	. . . .
. . . .	. . . .	. . . .	. . . .	. . . .

Reports to be exchanged [and filed] by . . . . . am/pm on the dates specified.

APPENDIX 3

Pre-trial review Questionnaire	In the County Court/High Court Queen's Bench Division
	Technology and Construction Court Claim No. . . . . .
	Last date for filing . . . . . with court
To	office.

. . . .

- The judge will use the information which you and the other party(ies) provide to conduct a pre-trial review.
- If you do not complete and return the questionnaire the judge may

  make an order which leads to your statement of case (claim or defence) being struck out.

  conduct the pre-trial review without it. You may be ordered to pay (immediately) the other parties' costs of attending.

. . . .

. . . .

. . . .

. . . .

A.   Directions complied with

1. Have you complied with all the   Yes   No
previous directions given by the Court?

2. If no, please explain which directions are outstanding and why.

Directions outstanding   Reasons directions outstanding

. . . .

. . . .

. . . .

. . . .

3. Are any further directions required   Yes   No
to prepare the case for trial?

4. If yes, please explain directions required and give reasons.

Directions required   Reasons required

. . . .

. . . .

. . . .

. . . .

B.   Experts

1. Has the court already given   Yes   No
permission for you to use written
expert evidence?

                                        (If no, go to section C)

2. If yes, please give name and field of expertise.

Name of expert   Whether Joint   Field of Expertise
                        Expert (please
                        tick if appropriate)

. . . .

. . . .

. . . .

3. Have the experts held discussions as directed?   Yes   No

4. Have they filed statements as directed following those discussions?　　　　Yes　　　No

5. Have the expert(s) report(s) been served and filed as ordered?　　　　Yes　　　No

6. Has the court already given permission for the expert(s) to give oral evidence at trial?　　　　Yes　　　No

7. If no, are you seeking that permission?　　　　Yes　　　No
(If no, go to section C)

8. If yes, give your reasons for seeking permission.

. . . .

. . . .

. . . .

. . . .

9. If yes, what are the names, addresses and fields of expertise of your experts?

Expert 1	Expert 2	Expert 3	Expert 4
. . . .	. . . .	. . . .	. . . .
. . . .	. . . .	. . . .	. . . .
. . . .	. . . .	. . . .	. . . .
. . . .	. . . .	. . . .	. . . .

10. Please give details of any dates within the trial period when your expert(s) will not be available.

Name of expert	Dates not available
. . . .	. . . .
. . . .	. . . .
. . . .	. . . .

C. Other witnesses

(If you are not calling other witnesses go to section D)

1. How many other witnesses (including yourself) will be giving evidence on your behalf at the trial? (do not include experts—see section B above)

2. What are the names and addresses of your witnesses?

Witness 1	Witness 2	Witness 3	Witness 4
. . . .	. . . .	. . . .	. . . .
. . . .	. . . .	. . . .	. . . .
. . . .	. . . .	. . . .	. . . .
. . . .	. . . .	. . . .	. . . .

3. Please give details of any dates within the trial period when you or your witnesses will not be available.

Name of witness   Dates not available

. . . .

. . . .

. . . .

4. Are any of the witness statements agreed?   Yes   No

(If no, go to question 6)

5. If yes, give the name of the witness and the date of his or her statement.

Name of witness   Date of statement

. . . .

. . . .

6. Do you or any of your witnesses   Yes   No
need any special facilities?

(If no, go to question 8)

7. If yes, what are they?

. . . .

. . . .

. . . .

8. Will any of your witnesses be provided with Yes   No
an interpreter?

(If no, go to question D)

9. If yes, say what type of interpreter e.g. language (stating which) deaf/blind etc.

. . . .

. . . .

D. Legal representation

1. Who will be presenting your case at the hearing or trial?   You   Solicitor   Counsel

2. Please give details of any dates within the trial period when the person presenting your case will not be available.

Name	Dates not available
. . . .	. . . .
. . . .	. . . .

E.   Other matters

1. How long do you estimate the whole of the trial will take, excluding judgment?   Minutes   Hours   Days

2. What is the estimated number of pages . . . . . (please give number). **of evidence to be included in the trial bundle?**

3. Please provide a case summary and proposals (agreed if possible) for directions to be given, by reference to the pre-trial review directions form.

Signed | . . . . |

Claimant/Defendant or Counsel/Solicitor for the Claimant/Defendant.

Date | . . . . |

THE OFFICIAL REFEREES SOLICITORS ASSOCIATION

EXPERT WITNESS PROTOCOL—VERSION 1.0

As issued by The Court Service for Technology and Construction Court—February 2000

The Official Referees Solicitors Association (ORSA) was formed to promote the interests of solicitors and their clients conducting business in the Official Referee's Courts and in related arbitration.

The Committee of ORSA believes that the relationship between solicitor and expert witness is of the utmost importance in view of the duties each owes to the court or other tribunal. This protocol has been prepared with a view to assisting clarity of communication and in order to provide a framework within which solicitors and experts are able to operate freely. It is not intended that this protocol should operate in a rigid way but it is hoped that reference to it will enable experts and solicitors to consider key areas at an early stage.

The publication of this protocol came out of the ORSA Response to the Issue Paper on Expert Evidence released by the Access to Justice Team in January 1996. ORSA hopes that this protocol will encourage independence and impartiality of the expert.

Not all of this protocol will apply to every appointment and there will inevitably be areas which the protocol does not specifically cover. It is intended to keep this protocol under review and comments will be most welcome. ORSA supports the Code of Practice published by the Law Society and acknowledges comments made by many bodies and individuals as part of the consultation process.

PROTOCOL

A. Selection

1. The solicitor shall supply sufficient information to the expert to enable the expert to confirm whether or not the issues, as identified by the solicitor, are matters on which the expert is competent to act as expert witness. The expert should be satisfied that he has the necessary resources to meet the requirements of the appointment, including the required timetable. ORSA encourages the appointment of experts who maintain active professional practices.

Conflicts and Confidentiality

2. The solicitor shall provide the expert with a list of relevant parties and the expert shall state whether or not he has any connection with any of the parties named or to be reasonably inferred from the list to enable the solicitor and the expert to consider whether any conflict of interest exists.

Information

3. The expert should normally expect to provide information about his expertise and experience and suitability for the role for which he is being considered together with details of his proposed basis of charge. If the solicitor intends to approach more than one person to discuss their potential suitability for appointment as an expert witness, he should inform each expert that he is one of a number under consideration.

Independence of Expert

4. In any selection and appointment process the solicitor should remember that a witness who is not selected or whose appointment is subsequently terminated may be free to accept an appointment from other parties. The solicitor may wish to ensure that documentation and information made available as part of any selection process is carefully chosen, commensurate with the requirement to provide relevant information, and that documentation is retrieved at the end of the process or of an appointment. The expert should be reminded that any documentation provided to him is subject to the rules of privilege.

B. Brief

5. As soon as possible after the expert has been appointed, the solicitor shall explain the client's commercial and legal objectives in a manner commensurate with the independence of the expert and prepare for the expert a brief which shall be in a form appropriate to the nature and complexity of the matter on which the expert is asked to form an opinion. The Brief will normally contain the following information:

— Party making appointment.
— Subject matter.
— Contacts.
— Nature of proceedings.
— Timetable fixed in any proceedings and current status.
— Pleadings in any action which has commenced.
— Details of other experts appointed by the party making appointment and others, if known, with field of expertise.
— In a large or complex matter the method by which experts are to co-ordinate their services. Is there to be a lead expert with whom other experts will liaise?
— Areas in which the expert is called upon to give his opinion.
— Specific issues on which the expert is asked to advise. In an appropriate case the solicitor should prepare a detailed Statement of Issues for the expert.
— Timescale within which the expert is asked to prepare:
    — initial review and advice on technical issues pleaded or assistance in preparing the client's pleaded case.
    — draft report for discussion and review of brief.
    — report for issue.
— Details of key documentation and details of location of all relevant documents. In a straightforward case appropriately bundled documents should accompany the brief but in a complex case the expert may be required to review documentation and the brief itself will contain only limited documentation.
— The brief should outline the principles of privilege and discovery.

6. On receipt of the brief the solicitor and expert should review the nature and extent of the brief with regard to the role of the expert and those of any other experts appointed by the solicitor. If the expert has been appointed prior to the solicitor's involvement, it is important that a brief is established jointly. The proliferation of experts should be avoided. The solicitor should be aware that there may be no need to appoint a separate expert in every relevant discipline and that a carefully selected expert may be able to cover more than one area.

7. The solicitor and expert should keep the brief under review at all times and advise each other of any material changes to relevant issues. The expert should not undertake work outside the brief without the prior approval of the solicitor.

8. The scope of the expert's appointment should be defined and the expert should be appointed in a way that will avoid costs being wasted.

9. The solicitor may wish to discuss with those representing other parties the matters on which expert opinion is required in order to assist and refine the brief.

Timescale

10. The solicitor and the expert shall agree the overall timescale and the programme within which the expert shall work. If either the solicitor or the expert becomes aware of any matter likely to affect that timescale, they should advise the other. The exact timing and sequence will vary from case to case. Consideration should be given to the extent of the expert's required attendance at any hearing. These issues should be discussed at an early stage.

Hearing Date

11. The solicitor should keep the expert advised of the timescale set in any litigation or arbitration or of any timetable which is to be met and of any changes that are likely to be made, including in the expected length of or dates of any hearing or trial.

12. The expert when advised of any hearing or trial date on which he is likely to be required to attend or give evidence shall make that date available and inform the solicitor if there are any pre-existing commitments likely to affect the expert's ability to fulfil the appointment.

13. Where the expert has pre-existing commitments the solicitor and expert shall work together in order that the interests of the client can best be served. The expert shall not take on new commitments which might interfere with his responsibilities under the appointment without first assessing the position with the solicitor.

C. Reports

14. The report should normally be issued to the solicitor as a draft for discussion and should be accompanied by any documents not originally supplied by the solicitor to the expert. The solicitor and the expert should discuss the format of the report, provided that the report remains the

independent product of the expert. It is wise for the solicitor and the expert to test the expert's opinions in the light of alternative facts contended for by the client's opponent.

15. When the expert's report has been finalised it will normally be exchanged by the solicitor and not by the expert. Usually simultaneous exchange is appropriate, but in certain cases sequential exchange may be required. The expert and the solicitor should discuss this early in the appointment. The expert's report and any copyright in it will normally be the property of the client.

16. The expert and the solicitor will need to review the status of the report if the underlying facts change or if the expert's opinion alters.

D. Without Prejudice Meetings

17. It is common practice for a tribunal to order the parties' expert witnesses to meet to identify those parts of their evidence which is in issue. There is no standard format for such meetings. What follows is intended as a guide.

18. Meetings of experts should normally take place before exchange of the experts' reports. The predominant view of ORSA is that, if exchange takes place first, it is more likely that "positions" are taken too early to the detriment of proper discussion at the meeting.

19. The meeting may be most effective if it is chaired by one expert and an agenda agreed in advance. It may also be of value for the experts to exchange key criteria which they wish to discuss, for example, Standards or Codes of Practice or methods of valuation. It is appropriate for the parties' solicitors in conjunction with their experts to identify matters in issue in order to determine items for the agenda. Lawyers and clients should not be present at the without prejudice meeting of experts. It is important that the meeting of experts addresses the matters of expert evidence that relate to the matters in issue in the proceedings. The meeting is not the place for the lawyer to "surprise" the other party's expert with a new theory or new documents.

20. Close liaison will be necessary between solicitor and expert and amongst experts in order to make the best use of the meeting. Normally experts of like discipline will meet together. Occasionally it will be appropriate to have meetings of experts in more than one discipline, usually following the initial meeting. For example: Architect, Structural Engineer and Quantity Surveyor, from all parties, might meet to discuss the nature and extent of remedial works contended for.

E. Notes of Without Prejudice Meetings

21. The expert should report to the solicitor promptly after the meeting and discuss any apparent agreement or narrowing of issues.

22. The expert should, in conjunction with other experts of like discipline, prepare a written note signed by each of them as to matters of opinion on which they are agreed. The note should, where possible, give brief reasons for the views held. It should be remembered that matters of fact are for the tribunal or the agreement of the parties and not matters for the experts to agree between them. Where not all experts can agree a particular point, limited agreements should be explored.

23. If areas of apparent agreement on matters of opinion emerge at a without prejudice meeting, it is good practice to record these promptly to ensure accuracy. It may be appropriate for the expert to reflect on the issues following the meeting. A solicitor should not instruct an expert to apply pressure upon experts of other parties.

24. The expert does not normally have authority to bind his client, but the solicitor should make sure that the expert is aware of the extent of the expert's authority and that matters which the expert agrees in a note of the meeting may be binding on him. It is good practice for the expert to ensure that all written notes of the meeting are marked "without prejudice" until clearly agreed by two or more experts.

25. The solicitor shall never impede the expert in reaching agreement or forming an opinion but can give guidance to the expert in formulating the note to reflect the matters in issue in the proceedings.

F. Expert's Duty and Reporting

26. The expert shall comply with the requirements of the brief and exercise the reasonable skill and care of a person of the expert's profession, occupation or experience in providing advice on the matters in issue. In giving evidence the expert shall act impartially and owes an overriding duty to the court or tribunal.

27. The expert shall not express a final concluded opinion until all relevant issues of fact have been considered by him. The expert will advise the solicitor if the brief appears incomplete or where the expert believes other information is likely to be available.

28. The expert shall advise and assist the solicitor generally, where appropriate, beyond the matters on which the expert is required to give a formal opinion. The expert's report should contain the substance of the expert's evidence which it is intended to give at the tribunal and should be prepared in a clear and succinct manner. The solicitor and the expert

should discuss the format of the report. It is not the role of the expert to make a finding of fact which is in issue. Where an opinion depends upon the facts which are in issue, this should be clearly stated.

29. The solicitor shall throughout the currency of the appointment keep the expert up to date with information and issues as they relate to the appointment. The expert shall keep an opinion under review and have regard to all relevant matters when advising and assisting the client and the solicitor. After reports have been exchanged the expert and the solicitor should consider the need for a supplemental report.

G. Fees

30. Fees and terms and conditions should be clearly agreed at the outset of an appointment. An appropriate breakdown, daily rate and hourly rate equivalent should be provided. Fees shall be inclusive except where survey, laboratory or other costs are expressly stated separately.

Payment of Fees

31. The expert and the solicitor should consider and agree whether the solicitor appoints the expert and is responsible for the expert's fees, or whether the solicitor acts as agent for the client by whom all invoices are to be paid.

Budget

32. The expert should normally provide a budget for various stages of any appointment where the work is identifiable. The solicitor and the expert should ensure that fees are proportionate to the value or importance of the matters in issue.

33. It should be made clear and agreed at the outset how regularly fee invoices are to be rendered, what degree of information they are to contain and whether they are to be sent to the solicitor or the client. The expert shall provide supporting information and keep accurate contemporaneous records sufficient to justify the fees claimed or as may be required in any taxation of costs or similar procedure.

Legal Expenses Insurers

34. The solicitor should always advise the expert in advance where the agreement and payment of the expert's fee is subject to the approval of legal expenses insurers and should immediately notify his expert of any ceiling on fees.

Legal Aid

35. If the expert is appointed in a case where the solicitor's client has a legal aid certificate in force the solicitor must advise the expert of the basis on which interim fees can be claimed from the legal aid fund and whether the expert is to be appointed on the basis that the expert's fees may be reduced on legal aid taxation. The solicitor shall advise the expert immediately of any change in the client's legal aid status.

Cancellation and Commitment Fees

36. Cancellation charges shall only apply if they have been discussed and agreed at the outset of the appointment and where the expert can establish that he has no other appropriate work to undertake. The expert should not normally charge a minimum or commitment fee. The level of charge, which may be on a sliding scale, should aim to compensate the expert for disruption and inefficiency in rearranging his diary at short notice and not aim to provide remuneration for the whole of the period cancelled.

Security

37. Where the solicitor has appointed the expert as agent for the client, the expert may request that the client lodge with the solicitor, or in a designated account, sufficient monies to provide reasonable security for the likely fees of the expert. The solicitor and the client will have regard to the financial status of the client.

FLOW CHART OF TYPICAL TECH-NOLOGY AND CONSTRUCTION COURT "MULTI-TRACK" ACTION

Civil Procedure Rules Overview

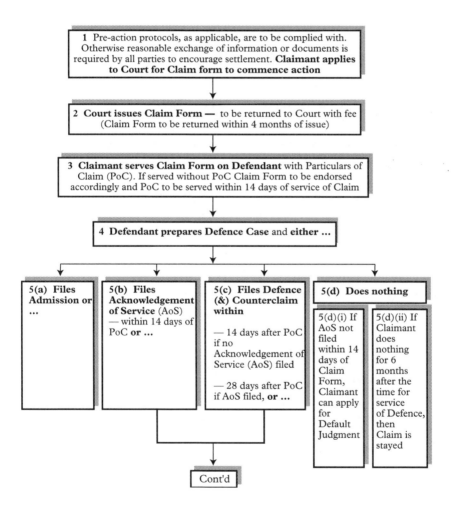

1 Pre-action protocols, as applicable, are to be complied with. Otherwise reasonable exchange of information or documents is required by all parties to encourage settlement. **Claimant applies to Court for Claim form to commence action**

2 Court issues Claim Form — to be returned to Court with fee (Claim Form to be returned within 4 months of issue)

3 Claimant serves Claim Form on Defendant with Particulars of Claim (PoC). If served without PoC Claim Form to be endorsed accordingly and PoC to be served within 14 days of service of Claim

4 Defendant prepares Defence Case and **either …**

5(a) Files Admission or …

5(b) Files Acknowledgement of Service (AoS) — within 14 days of PoC **or …**

5(c) Files Defence (&) Counterclaim within

— 14 days after PoC if no Acknowledgement of Service (AoS) filed

— 28 days after PoC if AoS filed, **or …**

5(d) Does nothing

5(d)(i) If AoS not filed within 14 days of Claim Form, Claimant can apply for Default Judgment

5(d)(ii) If Claimant does nothing for 6 months after the time for service of Defence, then Claim is stayed

Cont'd

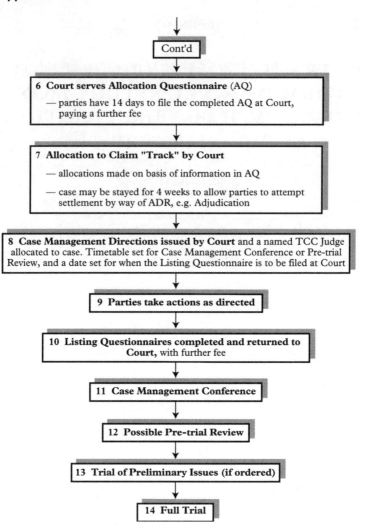

Cont'd

6 Court serves Allocation Questionnaire (AQ)

— parties have 14 days to file the completed AQ at Court, paying a further fee

7 Allocation to Claim "Track" by Court

— allocations made on basis of information in AQ

— case may be stayed for 4 weeks to allow parties to attempt settlement by way of ADR, e.g. Adjudication

8 Case Management Directions issued by Court and a named TCC Judge allocated to case. Timetable set for Case Management Conference or Pre-trial Review, and a date set for when the Listing Questionnaire is to be filed at Court

9 Parties take actions as directed

10 Listing Questionnaires completed and returned to Court, with further fee

11 Case Management Conference

12 Possible Pre-trial Review

13 Trial of Preliminary Issues (if ordered)

14 Full Trial

EXTRACT FROM RECOMMENDED FORM OF FINAL REPORT AND EXPERT WITNESS DECLARATION AS PUBLISHED BY THE INSTITUTE OF EXPERT WITNESSES

(Reproduced with the kind permission of The Expert Witness Institute)

xxxxxxxxxxxxx v. xxxxxxxxxxxxx
Title of action

xxxxxxxxx
Court reference number

Final report of . . . . **for the** **Technology and Construction Court.**

Dated:	*The date you sign your report and send it to your instructing solicitors.*
Specialist field:	*Your specialist field.*
On behalf of the Claimant/Defendant (or both if single joint expert):	*The name of the party to the action.*
On the instructions of:	*The name of the solicitors who have instructed you.*
Subject matter:	*A very brief description of the subject matter.*
Your	
Name:	. . . .
Address:	. . . .
Telephone number:	. . . .
Fax number:	. . . .
Reference:	. . . .

This format is only a **suggestion**. It contains the main elements you will need to consider but you will need to create your own personal format that will depend on your specialist field and the particular case.

The front page should be visible, preferably with a transparent plastic sheet, although this is optional. Do not use comb binders. Use A4 good quality paper, hole punched for lever arch file with a side binder. Find out from the solicitors who instruct you how many top copies are needed. Your report should be addressed to the court and not to the party from whom you received instructions.

Standard Header: *Report of . . . . (Expert's Name)*
Specialist field . . . .
On behalf of Claimant/Defendant or as Single Joint Expert.

Contents

Paragraph Number	*Paragraph Contents*	*Page number*
1.	Introduction.	
2.	The issues addressed.	
3.	My investigation of the facts.	
4.	My opinion.	
5.	Statement of compliance.	
6.	Statement of truth.	

Appendices

1.	My experience and qualifications.	
2.	Documents that I have examined.	
3.	Details of any literature or other material I have relied upon in making this report with copies of important extracts.	
4.	Photographs and diagrams.	
5.	Chronology.	
6.	Glossary of technical terms.	
7.	Other.	

This contents page is useful even if the report is short. In longer reports the contents page may need to be more detailed so that the reader can easily find their way around the report.

Report

1. Introduction

1.01   *The writer*

I am . . . . (*full name*). My specialist field is
. . . . *and give a short summary of the most
important qualifications and experience. No more than three lines.* Full details of
my qualifications and entitling me to give expert opinion evidence are in
appendix 1. *It is necessary to have these full details as you may be cross-
examined on them.*

1.02   *Summary of the case*

The case concerns *give a short outline of the case.* There is a short
chronology of the key events in appendix 5. I have been instructed to *say
briefly what you have been asked to do.*

1.03   *Summary of my conclusions*

This report will show that in my professional opinion *give your conclusion. It
is good practice to put an executive summary at the beginning so that the reader
knows the direction of your analysis. The Civil Procedure Rules require your
report to contain a summary of the conclusions.*

1.04   *The parties involved*

Those involved in the case are as follows:

*List the people and organisations you refer to in your report with a short
description of each. This can be very useful for a judge.*

1.05   *Technical terms and explanations*

I have indicated any technical terms in **bold type.** I have defined these
terms when first used and included them in a glossary in appendix 6. I
have also included in appendix 3 extracts of published works I refer to in
my report and in appendix 4 there are diagrams and photographs to assist
in the understanding of the case.

2. The issues to be addressed

*2.01 Set out the issues you will address in your report. Number each issue as you
will refer to each in your opinion in paragraph D. Do not give your opinion here.*

Give a statement setting out the substance of all material instructions (whether written or oral). The statement should summarize the facts and instructions given to you which are material to the opinions expressed in your report or upon which these opinions are based. Remember section 3 will give you details of your investigation of the facts.

3.   My investigation of the facts

This section establishes the foundation of fact upon which you will base your opinion. The starting point is "I do not know, but let me see what the facts are". Set out the facts of the case as you see them. Identify the sources of these facts. You must distinguish fact from opinion. Also distinguish facts you have been told and those you personally observed. This paragraph is purely factual. Paragraph 4 will deal with your opinion.

3.01   Documents

Identify the important documents for the judge. Remember appendix 2 contains a list of the documents you have considered with copies of the really important documents.

3.02   Interview and examination

Give details of any interview and examination you did. Give dates and times. Say if anyone else was present. There may be none.

3.03   Research

Give details of any research papers you considered. Remember appendix 3 contains a list of published works you refer to and has copy extracts. Lord Woolf has recommended that as an expert, you should give details of any literature or other material which you have used in making your report.

3.04   Tests and experiments etc.

Give details of any experiments you did to prepare for the report. You should say who carried out any test or experiment which you use in your report and whether or not the test or experiment has been carried out under supervision. Give the qualifications and experience of the person who carried out any such test or experiment.

4.   My opinion

Go through each issue identified in paragraph 2, link these to the facts from paragraph 3 and then give your reasoned argument for the opinion you come to.

*Facts, analysis then argued conclusion. It is useful to use the word "because ..."
to identify the reasons why you have come to your opinion.*

*Remember the reader of your report does not have your knowledge and expertise.
He needs to have your thinking* **explained***. Avoid the word negligence as this is
a legal term. Let the judge make the decision, so just give your professional
opinion. Do not give a legal opinion.*

Where there is a range of opinion on the matters dealt with in your report:

    (i) summarise the range of opinion, and
    (ii) give your reasons for your opinion.

5. Statement of compliance

I understand my duty as an expert witness is to the court. I have complied
with that duty. This report includes all matters relevant to the issues on
which my expert evidence is given. I have given details in this report of any
matters which might affect the validity of this report. I have addressed this
report to the court.

6. Statement of truth

I believe that the facts I have stated in this report are true and that the
opinions I have expressed are true.

Signature . . . . **Date** . . . .

As an alternative to items 5 and 6 above the EWI have published a model "Expert's
Declaration", together with some guidance notes. This alternative statement reads as follows,
to be completed by signing and dating as above:

Expert's Declaration

1. I understand my overriding duty is to the court, both in preparing
   reports and in giving oral evidence.

2. I have set out in my report what I understand from those instructing
   me to be the questions in respect of which my opinion as an expert is
   required.[*]

3. I have done my best, in preparing my report, to be accurate and
   complete. I have mentioned all matters which I regard as relevant to the
   opinions I have expressed. All of the matters on which I have expressed
   an opinion lie within my field of expertise.

---

[*] The point of this is to ensure that the expert is directing his/her opinion to the relevant
issues. Experience shows that unless this is done, much time can be wasted on the wrong
question.

4. I have drawn to the attention of the court all matters, of which I am aware, which might adversely affect my opinion.

5. Wherever I have personal knowledge, I have indicated the source of factual information.

6. I have not included anything in this report which has been suggested to me by anyone, including the lawyers instructing me, without forming my own independent view of the matter.

7. Where, in my view, there is a range of reasonable opinion, I have indicated the extent of that range in the report.

8. At the time of signing the report I consider it to be complete and accurate. I will notify those instructing me if, for any reason, I subsequently consider that the report requires any correction or qualification.

9. I understand that this report will be the evidence that I will give under oath, subject to any correction or qualification I may make before swearing as to its veracity.

I believe that the facts I have stated in this report are true and that the opinions I have expressed are correct.

Guidance Notes

1. *The declaration should be considered carefully by the expert. Signing it is not a routine matter. If any part of it requires modification for a particular case, it should be modified accordingly. Thus in some cases, an expert's instructions may limit the scope of the report and paragraph 2 may require modification accordingly.*
2. *The declaration is appropriate only for civil cases.*
3. *The declaration is not about ethics, but about responsibilities.*
4. *The declaration is only appropriately associated with the final report for exchange.*
5. *The declaration should be served as an appendix to the final report.*

Appendix 1

Details of my qualifications and experience.

Appendix 2

Documents that I have examined, with copies of important documents.

Appendix 3

Details of any literature or other material I have relied upon in making this report with copies of relevant extracts.

Appendix 4

Photographs and diagrams.

Appendix 5

Chronology.

Appendix 6

Glossary of technical terms.

Appendix 7

Other.

Have a separate front sheet for each appendix, unless it is a very short report.

INDEX